ON HALLUCINATION, INTUITION, AND THE BECOMING OF "O"
by Eric Rhode

When Shakespeare's Richard II breaks his "glass", his reflection fragments and he is separated from his immortal celestial god–king self. How is the myth of the king's two bodies maintained? How exactly does the self as actuality co-exist with the self as potentiality?

A curious phenomenon explored by the anthropologist Claude Lévi-Strauss is that two parts of the self, or two individuals, or two groups in a village can conceive of the space–time situation that they inhabit in quite opposing ways, so that they fail to recognize that they exist in different dimensions.

Consider, as W.R. Bion invites us to do, the observer who looks through the piece of glass on the other side of which Picasso paints. The observer might be looking through a window or into a mirror. Fearing his own self-envy, he fails to realize that the "Picasso" in the mirror is his own potentiality, speaking in a language of signs whose dimensions he cannot be in touch with. The observer and Picasso are reciprocals, isomorphs, binary functions. An unknowable code as mediator activates them into some possible exchange of meaning. In this case, the mediator is the "invisible" piece of glass – which in certain circumstances is fragmented. The theme of this book is: *What happens when the glass breaks?*

The tension between the mediator and the reciprocals is such that either the mediator is destroyed, like a meteor entering the atmosphere, or the space–time conditions disappear in which the reciprocals can take on being. In order to sustain the conditions of space–time, the mediator (as a god or priest–king) has to be correlated with some act of sacrifice. The mediator has to be dismembered and to become inaccessible to those to whom the concept of eternity (or existence without extension) is unthinkable. The mediator cannot continue to exist in space–time. He vanishes into light. But conversely the reciprocals cannot exist outside space–time; and possibly they cannot see the strangeness of their condition

ERIC RHODE

ON HALLUCINATION, INTUITION, AND THE BECOMING OF "O"

First published 1998
Republished in 2018 by Apex One
7 Hillsleigh Road
London W8 7LB

Copyright © 1998 & 2018 by Eric Rhode

British Library Cataloging in Publication Data

A C.I.P. for this book is available from the
British Library

ISBN 978-0-9935100-6-9

Edited by Communication Crafts

Designed by Bradbury and Williams

Other books by Eric Rhode

Tower of Babel: Speculations on the cinema

A History of the Cinema: From Its Origins to 1970

On Birth & Madness

The Generations of Adam

Psychotic Metaphysics

Plato's Silence: A Study in the Imagination

Notes on the Aniconic: The Foundations of Psychology in Ontology

Axis Mundi

On Revelation

Silence and the Disorder of Tongues

Himalaya

Table of Contents

PART THREE.

Transformation in Hallucinosis and the
Institution of Divine Kingship

PART FOUR

The Play Shakespeare Did Not Write

FOREWORD

Gilead Nachmani, PhD

Many years ago, when I first began reading Bion, in particular, *Second Thoughts* (1967), I was struck with the sense of organization that Bion saw in the psychotic personality. The very notion of organization in psychosis was novel, and challenged my thinking at that time which presumed that madness and organization were incompatible. That there could be pattern, order, method, and sensibility in psychosis was revolutionary to me. The bizarre object was created by a person, it was not some unaccountable phenomena akin to what might happen across an event horizon in astrophysics. Basically the idea offended and frightened me, but I kept returning to it. (Perhaps it kept returning to me.) What struck me the most was that Bion was such an exquisite observer, and it was his ability to sense and observe rather than rush to "interpret" which cultivated an analytic relationship in which patterns could emerge even in "madness". It was not the need to create closure so much as the ability to be without preconception that was essential to his definition of psychoanalysis. I was impressed by what he saw, and how he came to know what he saw. This revolution in my thinking again occurred when I listened to Meltzer talk about autism and adhesive identification.

Several years ago, while reading Bion's *Cogitations* (1992) one idea at a time, I thought that psychoanalysis was on the verge of creating some equivalent of an anatomical text of the unconscious, or an unconscious grammar. Through a sense of fascination with the title, I read Eric Rhode's *Psychotic Metaphysics* (1994) and discovered that he was working in that very domain. The book was quite an experience. It did not reveal itself to me with ease. In fact, my resistance to it was strong, and reading became a lively wrestling match in which I argued with the author in an imaginary dialogue, over many points. It was a type of reading to which I was not readily accustomed: I would read a chapter, think about it, argue about it, put it away, and come back and read it again. It was an invitation to an experience in learning which had not been frequent in my life. Rhode's work grabbed me and would not let go. He draws the reader into his work by engaging you. He cannot be read lightly without affecting the reader. To read him is to work along with him. It is not a style of writing, but a profundity of thinking that insists that you take your own thinking seriously in order to read it. That is Eric Rhode's signature. He directs his thinking to various other fields of thought with an intellectual ease that makes his insights appear obvious. Reading his work is like watching a ballet dancer "fly" – it looks effortless, but it is the result of many years of work to express such creativity.

Eric Rhode's most recent book is a scholarly adventure in post-Kleinian psychoanalytic thinking in which his own imaginative interests emerge with a strong influence from the work of Bion. In *On Birth and Madness* (1987), *The Generations of Adam* (1990), and *Psychotic Metaphysics* (1994), his incisive, curiosity-driven thinking develops from a type of phenomenological psychoanalytic consideration of families and their transformations when children are born; the illusions and meanings of family histories, the roles played by personal narration, the levels of meaning and interpretation which can be considered in the telling of one's story, and a study of the very nature of the organization of unconscious experience at the threshold of sensations becoming ideas and feelings. Together, these books comprise a complex journey from fundamental Kleinian and Bionian thinking into distant realms of thought as varied as mythology, critical theory, comparative literature, structuralism, and cosmology, to mention but a few. Rhode's gift is seeing the experiential common denominators, the unconscious phantasies, in disparate fields of thought and study, and then expressing his own ideas and work in relation to other schools of thought such as linguistics (Saussure) or structuralism (Lévi-Strauss). The seemingly disparate become vividly related through his insightful thinking, and we the readers become delightfully surprised and awed by his discoveries.

This is no small feat. In taking on the exploration of the nature of experience, Rhode delineates the microstructures of paranoid-schizoid thinking; and begins to formulate an unconscious grammar. The challenge is formidable, and to those familiar with his earlier work, his efforts are graceful, condensed, and deftly creative. His work evolves into a complex post-Kleinian and post-Bionian thinking: subtle, not introductory, logical and not general. This is not an earlier Kleinian Bion – a self-psychological object relations theory – although Rhode does make tracing his own thinking back to those apparent roots. The Bion here, is the exile, writing *The Dawn of Oblivion* (1979) from a psychological wilderness, a consulting room where the patient and analyst are incoherent, where both must wait for patterns to emerge from their incoherent void, where there are gaps and voids in their relationship. Rhode writes of a psychoanalytic relationship where the panics caused by gaps are better tolerated and where a patience and a curiosity are cultivated in the absence of something, and where intuitive truths are discovered. This volume is written for an open-minded reader, eager to see connections among other systems of thought besides psychoanalysis, such as critical theory, philosophy, literature, biblical studies and mythology.

In reading this book one learns through a type of intimate personal recreation in an intellectual playground, where the familiar toys are projective identifications, dreams, sessions, "gaps" and voids, "false perceptions", intuitions, and varied forms of hallucinations. How very true to his earlier writing Rhode remains in this volume where he gives substance to the imaginary, and then questions the need for substance. He writes that "thought is an idol". This is bold yet ingeniously simple. His writing is clearly developed from the work of Bion, but his contributions reflect his own creative insights and go beyond Bion. His elaborations are his own, in particular his ability to place psychoanalytic thinking within a broad intellectual body, as well as his ability to see latent psychoanalytic reasoning in literature, history, and mythology. He is an intellectual historian, applying the later work of Bion to the evolution of knowledge and knowing. He is like a Magellan of the unconscious, sailing off to map this mysterious internal world, in part with the conviction and confidence that maps do represent what is "in there", and in part, as the fearful narrator of a journey over the edge and beyond the horizon.

Readers familiar with the thinking of Klein, Meltzer, and Bion are already well informed about the structural aspects of the paranoid-schizoid position – a state of mind committed to the creation, preservation, and location of experiential structure. With regard to these early and some times primitive experiences, Bion referred to two vertices, medical and religious. The medical vertex is characterized by an idealization of continuity in which experience is defined in part by spatio-temporal values. Implicit in the medical vertex is the belief that everything can be answered. If the medical vertex represents the organization of anatomy (the corporal body and through transformation the *body* of knowledge), then a gap is a hole in the continuity of the body. From a medical vertex, this gap is "nobody there", damage, and catastrophe. Considered from a religious vertex, the body is "used as a sign language for other powers", and the gap need not be a representation of an absence of continuity, but access to a "transcendental and supernatural order". In the religious vertex, the mind connects dissimilarities, in order to bring out their incongruity. From the medical to the religious there is a sea change, a formidable shift in the quality of thinking from the knowable patient in the consulting room to the mystic, where religious vertex is concerned with radical dissimilarities. Rhode states that "... a system that cannot be disabled is a religious system". The forms that come out of the gap, out of the void, do not differ from the "embodied medical world in quantity, but in quality". Thoughts from the religious vertex are qualitatively different, and the continuity of facts do not apply. Rational "knowledge" does not work there. Rational knowledge applies to what is not in the void. In the medical vertex, this discontinuity is perceived as meaningless, perhaps even destructive. In the religious vertex, discontinuity, voids, gaps, and holes can be the very source of meaning, and it is in this religious vertex where Rhode concentrates the work of this book. The early thinking of children occur along the religious vertex, with the medical vertex acquired later. The importance of our earliest thinking is religious and is the stuff of how one first comes to view the world, the cosmos. Herein lies the wealth of Rhode.

The religious vertex emerges from an experiential void that reveals two types of hallucinations, one type representing being, the other type representing non being. Implicit in the medical vertex is the dogma that if there are gaps in knowledge, facts can be found to fill them. If science is based on the relationship of similarities, religious thought is based upon radical dissimilarities. "Narrative thinking is a defence against the use of intuition".

Much structural psychological thinking has been done considering the nature of projective identification. By comparison, less definitory work has been done on the phenomenology of hallucination and intuition. These are the focus of this book. By making distinctions between the two vertices, but not pitting one against the other as a "true" foundation of knowing and meaning, Rhode creates a space for his exegesis of hallucination, intuition, and becoming "O". He explores modalities of unconscious experience, forcing the reader to re-think the nature of psychoanalytic work. What is the nature of not knowing? What are the experiential bases of the epistemology of not knowing? Hallucination, intuition, and becoming "O" are the experiences which Rhode explores, bringing clarity and complexity to the nature of knowing.

"Hallucination differs from many forms of projection. It operates through sensation rather than feeling – although both hallucination and projection are a mixture of sensation and feeling." Hallucination is directed toward filling the perceived gap in the object. It plays with disappearance. Projection need not be sensitive to the object it enters, but hallucination is sensitive to absences in the object, as well as absences that *are* the object. Hallucination is a way of conjecturing (cognition, not panic) about gaps as types of catastrophes, or a hiatus in sensation. It operates by psychic contact. It fills the gap, as a reflection fills a mirror, insight "dawns" through the intuition. Insight emerges as a pattern after the gap is noted.

Originally, Bion's writings considered hallucination to be a result of a catastrophe in which the infant has not found a mother in reverie – a container. What the infant found was a gap when it needed continuity. What then resulted was psychotic panic – nameless dread. Rhode writes that "hallucination is apparent when the oscillation between the world as text and the world as absence of text become unpredictable.... If hallucination is other than destructive, or other than evidence of deficiency, then not everything disappears nor is everything lost when reference is lost". Not every gap is experienced as nameless dread. It is this supposition which is the *segue* into intuition and becoming "O". In the developing mind what is perceived to be present is fundamental to growth and security. Where does the perception of *no thing* lead? That is the journey of this book.

Rhode's exegesis of Bion's developing formulations of hallucination is a masterstroke. He traces hallucination from Bion's work in schizophrenia, to the ability to imagine alternatives, to the idea that hallucination represents the loss of reference; "it replaces nothing", to the idea of representing the inconceivable, and intuition.

References

Bion, W.R. (1967). *Second Thoughts*. New York: Basic Books.

Bion, W.R. (1979). *The Dawn of Oblivion*. In *A Memoir of the Future*. London: Karnac Books, 1991.

Bion, W.R. (1992). *Cogitations*. London: Karnac Books.

Rhode, E. (1987). *On Birth and Madness*. London: Duckworth.

Rhode, E. (1990). *The Generations of Adam*. London: Free Associations Press.

Rhode, E. (1994). *Psychotic Metaphysics*. London. The Clunie Press and Karnac Books.

PART ONE

The Caesura as Transparent Mirror: W. R. Bion and the Contact Barrier

1. THE DEFINITIONS OF MIND AND BODY[1]

The other day, as I had a first session with a new patient, I became aware of how I was clinging to his speech, as though moving by touch along a surface. I was conscious of the way in which his sentences were constructed. They were put together like bits of mosaic. The joins between the mosaic bits might have been gaps, blurs, disappearances of themes, and half themes. Esther Bick (1968) and Donald Meltzer and colleagues (Meltzer, Brenner, Hoxter, Wedell, and Wittenberg, 1975) have described a type of identification that they have called adhesive. My contact with this mosaic surface was adhesive.

At the same time, I recollected another type of response to a patient. Obviously there are many ways of responding to a patient but these two responses came together. I recollected how W.R. Bion had said that it was important to put up with the experience of a session and to observe the facts *in a state of not knowing* until a pattern began to emerge. This is not clinging to a surface, this is letting yourself go into deep space, the "not knowing" of a session; sometimes, as though you were at one with a dying or dismembered being.

Later I thought – as I often had thought before – how important and how strange Bion's formulation was. After all, he does not say you observe and observe until you *see* a pattern, which makes sense in a cause and effect way. He says: put up with something, and observe the thing you put up with, and then with luck and in time, and perhaps as a *non sequitur*, you may be aware of an emerging pattern. But a pattern that emerges from where?

Bion came to his view of how one should work by way of a crisis in confidence. The crisis brought about changes in his way of thinking. I shall illustrate this change with a fragment of clinical material. Over the years the meaning of this fragment underwent a change in Bion's mind, or so I infer from the evidence I am going to present. I do not know whether Bion himself was aware of this particular process of transformation.

Bion (1979) describes the crisis in *The Dawn of Oblivion*, which is the third book in his novel *A Memoir of the Future* – or rather Bion has a character called "Psycho-Analyst" who describes a crisis that sounds not unlike Bion's own experiences.

The character called "Psycho-Analyst" says:

> I found it difficult to understand Klein's theory and practice though – perhaps because – I was being analyzed by Melanie Klein herself. But after great difficulty I began to feel that there was truth in the interpretations and that they brought illumination to many experiences, mine and others, which had previously been incomprehensible, discrete and unrelated. Metaphorically, light began to dawn and then, with increasing momentum, all was clear [...]. One of the painful, alarming features of continued experience was the fact that I had certain patients with whom I employed interpretations based on my previous experience with Melanie Klein, and though I felt that I employed them correctly and could not fault myself, none of the good results that I anticipated occurred (1979, pp.121–122).

The chance reading of three texts had him persist in his work. Let me list these texts quite summarily.

1. He re-read Freud's obituary of Charcot, in which Freud stated that he had been impressed by "Charcot's insistence on continued observation of facts – unexplained facts – until a pattern emerged".
2. Elsewhere in Freud, he once more read Freud's "admission that the 'trauma of birth' might afford a plausible but misleading reason for believing that there was a caesura [i.e. gap] between natal and prenatal. There were other impressive 'caesuras' – for example between conscious and unconscious – which might be

similarly misleading" (p.122).

3. He re-read John Milton's evocation to light at the beginning to the Third Book of *Paradise Lost*. "I re-read the whole of *Paradise Lost* in a way which I had not previously done, although I had always been devoted to Milton. This was likewise true of Virgil's *Aeneid*" (p.122).

A quotation from Milton essentially describes what Bion calls the religious vertex. "The rising world of waters dark and deep [are] won from the void and formless infinite" (cf. 1965, p.151).

The literary critic William Empson (1961) has written that Milton's *Paradise Lost* put him in the mind of the brutal and splendid West African sculpture of Benin. "I think it horrible and wonderful; I regard it as like Aztec or Benin sculpture, or to come nearer home the novels of Kafka, and I am rather suspicious of any critic who claims not to feel anything so obvious" (p.13).

How is it possible to move from Freud's conception of mind and thought as arising out of the biological processes of body – as in his famous dictum that the ego is body ego – to the truly barbaric and patriarchal suppositions of Milton's *Paradise Lost*, in which it is claimed that the material as well as the ideal universe arises out of a void?

We put up with the void or silence out of which the session arises, as though faced by first creation. This might be evidence of a primitive civilization, a primitive catastrophe, or perhaps both.

Bion indicates that in every session there are at least two vertices, or points of view, of a global nature. The two vertices are the medical and the religious vertices. Both are essential to the creating of the dimension in which psychoanalytic thinking occurs. *Transference will founder if the couple in therapy damage or degrade one or other of the vertices*. If you can experience the two vertices in the room, you may experience them as creating the imaginative space out of which the thinking of psychoanalysis arises.

Both the vertices operate in the same way: they unfold like a chain. They resemble the ancient world's view of the cosmos as a great chain of being, as in Arthur Lovejoy's (1936) description of it. They start at some certain point and move out to the edge of intuition: what the ancients thought of as the end of the world. In their chaining they are a rudimentary form of rationalism, although it may be more accurate to say that in their structure they are like music.

The medical vertex begins from an idealized conception of the body as a whole entity. (Actually, it begins as a way of coping with the crisis of epidemic.) Body discloses itself as male and female versions of itself. The religious vertex begins from the void; and the void emanates two types of hallucination. One type of hallucination represents being, the other type represents non being. Both vertices carry within them an intersection. Bion thinks of it as the contact barrier. It contains zero function. Zero function is auto-destruct: definitions destroy themselves as they form.

In the religious vertex "gaps", which is what I want now to focus on, have a different meaning from "gaps" in the medical vertex. They can be indications of the becoming of "O", a mode of internalization that cannot be known and only inferred as a variable.

In the medical vertex there is an idealization of continuity. The concept of duration is viewed as fundamental to the notion of "experience". There is trust, to the point of credulity, in the postulate that the fact of succession in space and time is a basis for truth. Discontinuity tends to be related to the meaningless, even to the destruction of meaning. In the religious vertex, on the other hand, discontinuity may be a source for meaning.

I now want to look at some clinical material taken from Bion's writings concerning discontinuity and to show how his views on discontinuity changed over the years. Starting from the medical vertex, Bion describes discontinuity in terms of psychotic "gaps". With the passing of time, his concept of gap changes from a medical to a religious vertex reading – by way of a particular incident. Over the years his imagination was able to transform remarkably the meaning that a certain patient conveyed to him concerning some holes in a pair of socks.

At the Eighteenth International Psycho-Analytical Congress in 1953, Bion gave a paper called "Notes on the Theory of Schizophrenia". In his paper Bion referred to a patient who said to him, "I pick a tiny piece of skin from my face and feel quite empty". Later the patient said, "I do not feel able to buy any new clothes and my socks are a mass of holes" (in 1967, p.28). Whether intentionally or not, the patient made a link between the idea of skin with holes in it and the knitting together of holes that may result in a pair of socks.

At the time the patient made these remarks, Bion was put in mind of one of Freud's papers, *The Unconscious* (1915). In *The Unconscious* Freud writes about a patient who presented similar worries concerning skin holes and other forms of skin disturbance. Freud refers to papers by two of his colleagues, whose patients had been preoccupied by holes in skins and socks.

When Bion first heard his patient make the (perhaps) unconscious link between skin holes and sock holes, he was inclined to take up the link – as Freud once had done – from within the medical vertex. Now the medical vertex operates from some notion of continuity, tactile skin continuity, if you like. It is opposed to knowledge derived from the void. It assumes that if there is a gap in knowledge this gap can be filled because somewhere there is a dictionary, call it history possibly, which can fill any gap. Implicit in the medical vertex is the belief that everything can be answered. It conceives of experience as primarily an embodiment. It has no place in it for a concept of unknowable internalization – a concept of unknowable becoming. It quantifies life as an idealized span of time that everyone has a right to. It sees tactile continuity as a form of legitimized boundary. Skin holes and sock holes are signs, whose meanings lie in some master dictionary which is to hand, in the form of various types of classification: some being derived from psychiatry, from medical lore itself; others, like the theory of the complexes, being derived from Greek literature or from Greek idealism.

Working within this vertex, Bion thought that his patient had made a hypochondriac or phobic assertion and had given voice to unconscious phantasies concerning the sensation of somebody's body, perhaps even his own body, body being a form of universal grammar. He thought to "explain" the patient's experiences by referring to the psychiatric literature, as though it were an equivalent to *Fowler's Dictionary of Modern English Usage*. But then Bion came into contact, or rather failed to make contact, with a patient to whom this approach made no sense. Bion found that none of his uses of previously tested theory had any effect in helping him make contact with the patient. In the meanwhile, the patient had begun to find (in a comparable failure of reference) that his ability to use language in the sessions had lost any meaning. He spoke in disjointed clauses, then single words, then stopped speaking. Body and language and the language of the body seized up. Both men were reduced to giving up any pre-established notion of continuity. They had to put up with each other and to endure silence.

And of course the silence was a version of the skin and sock type of gap. A sophisticated person might have said that the gap represented the discontinuity implicit in the concept of continuity. Or that the gap represented the inconceivable, a truly metaphysical concept. But this is to leap ahead.

You have to wait and put up with considerable discomfort if you wish for the inconceivable to speak to you. In such a context, of waiting for the inconceivable to speak to you, the body-centred thinking of the medical vertex loses some of its power. The classifications of anatomy are important: it is one among two possibilities that the experience indicates. The other possibility is of body used as a sign language for other powers.

In later years Bion believed that the only person he could learn from was his patient, even though the patient might present himself as a void or gap or a text full of blanks. Theories concerning other patients could only get in the way. Bion thought that it was evidence of tiredness in a session if he got a rush of theories to the head. He had to put up with the facts until the pattern emerged. His crisis began to modify when he recognized that certain patients were using projection in their sessions not to intrude or to destroy somebody or something, but as a means of preverbal communication, sometimes of a pain that they could not tolerate; or that they were entering into states of hallucinatory modulation between the senses in a way that put Bion in mind of mathematical computation: that is, of a high cultural achievement.

Fourteen years after his initial public reading of "Notes on the Theory of Schizophrenia", Bion re-published the paper in 1967, in a collection of papers called *Second Thoughts*. His outlook had changed. Adding a commentary to the paper, he asserted that there was "no satisfactory psycho-analytical model" for the experiences of his "On Arrogance" patient. He felt that his patient's "[...] 'mental boundary' had lost an important part of itself through his destructive attack on it. He was now attacked by the 'hole' which was part of his mental skin [...] a residual after he had wrought his destruction" (p.142).

Bion gives a dramatic or mythic description to psychic talion. You attack your skin, as though it were the skin to someone's mind, and the damaged object then attacks you. Bion asserts that in order to extend "psycho-analytic theory to cover the view of mystics from the *Bhagavad Gita* to the present", he wishes to claim that his patient had "an attitude to the persecuting holes which ultimately showed features [that] we find in a religious attitude to idols" (p.145).

In terms of concrete thinking, gaps are idols and idols are gaps. Some people seek to personify and name the gap, perhaps as a nameless dread. The continuum, and any conceivable break in it, begin to separate: the continuum transforms into the immanence of the natural world, while the break in the continuum gives utterance to a transcendental and supernatural order.

In *Paradise Lost*, John Milton has asserted that you can only apprehend psychic reality by first forfeiting sensation; that is, bodily knowledge. As a ritual instance of this knowing of the gap, John Milton refers to the need for actual or symbolic blindness as a prerequisite for psychic knowledge. Are blind visionaries of the kind that Milton describes similar to foetuses in whose optic pits eyes have not yet formed? This is a medical-vertex question that fascinated Bion in his later years. At the same time he asks the religious vertex version of this question: Is Miltonic "blindness" the means by which the gap transforms into the contact barrier?

In Bion's thought the gap has now become the void, the formless infinite, something that he describes as the nameless "O". Milton's "rising world of waters dark and deep [are] won from the void and formless infinite" (cf. 1965, p.151).

I find it helpful to link the John Milton quotation to the two themes taken from Bion's reading of Freud: the need to tolerate the facts of a situation until a pattern emerges, and the belief in an implicit integrity between pre-natal and post-natal types of knowledge. In the religious vertex, mind operates by yoking together dissimilarities often in ways that bring out their incongruity, as in the violent yoking together of heterogeneous ideas in seventeenth-century "metaphysical" poetry.[2] Milton's theory yokes together dissimilarities in a manner that someone concerned with the importance of tactile continuity may find incomprehensible.

If science is concerned with the relationships of similarities, as in the relationship of grain and bread, which entails a knowledge of subtle and sometimes inaccessible processes related to biology, agriculture and cooking, then religious thought is concerned with radical dissimilarities, like the relationship of an incarnated and murdered god to a piece of bread, or the relationship between Mosaic stone-tables, on which are carved a cosmic blueprint, and a void out of which the stone-tables emerged.

The forms that are wrested from "the void and the formless infinite" do not differ from the embodied world of the medical world in terms of degree; they differ in kind. And there is no dictionary, or corpus of established definitions, by which they can be squared with one another. Any break in continuity of touch is disturbing enough; but the state of disturbance is increased by the fact that the discontinuity gives rise to a type of experience that continuity has not prepared it for: a primordial experience in which we know gaps as idols rather than as absences. Bion shows his readers that these idols might be icons: that they incarnate something, rather than act as delusional defences against nothing. The principle of sufficient reason *can* apply to hallucination.

Certain countertransference responses need time; they may come to mind long after a therapeutic relationship has ended. Seven years after the publication of "Notes on the Theory of Schizophrenia" in his book *Second Thoughts* – exactly twenty years after the first reading of the paper in public – Bion returned to the experience of the socks with holes in them in his *Brazilian Lectures*, and he gave it an interpretation which owes as much to Milton as to Freud's posthumous appreciation of Charcot. He says:

We might look at a pair of socks and be able to see a mass of holes which have been knitted together. Freud [...] said that the patient had a phobia which made it impossible for him to wear socks. I suggest that the patient did not have a phobia of socks but could see that what Freud thought were socks were a lot of holes knitted together (1973 [in 1990, p.21]).

Bion then imagines "[...] a penetrating beam of darkness [which is] a reciprocal of the searchlight". (This is a version of John Milton's act of self-blinding.) He continues:

The peculiarity of this penetrating ray is that it could be directed towards the object of our curiosity, and this object would absorb whatever light already existed, leaving the area of examination exhausted of any light that it possessed. The darkness would be so absolute that it would achieve a luminous, absolute vacuum. So that, if any object existed, however faint, it would show up very clearly. Thus, a faint light would become visible in maximum conditions of darkness [...]. Suppose we are watching a game of tennis, looking at it with increasing darkness. We dim the intellectual illumination and light, forgetting imagination or phantasy or any once-conscious activities: first we lose sight of the players, and then we gradually increase the darkness until only the net itself is visible. If we can do this, it is possible to see that the only important thing visible to us is a lot of holes which are collected together in a net (1973 [in 1990, pp.20–21]).

Losing contact with the world by way of sight, losing the ability to use eyes as though they were a way of touching or being touched, arouses a premonition filled with dread. How can it be related to visionary truth? The premonition is one of having to meet the psychotic element in ourselves (or others) without the intermediary of the contact barrier; or it may be concerned with acts of mutilation, again of oneself or of someone other. Or it may be concerned with the act of falling asleep and of losing the world of sense knowledge and possibly discovering the world of dreams.

The couple who play tennis, the primal couple perhaps, disappears;

or rather an image disappears, as its underlying meaning comes to the fore, a glowing reticulation, an indication of thought's concealed syntax that the non psychotic parts of the mind do not see, a primal articulation that spills out of mind into the universe as a cosmology. In awe we release primal articulation into the significance and beauty of the night sky filled with stars.

In terms of the medical vertex, the reticulation is an idol: a delusion that insulates thought from a dread of the void. In the medical vertex, hallucination is an idol. In terms of the religious vertex, the reticulation is an icon. It arises on the boundary between life and death. It is agent for the experience of the gap in the transference. I know the reticulation most familiarly in daily life in my pleasure in music. I said to a musician who inclines to psychosis, "music arises on the boundary between life and death" and he answered – "of course". The reticulation is the contact barrier: a means of making contact, or of touching, the inconceivable. In *The Dawn of Oblivion*, Bion writes, "It was as if, literally as well as metaphorically, light began to grow, night was replaced by dawn" (p.122).

The world that I know spatially may not be the world as it is, because erroneously I derive phantasies of the world from my senses used as touch. Even the sight of a glowing reticulation is not secure. Bion recalls that mankind for generations misguidedly believed that Euclidean space was the only type of space to exist. But the fact that sensation is used to realize a certain kind of space does not entail that it is the only type of space that might exist.

Bion refers to the extreme capacity for observation that is natural to some patients.

> Just as it is natural for me in my gross, macroscopic way classically to see a pair of socks, this kind of patient has a visual capacity which is different, making him able to see what I cannot see [...]. We must be able to see that it is a pair of socks, or a game of tennis, and at the same time be able to turn down the light, turn off the brilliant intuition, and see these holes, including the fact that they are knitted, or netted together [...]. I would like to consider the category "psychotic" and suggest that it is too gross, too macroscopic. If we look at it more closely,

in detail, in the way we would have to look at a game of tennis, or a pair of socks, we can see that there may be *insane* psychotics and *sane* psychotics. It might be possible to help the insane psychotic to become an efficient psychotic (1973 [in 1990, p.21]).

He adds: "It depends on a certain flexibility of mind in all of us who concern ourselves with the human mind" (p.22).

The theme of reticulation is implicit in the "On Arrogance" paper. At the time when patient and therapist were most unable to be in touch with the other, Bion recollected the figure of the sphinx in the play of *Oedipus*. The sphinx is an otherworldly being who destroys stability in the human mind by the riddles it asks. As a persecuted representation of the contact barrier between patient and therapist (contact barrier collapsed into beta screen), the sphinx becomes the interface between them both and shows a different aspect of itself to each of them. "It is as if the psycho-analyst whom the patient is attacking had a 'skin' which floated off him and now occupied some position between the psychoanalyst and the patient" (1967, p.160).

The sphinx comes into being when thought, in its hunger for omniscience, seeks to convert the becoming of "O" into knowledge. This is the fundamental meaning of Oedipus's transgression; he fails to perceive that the intersection of the cross-roads, like a family tree, might restrain him from crossing certain boundaries. The reticulation arises like grace when thought is defeated in its craving for omniscience and transformed by the becoming of "O".

In order to discover how Bion relates the figure of the sphinx to the theme of reticulation, and to see how he was able to evolve the relationship into a more significant order, it is worth looking to another image, taken possibly from another patient (although it might be the same patient). We have to relate skin, reticulation, sphinx and primal water to a certain conception of clouds as premonitions of thought. Bion invokes the image of a "cloud of unknowing" from the writings of a mediaeval mystic. The cloud is made up of particles and is a form of reticulation.

In his paper "Attacks on Linking" (1959), Bion describes a patient who intuited a blue haze in the room one day, and on the next day intuited two shapes in the room which Bion called "probability clouds". Bion believed that the patient was hallucinating. At this stage in his thought, working within the medical vertex, Bion conceived of hallucination simply as a means of evacuating rubbish; he did not think of it as a form of sign language that can enable functions of internalization as well as of evacuation – Bion had not yet linked hallucination to the influence of "O". Nor did he relate the haze or the two shapes to some apprehension of a gap that might have been idolized, or even iconicised. Later in the same session the patient announced that a piece of iron had fallen to the floor. The patient entered into a series of convulsive movements which led, by way of an interpretation, to sensations in which he believed he was dying. (Was he falling into the void?)

Keeping to the medical vertex, Bion understood the clouds as marking the patient's attempt to eject a capacity for judgment which he had smashed into pieces; the patient wanted to eject his own smashed-up understanding of the therapist as a persecutor.

> His suspicion that the probability clouds were persecutory and hostile led him to doubt the value of guidance they afforded him [...] such as that a fact was an hallucination or vice versa [...] or would give rise to [...] delusions. The probability clouds themselves had some qualities of a primitive breast and were felt to be enigmatic and intimidating (1967, p.100).

In a later book, *Elements of Psycho-Analysis* (1963), Bion's conception of probability clouds has begun to change. He no longer emphasizes their functions as representations of damage; he began to see them as evidence of insight into the unconscious syntax of the mind.

He relates them – by way of Elliott Jaques' (1959) theory that an unconscious reticulation, or schema, is the necessary ground to the capacity to work – to the sphinx in *Oedipus*, whose meaning in ancient Greek is "tight-binder". The ancient Greek understanding of riddles as being etymologically similar to woven rush baskets heightens the parallel between failures in knowledge and qualities of reticulation (Onians, 1951, p.369).[3]

At this stage in the evolution of his thought, Bion (1963) is concerned to see the clouds as factors in the symbolic transformations that occur on the threshold between the paranoid-schizoid and depressive positions – as in Melanie Klein's formulation of the two positions. He writes of the clouds as made up of particles. The particles may come together, as depressive symbolization begins to take shape, or they may be fragmented and dispersed (p.42). Bion takes further the idea of probability clouds in *Transformations*, which was published in 1965. They are now like an understanding of skin as emanation. The confused nature of this image suggests that it requires the religious vertex to make sense of it. The medical vertex cannot categorize it.

Bion (1965) asks whether the "tension" of an idea in a session is able to appear visually as a probability cloud, or whether such a view is a form of thinking by metaphor. The distinction between hallucination and nonsensory intuition no longer has much application for him, in part because his attention is turned to the idea of preconception rather than to the idea of realization.

> As [the patient] lies on the couch and I sit [beside him], I imagine that a cloud begins to form rather in the way that clouds can sometimes be seen to form above a hot-point on a summer's day. It seems to be above him. A similar cloud may be visible to him, but he will see it arising from me. These are probability clouds (p.117).

The clouds, like John Milton's rising world of waters, mark the first indications of the infinite as yielding up diaphanous and translucent forms.

Living within the medical vertex (which for much of the time I am happy to do), I may set too much store on the reassuring tactility of bodies. But the importance I attach to touch and to sensation as forms of knowledge and communication can result in an over-valuing of the idea of specificity in configuration: the idea that since I inhabit my body, as a people inhabits a country, I can lay claim to sovereignty over my body. To some extent, this is a fair claim. Reasonable people do not want to have their bodies violated. But you have to violate your body to the extent of submitting to Miltonic psychic blindness in order to see the truth. On this point mind is not bounded in the way that body is. The eyes of the mind are not constrained by the idea of Euclidean space.

Contact barrier theory presumes that all forms of space–time assertion are of variables perceived – if such a perception is possible – from the viewpoint of the void. I should say that this is *not* Bion's container theory, which belongs to the medical vertex. Indeed Bion's medical vertex theory of containment and his religious vertex theory of truth are incompatible yet inseparable. In order to survive as a therapist, the therapist has no choice but to respect the existence of both vertices in the consulting room.[4]

Notes

First published in the *Journal of Melanie Klein and Object Relations*, 1997, 15(1): 77–89.

2. [Samuel] Johnson, who employed the term "metaphysical poets" [remarks] that "[...] the most heterogeneous ideas are yoked by violence together. The force of this impeachment lies in the failure of the conjunction, the fact that the ideas are yoked but not united [...]" (Eliot, 1921, in 1953, p.283).

3. "Your account of the origin of the 'Sphinx' being a word meaning 'tightbinder', and the link you made to a tightly woven rush basket sparked a memory in me from childhood of a garden implement like a large-scale sieve, which in my family was called a 'riddle'. With the help of an etymological dictionary, I now discover that this was not an idiosyncratic meaning but a late English usage. The dictionary meaning is given as 'A coarse meshed sieve used for separating chaff from corn, sand from gravel, ashes from cinders [...]'. I wonder if the function of a riddle, which is designed to allow certain elements to pass through it and others not, sheds light on the contact barrier you spoke of" (Alf McFarland, private communication, 1994).

A similar account is given for the fact that like comes together with like in Plato's *Timaeus*. Plato conceives of space as "a Recipient which affords a basis for images reflected in it, as in a mirror [...]. Space is the 'room' or place where things are, not intervals or stretches of vacancy where things are not; and if he admits any void at all, it is only as the interstices which the particles cannot traverse [...] (58a, B). The notion of irregular particles rests on the simile of the winnowing-basket [...] woven of basketwork [...] a wide shovel-shaped basket, high at one end and flattened at the other, held by two handles projecting from the upper rim at the sides [...]. The contrast is between the density and heaviness of the corn and the lightness and fine texture of the chaff. It is to these qualities that the separation of like to like is due, not to differences of shape or size. In the application, it is things of like quality that come together. These things are the 'vestiges' of fire and the rest, before any shape has been given to them" (Cornford, 1937, pp.200–202). This description is suggestive of the particle constituents of the alpha and beta elements.

4. Darkness in the tropics floods the sky just after sunset and reveals the glowing reticulation of the stars and the planets. The configuration of the sky by day, as the tennis-net, is an after image of the sky at night. Imagine "night" and "day" to be the names of the two groups who make up the inhabitants of a village. Lévi-Strauss (chapter 5 *infra*) describes village moieties that in all likelihood should be unable to live together. "Night" and "day" might be the names of the moieties. Each of the moieties has a view about the geometry of their shared living space, and these views are in conflict. An overlap between them evokes a third configuration that synthesizes elements from the conflict, so that the moieties can live together in a misconception of coincidence.

A couple similarly may have divergent conceptions of the mental space that they share; and yet out of overlap an idea of a baby may arise that reconciles the divergent. In myth at least, "night" and "day" exist outside time as two incompatible spatial configurations. But "night" and "day" when coupled may have, as an imaginary infant, the idea of an *alternation in time* that allows them to co-exist. An idea of this kind characterizes the function of the Pharaonic king–priest, whose existence acts as a bridge between synchronistic thinking of myth and the diachronic thinking of history.

2. A SYSTEM THAT CONTINUES TO FUNCTION HOWEVER DAMAGED IT MAY BE

> When an European has been living for two or three years among
> savages, he is sure to be fully convinced that he knows all about them;
> when he has been ten years or so amongst them, if he be an observant
> man, he finds that he knows very little about them, and so begins to
> learn (Codrington, 1891, p. vii).

Bion evokes the alienation and loneliness of the depressive threshold
in his paper "On Arrogance" (1957). In place of a contact barrier
experience, the transference faces him with the disjunction of a
zero function out of which contact barrier and beta screen arise.
The theories that he had been trained on, the familiar intellectual
topographies, no longer facilitate contact between him and the
patient. There is no coincidence, no intersection, no contact barrier.
He and the patient are disabled. There is blankness, hiatus and the
missing of some dimension. The patient seems to lose the ability to
construe sentences. He speaks in disjointed phrases; and when syntax
lapses, he loses words altogether; he is reduced to making noises. Bion
is faced by the choice of maintaining a perspective in which he sees
the patient as entered into a state of deterioration, or of relinquishing
one perspective for another, in which the patient enters an area of
experience that Bion is not in touch with.

The disagreeable experience that the patient and Bion undergo is
not related to deficiency. It is an intrinsic transference modality that

this particular patient–therapist combination has brought into the open. Bion's translation of the experience into myth – he compares it to Oedipus' meeting with the sphinx – places it within a recognizable, if incredible context. "What have we let ourselves in for?" is the implicit question raised by both patient and therapist. The daunting and incredible aspects of the transference – transparently close to acts of suicide and murder – encourage patient and therapist to enter into a collusion against it. Transference, as the intersection at which two beings coincide, or fail to coincide (as happened to Oedipus when he reached the cross-roads), is a rite of passage that contains or fails to contain a zero function that is inseparable from the premonition of annihilation.

One day the patient spontaneously raised the question as to why Bion was able "to stand it". The remark turns out to indicate a primary fact about the nature of the alienated state:

> [...] the sessions continued much as before. I remained at a loss until one day, in a lucid moment, the patient said that he wondered that I could stand it. This gave me a clue: at least I knew that there was something I was able to stand which he apparently could not [...] (1957, in 1967, p.90).

What was it that Bion could stand? Bion's hypothesis was that he was trying to put up with a projection that was preverbal, preconceptual and pre-epistemological and that his mind was untrained to deal with it. In meeting his patient he had met his imaginary twin, but without a contact barrier to protect them from each other.

Therapist and patient may embody different space-time schemes. Some belong to the past, some to an unimaginable future. The therapist who thinks to convert the patient to a psychoanalytic point of view, whatever that may be, is no different from the missionary who seeks to convert the native to his views with little concern for the roots that the native has in a different culture. The native who hopes to convert the missionary may have a zeal that is similarly unimaginative.

Faced by breakdown in himself and his patient, Bion could no longer believe in duration as an unconsciously shared experience. The transference has chopped up the fabric of history and sewn it together again in the form of a motley, the patient and therapist as a single unit. The transference is without regard for the belief that civilizations are sequential. The intersection has become the place where two civilizations, whose frontiers should never meet, have come together. This is an intersection that requires the religious vertex to make sense of it.

The imaginary twin embodies an ontology that leaves all epistemological ventures into its territory in disarray. It sees space and time as negations. It might agree with George Kubler's proposal that if a contemporary man went into the past *he would not be seen* and that if he went into the future *he would be wiped out instantly*, like an Inca horde faced by the conquistadors (1962, pp.64–65). Signs originate in circumstances that respect neither historical sequence nor temporal and spatial duration.

> What it was that the object could not stand became clearer in sessions where it appeared that in so far as I, as analyst, was insisting on verbal communication as a method of making the patient's problems explicit, I was felt to be directly attacking the patient's method of communication [...]. What I could not stand was the patient's method of communication (Bion, 1957 [in 1967, p.91]).

Neither could stand the other's means of communication. Some accretion between them, the sphinx, quelled them both. The transference was speaking to them through the incongruence of the sphinx, and the incongruence of the sphinx arose from a failure in coincidence. There was beta screen, and no evidence of a contact barrier, no possible link, except disembodied pain, between Bion's desire for knowledge and the ontological and anti-epistemological condition of the patient.

The patient had lost his syntactical skills because grammatical thinking had no relationship to his needs. He was living out a theme that Descartes was familiar with. Pain in therapy is often as dissociated from systems of meaning as is a referred pain from an actual limb. The patient has to locate a certain pressure, possibly a pain, by discovering it in somebody else, whose status in reality is uncertain. He articulates empty structures that appeared to be inseparable from structures of meaning that might be full. By way of the "beam of darkness" the therapist has to elicit the significance of the pain.

The patient and the therapist assume the existence of a phantom limb in order to locate a pain. The phantom limb may take the form of a dream brought into being to contain the zero function. A conviction that phantom limbs exist as icons of the void, and not as idols, may undermine the therapist's confidence in time and space as formal rules of the mind. The patient who loses his capacity to speak in sessions appears to descend beneath a surface into an environment that is not known about and that is possibly unknowable. The surface could be an interface between water and air. The imaginary twin then exists in a submarine place and is a creature of water and air. It is tempting, if erroneous, to place this relationship of earth creature and water creature as existing on either side of a contact barrier in successive space–time and to think of the imaginary twin as a foetus.

> I would like to see the state of hallucinosis treated with the kind of respect that we expect to accord neurosis, dreams, nightmares and other mental phenomena; we can then hope to learn more about it. I would like to say to the questioner: don't bother what I think about it, but have a good look at it when you feel that you have a chance of examining a state of hallucinosis (Bion, 1973, [in 1990, p.204]).

In *Elements of Psycho-Analysis*, Bion writes about a patient who gave up speaking – it might be the same patient as the one he writes about in the "On Arrogance" paper. "Writing" of a hallucinatory kind precedes not only talking but thinking.

> His actual speech was incomprehensible [...]. It became more meaningful if I thought of it as a doodling in sound, rather like tuneless and aimless whistling [...] an undisciplined pattern of sound [...] [that] the patient believed he could see, because the words and phrases that he uttered were believed by him to be embodied in the objects in

the room [...]. The objects were being used as signs to make thinking
possible about objects that were not present [...] as a mathematician
might employ mathematical notation to solve a problem (1963, p.38).

The patient doodles vocally; he translates "words and phrases"
into objects in the room. The mystery of this embodiment can be
approached if the abstractions of speech and the concreteness of
embodiments are described as "signs". The patient experiences the
doodle as a thing in his mouth or as a musical articulation. He uses
the objects in the room as signs, as a voice uses sounds, as a non-
conceptual means of articulation. The choice between one sense
rather than another, or between one sense-mix and another, remains
undetermined.

In contrast to the therapist's culture of endurance, of persisting
through space and time, the patient enacts doodlings or hallucinatory
transformations that belong to a sonic culture of modulation, of rocking
and breathing, a culture in which there is an unstressed unfolding.
Space–time considerations are distant (as though transformations,
belonging to air and water, were perceived as the night sky might be
perceived from deep within the ocean).

Like the notations of music and mathematics, the concealed
language that appears though the hallucinatory transformations
requires space–time, if at all, in ways that are not consonant with
the transformations of personality in tragic action. Tragic action is
saturated with intuitions of space and time, and the personality
knows transformation as stress, while the self that hallucinates
knows continua and gaps that have to be filled by the continua of
hallucination. The gap belongs to the two-dimensional logic of the
continuum: it is a precursor, as sign, for the experience of loss and
mourning. It may be an un-metabolized object, such as an infant
senses in its mother's mind: the dead baby that has not been thought
about or mourned and that is known as a blankness where an
interchange might have been.

Projection crosses great distances in space, however seemingly
unlimited the space. It travesties tragic action; it is extension without
endurance. Descartes' principle of inertia applies to it as well as it

applies to physical bodies. It needs to cross total space and to make contact with the wall that surrounds the Ptolemaic conception of the universe as a circular walled city (as though the wall were the entity inside the other person, to which the bits of the self in projective identification attach themselves). It has a built-in expectation of the wall, but it is unable to imagine that anything lies beyond the wall. Its absence of spatial imagination, compounded by its spatial dexterity, may lead it to tilt into the surface of the wall. Potentially the absolute length of the cosmos that a projection has to traverse is measurable in time, but projection operates in a system in which the concept of time is unformed.

Hallucination differs from many forms of projection. It operates through sensation rather than feeling – although both hallucination and projection are an admixture of sensation and feeling. It is directed towards filling gaps in the object rather than of intruding into the object in a gap-making way. It seeks to fill the space where an object has disappeared. It plays with the idea of disappearance. Projection need not be sensitive to the object it enters, but hallucination is sensitive to absences in the object as well as to absences that *are* the object. It is a way of conjecturing about gaps as types of catastrophe, or hiatuses in sensation. It operates by psychic contact. It fills the gap, as a reflection fills a mirror: the mirror reflection, as it were, is a hallucinatory projection onto a gap. It explores and defines the existence of the gap, as though to exorcise the gap of meaning. The presence of the gap precipitates the need to enter into computation, in the same way the presence of dead ancestors as in certain cultures incites the computation of professional diviners. The gap, and the hallucinatory need to fill it, are similar to an excitation in processes of identification.

The collapse of any belief in the usefulness of lexical reference in psychoanalytic thinking discloses an underlying system that continues to operate under any circumstance. For Bion, the underlying system consists of a non-ideological commitment to practise observation and to put up with an experience that can be close to unendurable. For the patient the underlying system depends on the therapist's capacity to tolerate the transformatory powers of a projected hallucination.

Crucial to the system that persists is the notion of a void out of which sign language arises. The void precipitates the functioning of hallucination and projection as incipient modes of relationship by way of the contact barrier.

3. "THE POWERFUL INANITY OF EVENTS"

Ferdinand de Saussure gave three series of lectures between 1906 and 1911 on the nature of speech. They were edited after his death in 1913 into a book called *Cours de linguistique générale* (1916).

Saussure opposes speech to written language. His understanding of speech as a phenomenon of the here and now is informative about the transference significance of the experience that Bion underwent with the patient of the "On Arrogance" paper. Bion discovered a new dimension to "observation" by discarding the postulate that the meaning of the "contact" between patient and therapist must depend on some reference to a lexicon or encyclopaedia that one, or both, of them might have. A "breakdown" in communication revealed that beneath the communication lay sign functions of hallucinatory projection and modulation that belonged to an immutable system.

A "system continues to function, however damaged it may be" – Saussure is referring to the nature of speech (p.124), but his generalization holds true for the transference. Elements of the transference can undergo transformations that do not affect the system in which they operate. In distinctive ways, Saussure and Bion postulate that sign systems are able to continue to operate, whatever the circumstance, because the process of transformation, on which they rely, is activated by the "emptiness" of an unknowable variable. Insight in psychoanalysis "dawns" through an intuition concerning the presence of "O".

Transference depends on the fact that breakdown is not a transferential anomaly. Icons or idols would not appear if there were no void to bring them into being. The principle of sufficient reason (whatever it is that validates icons) manifests itself by way of transferential breakdown. Patient and therapist may think to reach the principle of sufficient reason by turning to mechanical knowledge: cause and effect theories, or theories in which the concepts of continuity and succession are accepted uncritically (pseudo-biological and pseudo-historical theories), but knowledge of this kind tends to disintegrate. A therapist will be released from rigidity if something or someone in the room, perhaps the patient, is seemingly impervious to the rigidity. The therapist may discover powers of intuition that are stimulated by an observation of discontinuity.

A system that cannot be disabled is a religious system. Circumstances, whatever their state, are always ritual opportunities in a religious system. Claude Lévi-Strauss's theory of *bricolage*, which derives from Saussurian thought, is an example of such an opportunity. The *bricoleur* is like an odd-job man who "makes do" with whatever is to hand and is able, sometimes astonishingly, to use things intended for one activity to carry out another kind of activity. Picasso was able to convert a bicycle seat into a charismatic bull mask, and Picasso was probably Lévi-Strauss's model for the *bricoleur* as artist.

> His universe of instruments is closed and the rules of his game are
> always to make do with "whatever is to hand", that is to say with a set
> of tools and materials that is finite and heterogeneous because what
> it contains bears no relation to the current project or indeed to any
> project [...] (1962c [in 1972, p.17]).

Bion describes a film in which the spectator perceives Picasso on the other side of a pane of glass (the contact barrier) on which Picasso paints. Picasso represents the imaginary twin, who sees with the "eyes of the mind", by way of the contact barrier. Awed by the presence of the debris, the imaginary twin perceives the debris as an opportunity to make an idol that it can worship. It cannot conceptualize damage as such, since it does not have the concept of damage. The "fragment" of a dream that the waking self refers to is, to the dreamer who (like the *bricoleur*) has no concept of fragment, an interaction between image and oblivion as alternating as the configuration of stars and night sky.

Saussure takes the discussion out of psychopathology by a Kantian description of signs *as formal rules*. He opposes the idea of a *diachronic* system, or a system of successive signs, with a *synchronic* system, a system of co-existent signs. He observes that people seldom talk with an encyclopaedia to hand; they do not rely on a lexical reference, and in a sense they do not rely on memory or history. They interact in the present moment by way of an unknowable variable.

> It is sometimes said that nothing is more important than to know the origins of a given state; and that is true to the extent that the conditions that form a state illuminate its true nature and guard us from certain illusions; but that shows truly that diachrony is not an end in itself. Of diachrony, as of journalism, one might say that it leads in every direction, so long as one quits it oneself (p.128).

In Saussure's description, a synchronic system of co-existent signs entails an interaction between an unknowable code that Saussure calls *langue*, which is recognized by inference, and *parole*, or individual speech usage. *Langue*, explains Saussure, "is not complete in any of us; it exists only in the group" (p.30). "It exists only by way of the contract that exists between members of the community" (p.31). It is "an instrument created and furnished by the collectivity" (p.27), "a treasure deposited in the members of the community"(p.30). *Langue* relates to the Kantian formal rules of the mind. Like Jaques' concept of reticulum, or Bion's articulated glow elicited by a beam of darkness, *langue* is a "code" to sign use in general. It is speech, and it is transference, intuited as an unconscious group object, an autonomous and imperceptible institution. Bion's description of hallucination as a benevolent projection used in the service of exploring the spaces and surfaces related to cavities, is comparable to the co-existent sign system of Saussurian speech, in which the sign unifies an empty concept (a *morpheme*), known as "the signified", and an "empty" acoustical image created by the mouth (a *phoneme*), known as "the signifier".

> *Morphemes*, which signify, break down into *phonemes*, which are
> articulatory elements without meaning, and less numerous than the
> *morphemes*. When organized into systems, these "empty" *phonemes* form
> the basis of all language (Benveniste, 1952, p.62 [quoted by Lévi-
> Strauss, 1964, p.20]).

Signs are arbitrary.[1] They are not dependent on the substantial
existence of events and facts in space and time, nor on a nomenclature
that asserts that names equal things. Meaning in a system arises from
the way in which the system functions; there is no deposit of content.
The floating signifiers that are crucial to its function are without
content: but since they operate within a system in which meaning
depends on function, to describe them as a "empty" or "full" is beside
the point.

> In so far as they are not the actual objects about which he [the patient]
> is attempting to "think" [i.e. the things in Bion's consulting room], they
> represent an attempt to invent and employ signs. To that extent *this*
> employment of actual objects represents a degree of liberation from the
> state of mind compelled to employ actual objects (Bion, 1963, p.39).

In Saussure's understanding, the objects in the room have meaning
only as empty concepts that are bound to "empty" acoustical images,
or gaps. In the case of Bion's patient, the concept of an "object in the
room" is a reification of a gap.

    As an intersection, the contact barrier marks out licence from
prohibition and it is a foundation to the elementary structures
of kinship: but it also the vehicle for hallucinatory projection. In
equation with the intersection, thought is able to extend through
space and time, as though it were a Vespasian man, whose hands
and feet are in contact with the edge of the world, represented by the
circumference of a circle. "Instead of Kant's *a priori* determinants of
our psychical apparatus, Psyche is extended; knows nothing about it"
(Freud, 1941). The self as an axle is able to radiate through spokes
to the rim of the wheel. Projections extend to the limits of a cosmos
conceived of as a gap. Among the Zuñi people, the divisions of *pueblo*

space reciprocate a classification of attributes, climates and creatures by quarters into a seven-part system that consists of North, West, South, East, zenith, nadir, centre (Durkheim and Mauss, 1903 [in 1974 p.50 ff.]). The act of demarcation is an idea with the power to translate all nouns into adjectives as appendages to a self that is equated with a centre.

Hallucinatory projection as a system of co-existent signs is neither spatial nor temporal; it does not belong to time; and therefore it cannot belong to any conception of space that relates to space–time. In Saussure's terms, it would be false to describe hallucinatory projection as pre-verbal because all sign systems operate by the same means, whether they are available to verbalization or not. Hallucinatory projection is no different from other sign systems.

Saussure's description of speech as a system that continues to operate under any circumstance occurs at the end of the paragraph in which he considers the concept of zero function. In Czech, as in certain other languages, there can be losses in inflection (as in certain genitive formations) that do not diminish the effectiveness of language as an operational system. The loss is a loss only from the diachronic perspective and is accidental to the system's functioning. In terms of the synchronic, an absent suffix sets up a contrast with other inflections and in this way indicates a sign that is non material, unlike the signs that arise from inflected forms. In a notebook Saussure wrote: "No reason always to relate an acoustical figure to an idea. All that one requires is an opposition, and x/zero will do" (p.455, note 182). Acoustical figure means *phoneme*, the instrumentality of mouth and ear use, as well as the exchange of the sounds between them. Idea means *morpheme*, an empty concept, which may or may not be embodied, as in Bion's understanding of individual thoughts.

A reversal of the formula zero/x arrives at an isomorphic model for Descartes' depiction of referred pain. In place of the amputated leg, there is the zero of an absent leg, and the zero equals the non-material sign of the pain created by a phantom limb (as though the referred pain, and the phenomenon of the after-effect had in common some source in hallucination). The reciprocity of x/zero corresponds to Bion's interest in perspectival reversals. Psychologically it precedes the emergence of the inside–outside distinction, and it operates through the fact that opposites attract each other. If one of a pair of opposites does not exist, it is brought into being as part of the process by which the system survives deterioration.

Hallucinatory modulation is inherent in the aesthetics of music; the unfolding of a present pattern has to carry a past series of patterning with it, if it is to evoke consonance as well as dissonance in the listener. In the same way as the pressure of light can create an after-image in the eye, so the presence of a sign in a synchronic system can evokes a non-material sign as its alternative. Hallucinating about the presence of an absence, Bion's patient made contact with the code that activates hallucinatory modulation between reciprocals. The idea of succession has little place in proto-speaking of this type. It inclines to experience succession as an aspect of emptiness.

> Structural analysis accords history [...] that irreducible contingency without which necessity would be inconceivable. Any investigation that is entirely aimed at elucidating structures must begin by submitting to the powerful inanity of events (Lévi-Strauss, 1966 [in 1973, p.475]).[2]

In their separate ways, Saussure and Bion conceive of a space in which there is no notion of "inwardness" and that exists in logic rather than in time, and in which surfaces, or versions of the continuum, assemble out of a void.

Notes

1. Emile Benveniste (1939, in 1966, p.51) has proposed that the linguistic sign is not arbitrary because it conjoins concept, acoustic image and the thing itself. The *morpheme* is the soul to the *phoneme*. Thoughts look for an oral structure as though a mouth structure were a form of thinker. The architectonic movements of the mouth in speech is a version of the hallucinatory modifications of the senses. Alternately, thought and mouth are reciprocating functions without content until a code has them generate meaning. Similarly, the patient and the therapist are reciprocating functions without content until the transference moves through them and gives them

significance in the here and now.

2. The hallucinating "patient" might locate history in the endurance of the therapist.

4. THE RELATIONSHIP OF THE BETA SCREEN TO THE THEORY OF CATASTROPHIC CHANGE

Crucial to Bion's thought is the belief that the claims of truth are incompatible with bodily satisfaction. The beta screen theory is a paranoid-schizoid conception of the belief, while the theory of catastrophic change is a depressive conception of it. The idea of the beta screen is important to the understanding. When it is entered into and endured, it asserts certain facts about duration that cast doubt on the sovereignty sometimes claimed for the subject–object model of experience. The observation that it is a paranoid-schizoid system does not invalidate its use as a tool of thought. It is instructive about the emotionality out of which depressive understanding arises. It foreshadows the emergence in Bion's thought of a third factor in the subject–object model, the becoming of "O", that exposes the model as an inadequate basis for thinking about the mind.

The beta screen is an obduracy that arouses discord in any assumption of a concordat between mind and body, senses and sense data, self and other, subject and object. It attacks the sense of well being that the subject–object model can engender. Because it undermines the model's authority, it is believed to be inimical to the existence of mind. Thought is embarrassed by a presence within itself, at its source, of elements that are discomforting, intractable and inimical to peace of mind. Awkwardness in mind, rather than the selected fact, is the factor that reveals an otherwise unseen dimension. Water in certain streams is imperceptible because it is clear. If someone places a stick in the water, the effect of the stick is to stir up the water, so that it is perceptible. For Bion (1973), mental turbulence is valuable because it brings the imperceptible into sight (in 1990, p.23).

The Kantian conception of experience as grounded in the grid of space and time is one of the systems by which mind defends itself against the impact of truth. People unable to use space and time as modes of defence, who keep slipping out of the skin of being a personality in "their own day and age" are most prone to undergo catastrophic change and possibly to be creative.

The beta screen is a paranoid-schizoid misconception of a depressive phenomenon. In his earlier writings Bion describes it as though it were a vampire. It is able to appropriate qualities of personality, like cunning, while not having a personality itself. It projects states of confusion, without itself being a product of confusion. Stealthy in its manoeuvrings, it projects states of annihilation with unusual accuracy. It "has a quality enabling it to evoke the kind of response the patient desires, or, alternatively, a response from the analyst which is heavily charged with counter-transference" (Bion, 1962, p.23). It is "coherent and purposive [...]. [It is] intended to destroy psychoanalytic potency [...]. The patient [is] concerned to withhold rather than to impart information" (ibid., pp.22–23).

A patient dreamt that he was travelling down a river and was about to go over a weir. Bion (1980) observed with a certain jocularity that the patient said that he had never woken from a dream so fast in his life (p.42). The thought of going over the weir is a premonition of a beta-screen experience, in which sensations of space and time contract to zero. A Kantian, who wished to "save appearances", might propose that the patient was undergoing a nightmare – and specify that nightmares are not experiences. But nightmares are experiences in the same way as consulting room intuitions are experiences: they are not invalidated by the fact that they do not fit into patterns of succession. Dreaming occurs whether the dreamer is awake or asleep, and the laws of dreaming operate concurrently with the laws of Kantian contemplation. It is meaningful to think of "space" and "time" as having the properties of contraction.

Bion's patient assumed that it was possible to resolve difficulties related to the collapse of space and time, by jumping from the conventions of dreaming into the conventions of waking life. The implausibility of this belief is exposed if we reverse the situation and imagine someone who is awake and who jumps into a state of somnambulism in the expectation of escaping from the threat of riding over an actual weir.

The beta screen provides sensations of being telescoped, condensed and contracted. Certain African fetish sculptures evoke the types of experience that it categorises. The idealised intensity of these sculptures depends on a contraction of space. The beta screen also provides experiences of rarefaction. It is not an attribute of any patient. It continues to exist in the room when one patient replaces another. It is "out there", an outcome of transferential changes in coincidence between patient and therapist. It afflicts them both. It anticipates in a rudimentary way the becoming of "O".

In ancient Greek legends, the past exists beneath the surface of the earth, while the future exists in the sky. Can the past be similarly "placed" in the consulting room? Small votive objects, clay birds, child-modelled perhaps, have been found in ancient Minoan shrines dedicated to the goddess Athena. "In the chapel at Gournia, as well as in other places, small terracotta birds have been found with the house-goddess" (Nilsson, 1949, p.27). Icons are tokens for the future. A child might pay tribute to fertility, by touching and talking to such birds as hints of sky that have descended to the earth. Intuitions in the consulting room recall these birds. They are tokens of a new life.

> The ancient Greeks had no category for time. Cyclical time is a modern
> concept. It is we, and not they, who believe in a return of the seasons.
> In their thought there was return in space and not in time: there is an
> *eleusis*, an *anados*, seasons come "from below" and not from "yesterday".
> The perpetual movement of the universe depends on rhythm and
> not time, as in a dance [...]. The rhythm is always one–two, one–two
> (Daraki, 1985, p.166).

Narrative thinking is a defence against the use of intuition; and Bion brackets it – with the uncritical acceptance of the Euclidean conception of spatiality – as a prime inhibitor of the capacity for observation. Kant's argument concerning the significance of succession in space and time depends for its conviction on a beguiling narrative in which an observer watches a boat move downstream. Such a relationship of observer and landscape is only one among many options in the thought of a session.

A Beta Screen Conception of Certain Clinical Information

In an experience comparable to the nightmare of the weir, a man dreams of someone whose parachute might have failed and who is falling from a great height and then strikes the ground. He thinks that the falling figure as other than himself and that it is perhaps made of cardboard: the ground absorbs the fallen body. The dreamer is invaded by psychotic fears of disintegration at the prospect of an end of term separation; and an association to the dream reveals another aspect to his fears. In childhood he would look into a mirror and then think to separate from his own body, so that he was able to look at himself as he looked at the reflection in the mirror. Embodiment puts him at risk. He has to jump out of his body in order to be a reflection, and no more, like the reflection in the mirror. Traumatised in fancy, he lacks the capacity to think about his trauma. He knows phantasms instead: a mirror–mother who contains a retaliatory ghost–twin that works in alliance with the dead mother to destroy him. Someone (the rival's reflection) has escaped from the beta-screen by leaping out of the experience into rarefaction, and not by entering into alpha-element states. He, too, escapes a beta-screen attack by the disembodiment of a hallucinatory rarefaction.

In the transference the ground that absorbs the body is the breast as an object that absorbs impacted feelings (mainly of rage). The patient did not feel secure enough to be able to project rage into the therapist. He had just begun therapy; he behaved like a well-mannered institution child. Impacted feelings are beta elements, or by the fact of their being condensed they can be confused with beta elements. They are anti-imaginative. Imaginative thinking (suffering loss) would be too painful at this point and – as a contact barrier—cannot be tolerated.

Another patient says that one side of his nose has swollen up. He relates this experience to a footballer of declining powers, whose nose has swollen up on one side. By *footballer of declining powers*, the therapist understands the patient to mean that he is becoming less inclined to control the therapist's mind by beta-screen projections of a charismatically bodily kind, of which he is consciously unaware. The beta screen is diminishing in its power; or perhaps it is changing into the unknowable. The two sides of the nose as they seem to divide into two noses, one swollen and the other un-swollen, as in some womb-like mitotic cell division that operates outside of any understanding of space and time, marking the deterioration of the beta screen. The beta screen has begun to fall apart, and a proliferation of meaningless particles determines the capacity for thought. The patient may move into alpha function if a contact barrier can form.

An adolescent one-time drug addict talked about the glitter of lights in a distant mountain village seen at night and of a coveted piece of jewellery. These are particle impressions that render meaningless the luminosity of a mother's gaze. At the same time as the patient was describing these experiences, the therapist felt weighed down, by a series of thoughts concerning people whom he felt had been damaged by their lifestyles. Thoughts of this kind are beta-screen projections of which the patient was unaware. By putting them into the therapist, the patient was able to escape from the agglomerative powers of the beta screen and to approach the particle impressionism that marks the onset of the contact barrier.

The Contact Barrier

Freud describes the hypothesis of the contact barrier in his neurological writings as a synapse between neurones. A neurologist may be unaware of possible religious vertex readings of a neurological structure, while a religious contemplative may be unaware of possible medical vertex readings of a religious structure. Bion takes the neurological description and understands it as a structure through which phantasies have to pass in order to form. In a perspectival reversal of the vertices, Bion modifies the opposition, which is genuine, between the contact barrier as imagination and the beta screen as anti-imagination.

In Freud's view, the contact barrier modulates the information that it conveys to the neurones on either side of it, insulating the neurones from each other, as well as allowing for a communication between them. Stimuli may permeate one type of neuron but not another. Initially Bion thinks of the neurones as representing the relationship of unconscious to conscious thought. He personifies them as "foetuses" separated by a floating signifier, as a patient of a certain type in interaction with a therapist of a certain type, or as a genius painter who communicates with a spectator through a pane of glass. Implicit in his concept of foetus is the concept of the imaginary twin: but the imaginary twin does not exist within the biological space–time circumstances of the foetus.

The beta screen transforms the meaning of the concept of experience. It condenses and rarefacts, magnifies and condenses, without sequence. Over time Bion's views on the beta screen change, to an extent that he allows the concept to lapse. It is not a projection by the patient; it is a factor in the transference that the patient–therapist relationship activates and that is essential to the transferential dynamics of the depressive threshold. If catastrophic change is a stage in a developmental process and operates without the concept of duration, then the theory that claims that hallucination is meaningless may be erroneous because it is inconsequential.

5. BION, LÉVI-STRAUSS, AND HALLUCINATION AS A "PURE" CULTURE

As professed one-time Kantians, W.R. Bion and Claude Lévi-Strauss published complementary investigations in the 1960s into sign systems that are independent of the culture of literacy and to some extent opposed to it. Neither of them has given evidence of knowing of the other's work.

Renaissance intellectuals, steeped in classical humanism, and thinking of space and time as extensions of the self, and not as forms of the unknowable, might have taken the conventions of tonality and perspective, and other means of tempering or denoting, as evidence of a newly discovered world, and not of newly discovered conventions concerning a possible world. Involved in conquest, the humanist was intent on serving the needs of man rather than the needs of an unknowable God who was on the point of becoming a superfluous hypothesis. Jean-Jacques Rousseau (a formative influence on Lévi-Strauss) was later to trace the shadow of the abandoned God in the various cultures of psychotics, children and "savages". Out of absences in connection he was to observe a logic to arise that had no relationship to the notations of literacy. Lévi-Strauss discovers this culture of discontinuity to have existed extensively in Amerindian myth.

The conquistadors had thought to conquer America, as though to impose the text of tonality on an aural space filled with sounds that were close to imperceptible; but now a chromaticism intrinsic to tonality was about to destroy tonality itself. The chromatic culture that the conquistadors had thought to regulate by imposing on it the dogmas of a moribund musicality was articulated once more in the writings of Lévi-Strauss and his contemporaries. Amerindian myths, as Lévi-Strauss describes them, are not complete in themselves and they cannot be isolated from one other. They are formed like dreams. The concepts of totality and fragment are irrelevant to them. One myth weaves through another by way of *motifs*. For Lévi-Strauss, music is one of the outcomes of mythic thinking of this kind. He draws a parallel between Wagner's deconstruction of nineteenth-century narrative and his deconstruction of tonality by chromatic effects as myth-making activities that allow for the recovery of mythic thought.

The interactions of Amerindian myth reveal an unadulterated culture of hallucination. The Amerindians modulate through hallucinations with the insouciance of Bion's 'doodling' patient. So far as I am aware, Lévi-Strauss never isolates this way of thinking from other ways of thinking by referring to the concept of hallucination. He appears to respond to hallucinated thinking, as to music, as viable cultural systems. In *Plusieurs Oiseaux des arbres de Vie*, the ninth movement of his "Éclairs sur l'Au-Delà ...", the composer Olivier Messiaen creates through polyphony a multitude of bird sounds in a forest. Lévi-Strauss has an affinity to Messiaen. By the end of the four volumes of his *Mythologiques*, and by way of over 600 carefully investigated myths, Lévi-Strauss has converted the America of preliterate myth, from one end of the continent to the other, into a vast and phantom symphonic form.

Blind Matter and Empty Form

Kant's conception of the world is haunted. His *Critique of Pure Reason* provides a mature representation of the humanist world view of man as the legislator of nature and master of all that he surveys. But its descriptions of space and time as formal rules of the mind bring out, by the fact of their brilliance, an unease in any notion of stability. The *Critique* was published in 1781, at a time when social revolutions of various kinds were putting into jeopardy the humanist myth of man's sovereignty over nature. A French ethnologist, the late Roger Bastide, has compared Lévi-Strauss's view of the unconscious as an emptiness to Kant's description in the *Critique of Pure Reason* of "blind matter and empty form" (*une matière aveugle et une forme vide*). Kant writes:

> Without sensibility no object would be given to us, without understanding no object would be thought. Thoughts without content are empty, intuitions without concepts are blind (Kant, 1787 [in 1950, p.93).

> I successively descend from a sensation which has a certain degree to its vanishing point, or progressively ascend from its negation to some magnitude of it (p.184).

> The proof of an empty space or an empty time can never be derived from experience (p.205).

> An event which should follow upon an empty time – that is, a coming to be preceded by no state of things – is as little capable of being apprehended as empty time itself (ibid., p.221).

In the subject–object model, subject and object think to generate meanings between them. In the alternative model, empty space and empty time, as negations, originate meanings.

Melanie Klein understands the separation of subject and object to activate hallucination as a substitute for the object. Hallucination is a wish fulfilment. In his description of the disappearing tennis-net, Bion re-arranges the relationship of absence and hallucination to allow for a different conception of hallucination, by removing absence and hallucination from the subject–object model (1973 [in 1990; pp.20–21]). The beam of darkness (the domain of hallucination) has to impose a negation on plenitude; it has to create the space of absence in phenomena in order to assert its own kind of reality. If the idea (and actuality) of the dead did not exist, mind would have to invent them. In his novel, Bion assumes the role of a ghost to talk with the ghosts of his First World War companions (1977b [in 1991, p.422 ff.]). In one respect, he seeks to placate the dead, whom he describes as always invoking dread. In another respect, he seeks to immerse himself in the domain of the glowing reticulation. Hallucination of this kind is the imagination. The imaginary realm of the dead, so central a motive in preliterate thought, or the imaginary realm of the unborn babies, is no different from the space of the supernatural that Shakespeare gives accommodation to with total generosity in *A Midsummer Night's Dream*. A pregnant woman's reveries *about* her foetus and her reveries *with* the foetus, is hallucination as the idea of *a gaze in the womb*.

"Kant once said that intuition without a concept is blind, and a concept without intuition is empty [...]. One of those statements which, like a seed, germinates and turns into some kind of tree or forest" (Bion, 1987 [in 1994, p.132). The statement opens an alternative to the subject–object model of the world. Bion imagines a pressure on the spots where eyes and ears might be that stimulates sensations and even signs that have no relationship to the senses or to sense data. Such signs have the authority of the "other world", of the spirits, that Prospero for one would seek to constrain. Either there are no concepts to articulate this inversion of experience, or there is an excess of shallow meaning (1980, p.40).

In one type of hallucination "blind matter and empty form" are ghosts that cling to embodiment and employ a spectral language of the body. Certain hallucinations function by equating the part with the whole; they totalize every particular. They assume the existence of *non being*, and of a spectrum of sensation which, as a reflection of *non being*, is a spectral *being*. Hallucinatory sensation as an eerie light out of nowhere, arises from a setting in which mirrors reflect back and forth the image of a non-existent substance.

In place of the concept of coincidence (as in a coincidence of thought and feeling between two people involved in a transference), hallucination operates by an intuition of correspondences. (This is thinking by way of analogue, Bion's notion of oscillation. It is similar to the presentation of thinking in certain nineteenth-century French symbolist poems.) Correspondences include, with a certain self-consciousness, cross-references of a synaesthetic kind. They can be so intricate in combination that they require a mathematical skill to elucidate them; and Lévi-Strauss has called on professional mathematicians to work out some of the preliterate systems.

The Discontinuity of Symbolic Thought

As a scientific materialist who is conscious of the ways in which scientific materialism can be used in the service of misunderstanding, Lévi-Strauss has proposed that the theory of totemism is a projection onto preliterate peoples of a "positivistic" conception of the world that oversimplifies their systems of classification. Lévi-Strauss sees many of the preliterate systems as practising a logic of discontinuity that scientific materialism does not have the means to understand.

> A shift occurred from a stage when nothing had meaning to a stage when everything had meaning [...] at the moment when the entire universe all at once became significant, it was none the better known for being so. [...] There is a fundamental opposition in the history of the human mind between symbolism, which is characteristically discontinuous, and knowledge, which is characterized by a sense of continuity (Lévi-Strauss, 1950, pp.59–60).

The idea of a symbolism founded in discontinuity is similar to Saussure's realization that sign systems depend for their generation on the use of "empty" devices, and to Bion's conception of a religious vertex in which the void originates signs. While the medical vertex centres on the facts of embodiment and on the dependence of bodies on each other, the religious vertex centres on the facts of the sacrifice, which is a cultural construct that articulates the becoming of "O". Fundamental to the thought of Bion and Lévi-Strauss is the notion that coincidence (i.e. the intermediary in the sacrifice who joins and disjoins the cosmos) is a variable.

The victim in the sacrifice is denied all biological rights. Its body is reformed to fit some group belief concerning the identity of individual and cosmic embodiment. It is a coincidence between creation and destruction and it carries a group premonition concerning oblivion that is realized by the act of its being annihilated. In the same way as the hysteric loses any capacity to differentiate between the nature of bodily sensations and phantasies about them, so that the body in sacrifice is no more than a blueprint for phantasy; it assumes the function of enacting transformation in hallucinosis for the group. On a physical level, the body is butchered and eaten, either raw or cooked. Transformations in hallucinosis and transformations in cooking parallel each other on the psychic and material levels; in phantasy, they are examples of the uterine "cooking" that represents the procreative powers of a woman who is pregnant.

Monmanéki

The Tukuna myth that Lévi-Strauss classifies as M354 and names as "The hunter Monmanéki and his wives" typifies a type of disjunction reminiscent of certain juxtapositions in French surrealist thought. Underlying the disjunctions of myth is a sign language, in whose grammar disintegrative impulses work in a contrary phantom motion to processes of integration. Possibly all myths enact the creation and destruction of the cosmos as occurring in the here and now. In this myth, of which I give only an extract, the hunter Monmanéki enters into a series of five marriages. Two of his wives are associated with the subterranean world, while three of them are sky creatures. Using the anthropological distinction of endogamic and exogamic relationships, Lévi-Strauss considers the topographical meaning of the marriages, and the oppositional nature of the various wives. Conceiving of bodies as group phantasies concerning the nature of the cosmos and not as physical organisms, he thinks to see that Monmanéki weds the cosmos in five different ways when he weds his five different wives.

> One day Monmanéki has a sudden fancy to squat down to defecate directly over the spot where an earthworm was burrowing. She pokes out her head and said: "My, what a lovely penis!" Monmanéki looked and saw an attractive girl. He copulated with her and took her home with him, where she gave birth to a child. He goes out hunting. One of his grandmothers looks after the newborn, while his earthworm wife

clips at the roots of weeds. The grandmother accuses the wife of laziness and cuts off her lips. The wife is unable to ask for her child. "Humiliated by disfigurement, she disappears [...]". Monmanéki remarries a woman of his own people. Every time he goes to a landing-stage by a river some distance from his home, the body of his first wife divides into two sections: her abdomen and legs remain on the river bank, while her chest, head, and arms entered the water. She catches fish. Her torso crawls "on its hands to the bank and adjusts itself on the lower part, from which the spinal cord protrudes to the length of a finger" (1968 [in 1978, pp.27–28]).

The nature of the fourth wife's dismemberment indicates that Monmanéki has entered into a different contract with the cosmos. The fourth wife's deformity is neither a biological anomaly nor an Aristotelian failure in fulfilment. It is a metaphysical fact, arising from the act of sacrifice, which lies at an angle to naturalistic facts. In the *Upanishads*, the act of dismembering a horse concretely equates the horse with the cosmos, by the same power that allows a seer to look into the entrails of a sacrificed victim and to perceive the total plan. The act of sacrifice opens and reseals "the abyss of annihilation" (Burkert, 1983, p.38). Similarly in eating, the act of ingestion draws the whole world into the mouth of the sacrifice as well as submitting it to a process of chewing. "Months and halfmonths are his joints; days and nights, his feet; the stars, his bones; the clouds, his flesh. Sand is the food in his stomach; rivers are his entrails [...]" (*Brihad-Aranyaka Upanishad* [in Hume, 1931, p.73]).

By drawing the macrocosm out of the microcosm, Lévi-Strauss demonstrates how the division of the wife's body is analogous to the relationship of three of the constellations in the night sky: Berenice's Hair, the Pleiades and Orion. The dismembered parts of the wife extend through space to the limits of the cosmos; darkness and indefinite space pour into the spaces that are her bodily gaps.

Further, by way of another myth (from Guyana), in which a woman is partially eaten by fish and transformed into the constellation of Berenice's Hair – and by way of the fact that Berenice's Hair appears in October and is believed to cause the death of river fish –

Lévi-Strauss associates the story of Monmanéki to a class of myths that correlates various differentials to the changing quantity of fish in the river and to the life of the river itself. He gives evidence to associate deformity, and the decomposition of bodies in river waters, to a relationship between aquatic plants and the human lungs (1964 [in 1970, p.243]).

Clinical Example: Entrails as Exoskeleton, and the Unravelling of the Cosmos

A man dreamt of his uncle as unravelling at one of his shoulders. In a mode of bodily expression that is typical of a hallucinatory sign language, the uncle's body was an unravelling woollen garment. The dreamer associated the dream to the fact that the uncle had committed suicide some years before. The uncle's condition in the dream represents the dreamer's premonitions concerning the closeness of the depressive threshold. He wants to pick at it, as though it were a piece of loose skin. He fears that he will lose magical powers of omniscience and founder in the slough that exists between psychic death and psychic rebirth: he will be confused with his uncle and commit suicide. In omniscience he equates the cosmos with his entrails; if he loses his sense of omniscience, he and the cosmos will unravel.

A soothsayer, who dismembers the body of the sacrifice, has contact with a grammar that enacts fragmentation in order to unify the totality on an everything-or-nothing basis. In the victim's entrails the soothsayer sees all space and time. The victim's entrails *are* the architecture of the king's palace, as well as the maze of the stars; and their relationship to omniscience as fetishes equates absolute power (the divine right of kings) with bodily sensation. The cosmos is so bound to the victim of the sacrifice at its centre that there is no need for a "you" or "me".

An early instance of documented hallucination – collected by the French psychiatrist Esquirol (who is reputed to have coined the word hallucination) – concerns a sacrifice phantasy.

> She [Mme L] hears cries. She catches sight of a surgeon. He is carrying
> out on an examination on a woman. He lifts up a hand covered in
> blood. She believes that she sees steaming blood and intestines floating
> everywhere (Esquirol, 1838, p.128).

The hand removed from inside the body unpacks the contents of the
body, so that it can float in an "everywhere" that is "nowhere". The
surgeon's hand is an index that is capable of practising an omnipotent
series of mental enactments. On the assumption that the surgeon was
not disembowelling the woman, it would seem plausible to think
that Mme L's involvement in the series of enactments stopped her
from seeing what was actually happening. Conceivably hallucination
always has some relationship to the visceral and to the idea of the act
of sacrifice.

But Lévi-Strauss finds the theme of the sacrifice distasteful and its
grammar unsatisfactory. "The system of sacrifice represents a private
discourse wanting in good sense for all that it may be frequently
pronounced" (1962c [in 1972, p.228]). He avoids the theme of the
sacrifice; still, he would seem to write about it perpetually, creating
poetry out of a theme that outwardly he appears to avoid. He defines
the sacrifice as a bringing "together [of] two initially separated
domains through a sacralized victim (an ambiguous object, in effect
attached to both), and [an eliminating of] the connecting term"
(1962c [in 1972, p.226]).

Ambiguity (which like the contact barrier is an intermediary
between incompatibilities) and *extirpation* are attributes of a
personified middle that Aristotle wished to exclude from thought as
rationally inconceivable. "There cannot be an intermediate between
contradictories" (*Metaphysics*, 4.7 [in Barnes, 1984, p.1597]). The
description that Lévi-Strauss gives of the Amerindian conception of
the rainbow is an example of the otherwise excluded middle. Rain
links sky and earth in a positive sense; dry earth hungers for rain.
But the rainbow links sky and earth in a negative sense, and many
of the Amerindians dread it. It is a *bad* hallucination, a *bad* cloud
of unknowing that is related to theft in that it steals its iridescence
from the variegated plumes of certain tropical birds (or conversely

the birds steal their plume colouring from the rainbow). In one myth the rainbow is "the mother of diseases", whom someone chops into two parts and throws into a river. The two parts become twin brothers who hold up the separate ends of the rainbow. The rainbow twins destroy the entire world – apart from two women, with whom the twins happily live in perpetuity.

Rain and rainbow exist on the intersection between being and non being: one of them carries the positive aspect of this link, the other its negative aspect; in their positive and negative aspects they allow for the inference that two types of imaginary twin may represent them.

In a paper on cosmic symbolism that is not included in his many books, Lévi-Strauss (1957) has described the nature of the ambiguity–extirpation link as it occurs in the Hako, a carefully documented ceremony of the Pawnee tribe. The Hako is intended "to strengthen children" (Fletcher, 1904, p.17). It carries the meaning of dream and breath. The Indians say, "Everything speaks, the eagle, the corn speaks; so we say Hako – the voice of all these things" (p.18). In the first of three stages, the ceremony begins with the making of an *imago mundi*. A lodge is built on a piece of sacred ground. Within the lodge are signs representing the sky, the earth, stars and the four quarters. The celebrants construct objects to represent the state of ambiguous intermediacy. The lodge people construct the chimeras with a daring juxtaposition of materials.

> Mother Corn is an ear of corn (vegetable food), attached to a piece
> of buffalo skin (animal food and clothing), and raised on a plum-tree
> stick (symbol of fecundity) by which it is attached to the earth; yet
> the top part of the ear of corn is painted blue (symbolizing the sky)
> and is surmounted by a white feather (representing the clouds). The
> construction of the object relates it to sky and earth, mankind and the
> gods, nature and culture; it facilitates movement from one world to
> another (Lévi-Strauss, 1957, pp.52–53).

Such objects are beta element agglomerates, like the sphinx in the Oedipus legend. Their function reveals how relevant the sphinx is to a dynamic of the Oedipus legend. The intermediary in preliterate thought is a cosmic impress; it is more determined by the structure of the cosmos than by biological process; it informs the hysterical subject with a metaphysical significance.

Many of the Pawnees believed that the cosmos arose out of confusion. The first moment of creation reconciled the confused essences. The rite of making the chimera (alias the sphinx) enacts the first moment.

Rationality denies the intermediary value, since the excluded middle, if it exists (as it does in archaic cosmology) renders superfluous *magnitude* and *succession*, concepts on which the Kantian worldview depends. The beta screen as an intermediary is felt to be so threatening in part because it annuls Kantian concepts.

Much at the same time as Bion was working out his idea of the contact barrier, Lévi-Strauss described the variable intermediate object as a *floating signifier* and identified it as a recurrence in cosmic thought. In one series of Zuñi myths Lévi-Strauss discovers it as a messiah, a pair of twins, a trickster, a bisexual being, a married couple, a grandmother and a grandchild and in four-term structures, groups and triads (1955 [in 1977, p.226]). The excluded middle as floating signifier has the power to become any representation of being. In the third stage of the Hako, the figure of a giant is marked out on the ground. The giant's head is equated with the space on which the lodge is built. The iconography is similar to the *Upanishad* equation of horse and cosmos, in which the horse is the cosmos and the cosmos is the horse.

The Ternary Nature of Dualism

The fundamental point at issue between the rationalist and the one who hallucinates concerns the existence of the intermediary. Aristotle, as rationalist, denies that an intermediary can exist between contradictories: there is either yes or no; and there can be nothing in between. The one who hallucinates attempts to personify the "nothing". Describing the contradictories as twins who represent the coincidence in opposites of plenitude and negation and finding his bearings by using the twins as a binocular form of vision, he realises the relationship of annihilation and transformation in hallucinosis by personifying an idea of the third twin, the victim in the sacrifice, whose reality those who deny reality to hallucination would also deny.

In a paper entitled "Do Dual Organizations Exist?", Lévi-Strauss (1956) described villages in various parts of the world, whose inhabitants experience themselves as separated into two groups. Each group perceives the topography of shared village space in dissimilar ways; it is as though they were looking at different objects. Lévi-Strauss demonstrates how the geometry of this space is of a kind that allows opposing perceptions to exist without conflict. While Bion regards Euclidean spatiality as "convincing and misleading", Lévi-Strauss thinks that the misleading nature of such types of village space allows for social coexistence. Among the Winnebago (in Paul Radin's perception of them), members of the upper phratry imagine the village to be a concentric space with a diameter running across it; they think of themselves as existing in the south-west half of the circle; and they conceive of social relationships in terms of reciprocal exchange. Members of the lower phratry imagine the space in which they exist to be an inner circle within an outer circle; and that both phratries exist in the inner circle. They conceive of social relationships in terms of hierarchical exchanges. The outer circle is a buffer zone between the village and the wilderness that circles it.

Placing the model of the diameter-divided concentric structure next to the model of the circle within a circle structure, Lévi-Strauss infers that the circle within a circle structure is an intermediary between a diameter-divided structure and a triadic structure that comes into existence in the first instance as an inference. It is as though the conflicting conceptions of space projected into existence a third configuration, a phantom overlap that acts as intermediary to the conflicting configurations.

Bion has a similar proposal when he encourages the reader to discover an affinity between the nature of the phantom overlap and the nature of the after-light. In terms of the medical model, an observer who perceives an intense light, then closes his eyes, and perceives an after-light, thinks of the afterlight as a residue of the intense light impression. The after-light is as dependent on the intense light as a shadow is dependent on a certain relationship of light. But in terms of the religious vertex, the relationship of light and after-light is not one of binary subordination. The after-light is an intermediary between the intense light and the unknowable "O". Similarly, the circle within a circle structure is an intermediary (like the after-light) between the diameter-divided structure and a triskelion structure that is, when translated into Bion's model, an agent for "O". Lévi-Strauss describes it as having "no function except that of permitting [the particular] society to exist."

> It would not be the first time that research would lead us to
> institutional forms which one might characterize by a zero value [...].
> This is the problem posed by the existence of institutions having no
> function other than that of giving meaning to the society in which they
> are found (Lévi-Strauss, 1956 [in 1977, p.159]).

Kantian man thinks of himself as a subject that coincides with the world as object. He may have doubts; the noumena cannot be known, for instance, and a hidden formal organization in thought determines the nature of events. But in so far as he coincides with the world, Kantian man knows that, doubts withstanding, the world is instrumental to his needs, and he is able to fine-tune the instrument. His relationship to the world resembles the two-phratries village structure of the *Dual Organization* paper. He and his imaginary twin, as preliterate man, do not realize the extent of their opposition because they do not realize that each of them uses the contact barrier between them as a variable or floating signifier: the contact barrier signifies whatever they need it to signify. A misconception of coincidence occurs in this way.

Sensitive to the power of the "other", Lévi-Strauss does not think to possess myth: it possesses him, in the same way as he allows the sounds of music to possess him. In an essay on Jean-Jacques Rousseau, he writes that "when I hear music, I listen to myself through it [...] music lives itself through me" (1962b [in 1976, p.39]). In music and myth, the self does not use the instrument of understanding in a Kantian way; rather, music as an instrument of understanding determines the self and renders the subject–object framework redundant. "Music has its being in me, and I listen to myself through it" (1964 [in 1970,p.17]). By way of music, the listener discovers types of structure that are without a centre to them because they are messages from nowhere, like forms of cosmos that arise from the void. "If it is now asked where the real centre of the work is to be found, the answer is that this is impossible to determine" (1964 [in 1970, p.17]).

In a sense the culture of music has replaced the culture of myth. In much the same way, the culture of atonality has undermined the sovereignty of tonal tempering. For Lévi-Strauss, the transformation of myth into music occurred in seventeenth-century opera. J. S. Bach's *The Art of the Fugue* marks the watershed. Music has "completely changed its traditional shape in order to take over the intellectual as well as emotive function that mythical thought was giving up more or less at the same period" (Lévi-Strauss, 1978, p.46). So far as the imagination of Lévi-Strauss is concerned, the fact that *The Art of the Fugue* exists destroys any social utility that myth might have had.

Atomization

In his writing on schizophrenia, Bion describes a patient as smashing up thoughts into minute fragments; he may then join the smashed-up thoughts as bizarre objects. The act of smashing confirms the existence of a certain model in which parts have a relationship to the whole. It is not possible to verify the existence of this idea. It is an imaginative conjecture concerning an analyst's experience in a session. The object may turn out to be one that is dissolvable, rather than one that can be smashed. According to Charles Rosen, atonality arouses terror in certain people because its model is one of saturation and not demarcation (Rosen, 1975, p.70). The nature of fundamental constituents in the life of the mind is problematic; and Bion and Lévi-Strauss can do no more than broach the problem. Lévi-Strauss has written, with the avowed aim to shock, that "The ultimate goal of the human sciences [is] not to constitute but to dissolve man. [...] To study man one must learn to look from afar" (1962c [in 1972, p.247]). Bion has drawn attention to the idea that particles of thought can take on a depressive formation as psychic raindrops gathered into a cloud of unknowing.

Rousseau's understanding of the chromatic as a coloured pattern is similar to the Amerindian conception of the rainbow. Arthur Hyatt Williams (personal communication) has suggested that a rainbow may evoke dread as an emblem for a certain form of paranoid-schizoid configuration. "As a category of human understanding, [the chromatic] implies a conscious or unconscious apprehension of a coloured pattern" (Lévi-Strauss, 1964, p.280). Synaesthetic intuitions are inseparable from the dissolution of forms.

Reciprocity occurs in the villages of the *Dual Organisation* paper because no one is able to acknowledge the existence of misunderstanding. In *Totemism* Lévi-Strauss has described an inversion of this situation: agreement arises through an act that destroys the very fact of recognition. Lévi-Strauss describes cataclysm as a form of 'negativised being'.

> We imagine infirmity and sickness to be deprivations of being and therefore evil. However, if death is as real as life, and if therefore everything is being, all states, even pathological ones, are positive in their own way. *'Negativised being'* is entitled to occupy a whole place within the system, since it is the only conceivable means of transition between two "'full' states" (Lévi-Strauss, 1964 [in 1970, p.53]).

The opposite to the phantom intermediary that reconciles is the phantom intermediary that splits moieties, often as a thunderbolt. An Ojibwa myth recounts how the five Ojibwa clans of catfish, crane, loon, bear, and marten came into existence when six anthropomorphized supernatural beings emerged from the ocean and mingled with humanity. The six supernatural beings had to be reduced to five for the two series (of supernatural beings and clans) to complement each other. A gap had to arise from the act of reduction, so that thinking by metaphor, as in Bion's theory of oscillation, could find a space in which to operate. The sixth supernatural being, whose eyes were covered, yearned to look at the Indians but did not dare to do so. Eventually he could not resist lifting the veil from over his eyes: his unintended glare killed instantly one of the human beings. His intentions had been friendly, but the glare in his glance inflicted death. His companions were forced to banish him, and he returned to the ocean (1962a [in 1964, p.19]). The originator of reduction is himself reduced (1964 [in 1970, p.53]): either he is denied the use of sight, or the nature of his sight is incompatible with the situation he has entered into, and he must destroy a member of a complementary series of beings. The supernatural being is a non-material sign that has the power to transform material signs (in the same way as Bion's dead war companions had the "occult" power to translate him into being a ghost). A closed system requires an operator that is alien to it, and of a different order from it, in order to bring about semantic transformation. The existence of classification is inseparable from an act of breakdown, in which the non-material signs of hallucination can form.

In a Tipokian myth, a god who races against the human beings, slips and then – feigning the state of being lame – snatches up many of the provisions of the feast. He stumbles when making an escape and drops four different fruits: a coconut, a taro, a breadfruit, and a yam – which are then held to be sacred because of their relationship to bodily parts of the various gods (1962a [in 1964, pp.25–26]). Underlying Lévi-Strauss's structuralism is a postulate that is fundamental to modernism as well as to psychoanalysis: that Kantian man was misled in thinking to have control over the world that he described.

The Weaving and Un-weaving of Relationships

Heraclitus endorses a certain confidence in rationality or logos when he says that the way up is the way down. Presumably he dissents from someone who says that the way up and the way down are not the same; or that if they are the same, that they are evidence of some process of un-weaving.

Two truisms stand in the way of understanding the anti-logos position. One is that *the world is as it is*; and the other truism is that *the concept of reversal is essential in describing the world*. Anti-logos thinking ignores these truisms. The way up and the way down, the way forward and the way backward are dissimilar. A canoe that moves down river requires a different length of time from a canoe that moves up river. Tallies, if they fit together, do so without reason, since there is no pre-established harmony. Something that moves in one direction may come apart from something that moves in the opposite direction. The concept of reversibility is implausible in a world in which the excluded middle is included as a variable and as a variable moreover that is liable to be destroyed. The world is a cultural construction, an act of *bricolage*; it is not what it seems to be.

> Sacrifice is an absolute or extreme operation that relates to an intermediary object. It resembles, while being opposed to them, the rites termed "sacrilegious", such as incest, bestiality, etc., which are intermediary operations relating to extreme objects (Lévi-Strauss 1962c [in 1972, p.225]).

Some cultures assume an affinity between the carving up of a bullock in the act of sacrifice and the classification of the various edible parts of the body and the rules that determine the assignation of women in marriage. "The methods for distributing meat in this part of the world are no less ingenuous than for the distribution of women" (Lévi-Strauss, 1949 [in 1969, p.33]). "In Ndembu culture, body is *prima materia*, undifferentiated substance, like a potter's clay out of which a culture fashions its meanings" (Turner, 1967, p.98). Body is a cosmic impress in the sign language of hallucination, as in the concrete equation by means of which the dismembered ritual state of a wife's body is no different from the formation of certain constellations in the night sky.

The wrought, even tortured surface of masks in initiation rites evokes negation as equal in its scope to plenitude. Two-dimensional and warped, masks are both intermediaries and variables in their ability both to link and to extirpate. They are the two sides of an intersection, and they imply that in the coming together of the two sides, the intersection marks an unstable coincidence.

Optic Glass: The Nipple–Tongue as Preconception

6. THE ROLE OF HALLUCINATION IN A MOTHER-INFANT OBSERVATION

One of the cultures of hallucination devolves around an attempt to establish correspondences as surrogates for a system of coincidences. Such cosmologies carry, as metaphors, an emotionality that otherwise would be without articulation. The tenderness of love in the mother–infant relationship draws attention to the nature of this quality of feeling.

It is not possible to find a compatible point between the concrete thinking of oral phantasy in the infant and the span attributed to maternal reverie. Concrete thinking and reverie – beta and alpha thinking – cannot be reconciled. The mouth that sucks has modes of awareness that are different in kind from the modes of awareness that it attributes to the nipple. I presume that the gap it senses between these kinds of apprehension is a source for intuitions concerning the tragic element in life.

An infant, observed in an infant observation, poignantly realized the nature of the gap. The latent failure in coincidence between the concrete nature of his oral phantasies and the culture of maternal reverie became a manifest failure at the time of his weaning. The observer of the infant informed the infant observation group that M's mother was about to wean him and she asked: does weaning mean the total end of the breast experience, or does it cover the state of transition between breast-feeding and spoon feeding? The question took on depth in the light of the circumstances that she then described.

M is seven months. He moves his hands in a circular and meaningful way, as though taking the outer world inside himself. He appears to have a robust sense of the relationship of the world outside him and of the world inside him. Since his earliest days, his mother has been inclined to retreat from his intensity; this is noticeable when she is feeding him. M does not reveal from his behaviour whether he is intimidated by the persecutory behaviour of an elder brother, although he has some reason to be intimidated. The environment of the family is one that is pain-avoiding and self-idealizing.

The weaning process begins. His mother seems to retreat from any evidence that he might be suffering. The first time the observer saw M being spoon-fed, she saw the spoon approach his mouth and she was shocked. She saw an M who was new to her, indeed an M who might have been the opposite of the passionate breast-attached baby that she had known. He shrank back and his face fell apart; saliva dribbled out of his mouth.

Certain members of the seminar group wondered whether M had recoiled at the hardness of the spoon. But the meaning of the incident depended on another incident, whose significance was to be realized later in the observation. M, it became clear, had removed from his mother the meaning of his mouth space, in which the passion and reverie of intimacy was in part located and projected it into his relationship with the observer. His mother was left to carry his jealousy at any intimacy. Very conscious of meaningful looks, he kept watch of his mother out of the corner of his eyes to make sure that he did not add to her jealousy. He gave the observer intense surreptitious looks, mingling desire and reproach. The mother adroitly managed to feed her two boys, without much emotional involvement in either of them. Her manner of feeding the boys, her unusual capacity for managerial juggling, carried the idea of some factor needed to keep the breasts alive as an illusion, as they "died" between mother and infant during the weaning process.

In part identified with this activity, M kept shaking a bunch of plastic keys. He shook them up and down with helpless impetuosity, as though regulating a breast that might be controlled by rhythm. But his attempt at regulation was ineffective, and he began to pull at his fingers as though pulling them out. The observer thought of him as being like a bereft old man.

The splitting off and projection of the capacity for symbolization into the observer, represented by the passionate mouth–breast attachment, had left M vulnerable to the projection into him of a state of incoherence, which the disintegration of the expression on his face reflects. He experiences the spoon as the function of discontinuity. Its "hardness" is a conception of beta elements, an intolerability in thought process, and not a material hardness; it is as though the softening powers of reverie exchange with a mother had been taken away from him. The oneness of the spoon, as against duality of the breasts invades mouth with impacted beta elements that communicate miscarriage, the tragic in an insupportable guise. Invaded by a ghost or anti-symbol, M becomes the ghost of miscarriage and falls apart. But what kind of ghost faces him? The hardness of the spoon suggests the impact of a poltergeist's missile.

The observer visits the family once a week, and she is associated with discontinuity (that is, of distances in space and time experienced as gaps); and in observing M, she opens herself to being the type of container for a certain type of benevolent experience. Infants often fall in love with observers for other than their personal qualities (although these may be loveable) because the observers carry a breast function that actual mothers may be unable to support. (The function, in fact, exists outside space and time.) Observing means being able to enter into a non-coercive reverie exchange with the other: attending to each other and letting the other be for the sake of being. This activity invites feeling of love.

The observer in this case is a suitable recipient for M's projection of a split-off conception of the good mouth capable of intimacy, the imaginary space in which a symbol may form. She carries an experience that he is in the process of losing, since it is equated with a mouth space that must suffer the loss of the breast as an object related to a disinterested yet loving glance; and if the experience contains within itself the magnitude of the imaginative, it does so because mouth is the site for an archaic equation of sensation with the macroscopic and microscopic alternations in magnitude of a mother's thought. Weaning can allow the equation to transform into processes of identification, and free process from the concrete thinking of mouth space.

Changes in scope of this kind enact an unconscious phantasy in the mother's mind concerning procreation. Her powers for reverie, as an ideal, are like the magnifying powers of a telescope that seems to extend into nowhere and to discover stars that have not been previously recognised. A way of describing the means by which the primal couple "know" a conception is to say that they draw a star into the orbit of human culture. Out of the unpredictable magnitude of archaic orality, as a model for passion, emerges the pain of quantification: loss is associated with a measuring of distance in space and time, represented by the presence of an observer who gives thoughtful attention to an infant, and yet comes and goes and stays for only a short time once a week.

Mouth Space and its Relationship to Magnitude in a Mother's Thoughts

A striking fact about the accounts that observers bring to an infant observation group is their evocation of a dream-like spatiality in the listener. One area of spatiality is related to the setting for the observation and the unusual psychic significance sometimes invested in the spaces and shapes of rooms and in the architectural configuration of the home. Another area of spatiality is related to the infant itself, which may be experienced as too close to be thought about or too distant to be focused on. On such occasions, observers can look at the baby as though in projective identification with some telescopic magnifier in a mother's mind that reaches out into the unknown and "discovers" a future life. The infant's eyes signal astral intimations; they are beings that yearn to be made actual. (A patient tormented by an image in a television program that showed a glass jar that contained pickled eyes associated the image to her own experience of having undergone without emotion a number of abortions.)

The heightened sense of spatiality is a function of infant orality.

Sucking is to know magnitude, an emotional attribute of the "other" that concrete thought requires the contact barrier to translate into meaning. The dynamic to the belief that concrete oral sensations are the whole world is the partial introjection of a mother's capacity for reverie. A phantasy of this kind is fundamental to archaic cosmologies. The evocation of such beliefs in the reverie of the infant observation group (the group uses the "eyes of the mind" as though they were a mouth) suggests that the modality by which the charisma of orality operates is twofold. The group are in concrete equation with a mouth space that in turn is in concrete equation with the powers of reverie of the maternal breast. The reciprocal relation of infant mouth space and breast depends on an equation between them concerning the nature of magnitude to space and time. Magnitude is an agent for reverie and passion. If it becomes attenuated as a determining factor in the measure of space and time in intimacy, it correspondingly intensifies with a lack of inhibition into absolute conceptions of an everything or nothing kind as a phantasy about the cosmos.

An effective weaning frees mind from the belief that thought depends on a "primal articulation": the belief that thought, as it develops, discovers the various forms of script – including geometric or perspectival mappings of sensation as facts in the world rather than as conventions. The concrete equation thinking characteristic of orality when it is charismatic indicates an existence of mind outside the constraints of space–time grammar. People with hypochondriacal sensations of a heart attack are inclined erroneously to locate their heart, and the source of heart pain, at a point beneath the left nipple. In unconscious identification, the infant in the self thinks of its mother's right breast as the site of the healthy medical-vertex baby who will fulfil its life through its body, while it thinks of the left breast as the site of "O", misconceived of as an abortion or some catastrophe linked to murder and suicide. The left breast "locates" two personifications in phantasy: the imaginary twin of the paranoid-schizoid position and the imaginary twin of the depressive position. One twin projects terror; the other twin is related to grief. The suffering and death of the second twin is capable of transforming through hallucinosis the *mundus* or mouth of oral thought into reverie. M's splitting off of the mouth–breast intimacy into the observer and his splitting off of the mouth–dying breast experience into his mother reflects a part-object split between two breasts. The mouth that realises the split possibly has no concept of the womb.

Lévi-Strauss fears that a chromaticism that is intrinsic to tonality is liable to overwhelm tonality by a process of saturation. The conditions of demarcation that determine tonality cannot make sense of a system that operates by saturation. A pain that is unacceptable because its nature is beyond understanding (it is as though it came from an alien environment) will be experienced as a form of indigestion in sensation (like the "hardness" of a spoon). The "hardness" of the spoon enacts depressive threshold phantasies of suicide and murder.

M and his mother interchange a conception of space, time and body, one triad of the mind. There are other triads. Miscarriage is a triad of body without space or time, an important conception in psychic reality, not an unfortunate deficiency. The tragic element is essential to any dimensionality in mind; it is not a superfluity.

7. "THE COSMOS IS A MIRROR IN WHICH EVERYTHING IS REFLECTED"

Alexander Marshak (1972) became fascinated by the culture of prehistoric man while working as a scientist at the Kennedy Space Center. He was convinced that prehistoric man had the capacity to think as a scientist and that his thinking had the intellectual calibre of the thinking of colleagues at the Space Center. He perceived man-made markings on dusty neglected bones found in display cabinets in out-of-the-way museums in France; and he pondered on the meaning of the bone markings; and he understood them to be a form of literacy that registered planetary changes. He assumed them to be lexical signs for a body of sky-stored knowledge: prehistoric man had observed the "facts" *out there* and had made a notation *here*, on the bones.

An astronomer who reads the sky as a text might think in this way; but conceivably early man may have discovered a different relationship between the markings on bones and changes in the night sky. He may have thought of the markings and the changes as together making a scientific object, in the Kantian sense of an object that has an order of succession mapped into it, in which the formal rules of space and time are common to subject and object. Or he may have thought of the markings and the changes as making a religious object that reflects the need in concrete thought to find a representation for kinaesthetic sensations associated with a gap.

In Lévi-Strauss's account of the Amerindian myth of Monmanéki, a dismembered body and a certain configuration in the night sky are, at some fundamental level, thought to be the same. Early man may have seen the markings on the bone as a notation concerning events in the sky or he may have thought that he created the events in the sky by making the markings on the bones. Or he may have thought that any attempt to differentiate the markings on the bones and the events in the night sky as irrelevant to the uses he made of intuition. And he may have thought about his dreams in the same way as he thought about the markings on the bone. Dreams notate the mysteries of "out there" (actual life), or they may, by their coming into existence, generate the "out there". Or they may deny any difference between themselves and the "out there". Early man was possibly aware that he was involved in a discontinuous enterprise. The data before him (marking on bones, changes in the sky) had an insecure relationship to duration. The magical object that he created realises a deep perplexity between here and there and now and then, a space that the vertigo of annihilation was liable to fill. Neither the markings on the bones nor the events in the sky were readable. They were not a translation of a three-dimensional occurrence into a script.

The thought-sensations in M's mouth are concrete. Out there, and yet inside him, is a mother's emotionality that he seeks to comprehend. There is a gap between the events associated with his mother's emotionality and the attempt in oral phantasy to comprehend the "oceanic" nature of his mother's reveries. The gap between the concreteness of oral thinking and the intuition of something other than concrete thinking that M ascribes to his mother's reveries is identical to the preliterate conception of a telescope as an instrument that creates the world out of a state of vertigo.

The literate mind realises that the image of stars on a computer screen depends on a radio telescope, possibly connected to the computer screen, that trawls the immeasurable space of the night sky. But the preliterate mind doubts the existence of this relationship; and it is inclined to put its trust in the Cartesian distinction of the clear and the distinct. It knows the image to be clear, in the same way as it knows a pain to be clear in its effect, but it does not believe the image to be distinct, in the sense that it doubts any judgment that locates the sensation here or there. The preliterate mind cannot be sure that the sensation, like the pain, has a definite location. It is religious in its doubting of its capacity for judgment. It is concerned with validation rather than with verification. The image may be an icon: in which case the telescope transforms some prehensile and otherwise unknowable information into an embodiment. Or it may be an idol; in which case the information is an extension of the subject rather than the object, and any notion of otherness (as in the otherness of maternal reverie) can be disowned as a delusion of a narcissistic kind.

M has to suffer the discomfort of discontinuity if he is to relate the events in his mouth to his mother's emotionality. He cannot resort to lexical thinking. He cannot be like a literate person and put his trust in the talisman of ascertained knowledge. A religious object is paradigmatic; it invites comprehension; but it is divorced from any source of reference; and its clarity is a source of puzzlement. The taste of the Eucharist in the mouth does not inform the believer of its possible significance as a miraculous object, because a miraculous object is one in which cause and effect, sensation and meaning, are either dissociated from each other or concretely equated.

Scientific objects of a Kantian type are lexical objects. In Marshak's view, prehistoric man is a Kantian who seeks to elucidate data that is mapped into the skies and who works with the Galilean assumption that nature is a type of encyclopaedia. Kantian man restricts himself to methodologies that demonstrate that he is right to think of the sky as a text that awaits its readers.

Literacy isolates the literate from the instructive prudence of the illiterate. M is fascinated by the activity of reading, although he cannot read himself. He watches his father (and possibly his mother) read the *Financial Times*. He himself gazes at the pages of the newspaper, with the same look on his face as he has when he caresses his penis while in the bath. Gazing at a newspaper page controls the act of making babies. When given a child's book from the library, he is troubled by the fact that the turning of a page exposes its fragility (so that in relation to its spine, the book is as vulnerable in articulation as a butterfly's wing). He glances delinquently at his mother in the hope that he can tear out the page without her seeing him. He does not know as yet how reading as a form of defensive magic can place him in a seamless relationship to the object and allow him to be one who notates and who has no need to question the source in authority of the notation.

Concrete thought intuits process as proto-process; that is, as two states separated by a discontinuity. The discontinuity is a zero function, out of which may arise the sophisticated notions of contact barrier and the beta screen, by means of which one event transforms into another. In concrete (religious vertex) thinking, there is no becoming: there is a gap, sometimes associated with annihilation, sometimes with zero as a variable, sometimes with the unknowable. In defining the idea of a becoming of "O", Bion takes psychoanalysis to the core problem raised by the existence of the depressive threshold; the fact realized by Melanie Klein in her 1935 paper that the depressive threshold and (because of its significant role in any theory of meaning) all forms of transition, are inseparable from phantasies of murder and suicide.

The relationship between a "failure in coincidence" and Bion's perception of hallucinatory phenomena was not random. The discovery of the capacity to perceive the culture of the one who hallucinates depended on an insight related to a state of catastrophe concerning a "failure in coincidence". Hallucination as a mode of exploration is an activity similar to music; it arises on the frontier between life and death; and yet the ideologies of life or death cannot claim it for themselves. The incongruity of the meeting of Perseus and the Medusa on the frontier between life and death – he faces death from the side of life and she faces life from the side of death – underlies the incongruity of Oedipus's meeting with Jocasta at an intersection that elsewhere in the legend is represented by a cross-roads.

A Kantian thinks of someone who is unable to grasp the concept of succession or of magnitude as deficient. But a non-Kantian who senses a creative significance in hallucination might recognize the absence of these concepts as a stimulus to thought. "Failure in coincidence" is a positive syntactical device in the sign language of hallucination. In São Paulo, Bion (1980) alluded to the "caesura as a transparent mirror" (p.108). The "transparent mirror" has the "caesura" attached to it in the same way as "coincidence" has "failure in coincidence" attached to it. The coincidence, as a variable, is the mother in *pietà*, who grieves a murdered imaginary twin, and who carries the idea of the "caesura", or failure in coincidence.

In the concrete thinking of archaic cosmology, coincidence when it occurs is amazing. It is a form of contact barrier. It reflects images, as well as transmits them. The Amerindian sacred circle that unifies the cosmos "is a mirror in which everything is reflected" (H. Storm [in Coe, 1976, p.180]).

> The placing of the sacrifice victim within the smallest of a series of magical circles is the final ceremony in Vedic ritual (Hubert and Mauss, 1899, p.231).

Anyone who contemplates magnifying devices and perceives magnification as a form of discontinuity may be perplexed by an idea that is as imponderable as the concept of "deep time". An infant tests out concretely in its mouth the meaning of the incomprehensible psychic spaces of its mother's emotionality. Do these spaces make the meanings in its mouth or does its mouth make the world of its mother's emotionality?

The preliterate mind feels its way about an emotionality that it cannot transform. It is unable to make sense of telescopic or microscopic functions of the mind. A clear image, a paradigm, is yoked to an experience of the indefinite. Unable to grasp the concept of magnification, it translates intimations of the concept into a metaphor for states of yearning. By magic the optical device stretches out and incorporates an object that is imperceptible. Possibly each of the senses contains within its natural use an unacknowledged prehensile faculty. Yearning extracts something out of a nothing in a nowhere. A clear image appears in the consulting room, and the therapist discovers in it a coincidence of opposites, a sense of clarity yoked to a prehensile yearning for the indefinable that of its nature must be indistinct (and possibly related to murder and suicide).

The culture of hallucination that Bion faced conveyed no intuition of an underlying spectrum to the senses and no idea of succession by degree. The idea of coincidence, against which "failures in coincidence" might be measured, requires a system of continuities to be meaningful. Bion described certain "revelations" that passed between the imaginary twins as too "large" or too "small" to be tolerable and compared them to the experience of looking through the different ends of a telescope. "It is felt to be the 'fault' of the instrument that brings such objects together" (1975 [in 1991, p.57]). Hallucination focuses on radical juxtaposition. Its creativity is motivated by the need to create a centre where no centre exists. It discovers radical separations, where thought in the medical vertex would discover one substance. In the religious vertex, the way up and the way down are as dissimilar as the ascent to heaven or the descent into hell.

The sign language of hallucination reaches out through certain feelings and links into the medical vertex. Men and women who yearn to be parents are inclined, when they enter into an infant observation, to focus on the eyes of the infant they are observing. In the minds of those listening to their observations, the eyes of the infant seem to grow, as though they were agents for an imaginary twin perceived through a contact barrier. The cosmos is a mirror in which everything is reflected. Passion and yearning transform the bounded world by overriding any sense it may provide of continuity. The infant, as optic glass, magnifies the powers of insight so that it takes on the immensity of the sky.

In a certain African myth, a woman unable to have a baby will sing a song in which she expresses her desire to be turned into an eagle so that she can rise up and steal a baby from the sky. The baby, identified with the celestial world, is considered to be "a soft thing" and is related to everything that is soft. When newly born, it is liquid and labile and related to water. When its umbilical cord drops off, it begins to be a "dry" or solid being; it has entered the world and it has acquired status as a social being. Transitions between such categories as liquid and solid, soft and hard, damp and dry describe the infant's development and continue until it begins to grow teeth, the hardest of bodily parts. If it dies before dentition, its mother buries it secretly in a pot close to a water source. The infant is still a cosmic being without social status. It is related by water to the rain that falls from the sky and to the burial pot, which is analogous in form to the dome of the sky. If it has died before it has become a social being, it will be returned to the sky from whence it came (Zahan, 1995, p.33). This is a cosmic metaphor for the relationship of a mother and her newborn. It is cosmic because it is total. It is true of an intimacy in which the particularity of the infant is equated with the totality.

The failure of coincidence between Bion and his hallucinating patient brings into question any claims made by the culture of literacy to be an orthodoxy identified with truthfulness. Bion sought to read the meaning of the session. He thought the fact important that the session might have a lexical reference. He used his intuition as a telescope to track down information that he was sure was there, although it was not available to the senses. But something went wrong; there was awkwardness, frustration and the onset of pain. Preliterate mind looks into the sky and does not discover a text whose meanings are endorsed by the phantasy that the sky is a text. It discovers a plus and a minus hallucinatory world; and it reasons that the minus world of non being, of ghosts, of the dead, has an authority that is not given to the plus world of hallucinatory being, which is sometimes incomprehensible because it is a world of grief that hallucination has partly concealed.

The void yields up at least two types of creationism. Bion has discovered one type of creationism in Milton's *Paradise Lost* – and Zahan has discovered a similar type in African myths that link babies to the sky. By a series of transitions that moves from translucency and liquidity to opacity, dryness and solidity, the void puts out a world of substances. But the void also puts out another type of creationism: a world of minus substances, of disembodiments, of non being.

In their separate ways, Bion and Lévi-Strauss are concerned to qualify the view of truth that assumes that every event can be "read" in the way that texts can be read.

8. THE DISAPPEARING TENNIS-NET

The person who is awake will believe that he is speaking the truth when he says that he had a dream last night. How does he know he had a dream last night? (Bion, 1980, p.105).

The transference binds embodiment to the inner world by way of a form that Melanie Klein describes in terms of a possible progression between two positions. Bion brings out the structuralist implications of Melanie Klein's model by evolving the progression between positions into an oscillation between reciprocities. An unknowable code activates an interaction between the paranoid-schizoid and the depressive positions as reciprocal functions void of content that has them generate meaning. Bion discovers the existence of "O" in a state of dislocation and dismemberment. In Kleinian thought, grace enters nature by means of a similar state. One or more imaginary twins personify the state. Acknowledging the existence of the personifications draws attention to the importance of "O". Definitions of hallucination and intuition have different values when they are related to embodiment or to the becoming of "O".

1. Bion defines hallucination in his papers on schizophrenia as beta element evacuations that mark a deepening retreat into the spectral nature of the paranoid-schizoid position. The evacuations imply some identification with a mother who aborts babies, and/ or confuses babies with faeces.
2. In a contrary direction, hallucination as a function of intuition is

essential in activating movement across the state of dislocation that occurs on the depressive threshold. In the same way as the existence of a photograph implies the existence of a negative, the existence of the world allows mind to conceive of its alternative. The tennis-net, as the representative of the light of common day, depends for its being on the existence of the usually imperceptible glowing reticulation. The beam of darkness creates the space for hallucination as an essential stage in the entry into the depressive position.

3. The binary oscillation of hallucination relies on a conception of the world as text. Leibniz describes the world as text, or its equivalent, as the realm of nature. The investigation of hallucinatory functioning discloses that the text is liable to disappear (as well as appear) and that there is then a loss of reference.

4. Hallucination as representing the inconceivable "O" is, in Leibniz's terms, the realm of grace. Hallucination of this kind marks out the nature of doublings and unities in images. By its authenticity it exposes the sham in cloning and fetishism.

Bion imagines a tennis-net to disappear in a beam of darkness. The beam of darkness is a hallucination. It is not night in a fragmentary form. It is not an absence of light. It is not an alternative to the real world; on the contrary, the "real world" is an alternative to it. The impression of light is an alternative to the image of after-light. The after-light embodies a real if unknowable world. Although it has natural attributes, it is an object of grace. Hallucination creates a space for itself and brings about unpredictable changes in the space. The tennis-net appears in a transfigured form as a glowing reticulation. The space that the hallucination creates, and the transformations that occur in this type of space, cannot be related to some quantifiable source. Galileo describes nature as an encyclopaedia, as though the distinction of nature and culture had no meaning. Similarly, Bion's tennis-net is the world as text, a system with some presumed reference to a body of knowledge. But it disappears. How can nature disappear without everything disappearing with it? The tennis-net is a cultural object that is linked by way of the concept of sociability to the primal scene. Hallucination makes the primal scene disappear as an actuality in order to reveal its reality as a glowing reticulation; that is, as a mysterious and unknowable function of the inner world. Hallucination does not destroy the primal scene; it transforms its meaning as an *imago* in the mind. In this way, the idea of the primal scene reveals a kinship to the becoming of the unknowable "O".

In order that the type of hallucination represented by the beam of darkness should appear, hallucination has to press into being the convention of myth. Myth and rite are pretexts that allow hallucination to enter nature-as-text. Hallucination is apparent when the oscillation between the world as text and the world as an absence of text is unpredictable, or when alternation loses the fundamental patterning of positive and negative function. The radiance that attends the birth of a child carries another child with it as a shadow. The child born into nature is accompanied by a child that has been born into grace. The birth of more than one child at any time from any one mother (or, in myth, the birth of one child from two mothers) upsets this rhythm. Many tribal cultures over-estimate the power of twins because they believe that they upset the balance between two types of being (sometimes thought erroneously to be the balance between the world of the living and the world of the dead); they are unpredictable; they disturb supernatural forces that should be left undisturbed. Bion's theory of the imaginary twin as an agent for depressive change discovers a new meaning in this type of intuition. It is as though some harmonious relationship between conscious and unconscious had been upset, and the unconscious had taken over the place of the conscious.

The beam of darkness, a womb gaze that creates a psychic space in which a new life has being, is hallucination in a benign form. But if it is viewed as an unconscious take-over of the conscious mind, it can be seen to have a destructive guise. It invades textual space to fragment it and to replace the content of the space rather than transform it. In the Ojibwa myth that Lévi-Strauss categorizes as "the origins of totemism", the glance of a sea-god who has climbed onto land inadvertently kills off an inhabitant of the place, but the result is fortunate for those who did not mourn the dead terrestrial. It creates a space in which concepts can appear.

The Oscillation Between the World as a Text and the World as an Absence of Text

To read the text is to have a sense of mastery. The signs appear related to a system that is knowable. Conversely, Saussure (1916) assumes that in speech rather than in writing, thought is governed by an unknowable code that activates the reciprocity of two functions lacking content so as to generate meanings. The reciprocal nature of the two functions defends against an experience of the unknowable. When it breaks down, the effect is similar to the disappearance of a text. A radio telescope trawls through the spaces of the night sky, and an image of a star appears on a computer screen. Claiming to know the source postulates that the night sky is a treasury of knowledge that the mysterious functions of magnification and magnitude disclose. An infant who perceives oral sensation as related to the span of its mother's reveries may conceive of her span in the same textual way. The nature of the span is beyond its understanding, but it expects to be able to relate to it as a source.

But why should anyone believe that some treasury of knowledge exists in the night sky? This is a projection of culture onto nature. If the infant cannot link maternal reverie to some source, then it may doubt whether it will be able to validate any of its oral sensations. If hallucination is other than destructive or other than evidence of deficiency, then not everything disappears when nature disappears, nor is everything lost when reference is lost. The text transforms into something other; and the disappearing of the text can be a token of a glowing reticulation. The appearance and disappearance of texts may occur against a stable ground in which nature appears or disappears according to conditions that are unpredictable.

The ancient Taoists resorted to a system in which the presence or absence of a text acted as a displacement sign: the presence of text was an indication of status, the loss of text marked the degradation of the one who has lost it. Those who knew the texts were superior people, possibly gods. Only the highest gods were able to see the original celestial writings written in cosmic script [... and] only at times of an imminent catastrophe [...] can these texts be transmitted through a series of intermediary stages, to certain elected mortals (Bumbacher, 1994, p.2).

> Wang Lie [...] once ascended Mount Baodu at Hedong. Unexpectedly he caught sight of a rock-cave. It contained a stone plate, on top of which there were two scrolls of the *Su jing*, the scripture of simplicity. He took them up and wanted to read them but was unable to decipher the script. Since he did not dare remove the scrolls, he put them back but secretly copied a few dozens of its characters. He showed them to the famous Xi Kang [...] who recognized all the characters without exception. Together they went to the cave in order to inspect the original scripture, but although the path was discernible, the cave had disappeared. Xi Kang told his disciples that obviously Wang Lie was not ready to be given access to this scripture, therefore he could not find again the entry to the cave (*Shenxian zhuan*, cited by Bumbacher, 1994, p.7).

The texts exist in a celestial library, whose system of classification is undisclosed. They appear and disappear. Prediction is possible within the scope of each of the units; but the existence or the non-existence of the units themselves is unpredictable. Logically, a synchronic situation of this kind precedes the emergence of succession which takes the form first of diachronic myths, then of facts. Birth and death myths concerning appearance and disappearance practise a split between two selves, one of whom dies and one of whom is born, either at a time of birth or of death. The significance of the split is enshrined in the rite of the sacrifice. The divine king is a concrete equation representation of "isness" or being, and this is evident from the belief that he carries the meaning of being a vertical axial between the sky and the earth. The act by which he is murdered extirpates the vertical axial and gives rise to two types of hallucination. One is a binary oscillation between concrete representations of being and non being. The other is an activation (by annihilation) of transformation in hallucinosis. *Destruction: creation*, as the coincidence in opposites on which the cosmos is founded, entail that the destruction of the victim should activate cosmic re-creation.

The ancient cultures of the Middle East attest to the double birth and double death of heroes. The dying pharaoh hands over his living self to his *ka*, or double, whose arms are raised in a geometric form as though supplicating the skies.

The appearance and disappearance of texts has a direct link to phantasies of birth and death. Moses allegedly had two mothers: one was a Hebrew servant girl, the other was an Egyptian princess. He is born twice as are Dionysus and Osiris and Oedipus; and possibly he dies twice. He carries with him (as a double, perhaps personified as an imaginary twin) an experience of abortion and dislocation. The birth of more than one child at any time from any one mother upsets the perpetual rhythm of the universe. It may bring about transformation. In synchronic terms "Moses" is either two twins with a single mother, or a single child with two mothers. Mass and void, the appearance and the disappearance of the text, are versions of the two mothers. Moses reverses the relationship between the substances and the mothers: mass becomes an attribute of the dispossessed Hebrew mother, while the void is allotted to the Egyptian mother. The divine king embodies the act of binary oscillation. As the sacrifice, he is repository for doubt concerning the truthfulness of sensation. Which side of the oscillation represents truth? The divine king seeks to validate thc icon and to invalidate the idol.

Moses discovered on Mount Sinai "two tables of stone, written by the finger of God" (Exodus, 31:18 [cited in Bumbacher, 1994]). The writing and the mass of stone appeared out of the void: either the mass of stone appears out of nowhere, or it falls from the sky like a meteor, or it rises up from within the ground like the Hellenic *kolossus* that J.-P. Vernant has described (1963 [in 1983, p.305 ff.]). The relation between *mass: void* is death-inspired, concrete and exhibits fusion rather than link. It is not symbolic.

No cause and no sequence exist outside the visionary moment of text decipherment. No human eye sees the finger that engraves the stone-tables. Continuity, succession and duration belong to the

Golden Calf. The religious object arises out of an unknowable source; concrete thought depicts the unknowability as a gap. Moses may have thought of the markings on the stone-tables as a distillation of macrocosm into microcosm. The markings are as mysterious as the computer image of a star. The totality is a text whose meaning cannot be misunderstood. The image on the screen contains an unknowable object and an indefinable space. A star that died millions of years ago appears on the computer screen as a living presence.

> "The silence was such that you could have heard a pin drop". In actual fact no pin was dropped and there was no pin; but the intensity of the silence was of a kind that everyone heard the sound of the pin that dropped. If we all became as silent as possible and then noted what we heard in the perfectly silent group, that would give us some idea of what the embryo might be aware of [...]. The person who is awake and conscious knows what he saw or heard or experienced in a different state of mind from when he was asleep (Bion, 1980, pp.104–105).

A group in silence intuits the existence of an object. Sense information intensifies or it is attenuated. Sensations of condensation or of rarefaction occur. The "optic glass" through which the group perceives the object is a variable. Durations in space and time disappear, and the hallucinations arising from the beta-screen assume a certain significance. An aural hallucination can counterpoint the intensity of silence; a spatial hallucination can exist in counterpoint to an experience of darkness.

A membrane comes into being, "high waters" that arise from the indeterminate. On the membrane, as though on a map, appears a clear configuration. Around it is the gap, a discontinuity hallucinated as un-girding water, an attenuation of appearance. In one instance: the cardinal points of the compass support "horizontal space in the manner of a pelt suspended at its four comers" (Wheatley, p.457, f. 20). In another instance: " [...] the four horizons were projected outwards to the cardinal points of the compass, thus assimilating the group's territory [...] to the cosmic order" (ibid., p.418). The Brahmans describes an assimilation of this kind as the "grounds of space" (ibid.).

Early humankind, contemplating markings on bones, as Moses contemplated the script on the stone-tables, may have had no notion of a here and there; and an absence of spatial reference that may be true of inspiration in general. The gap unfurls the continuum as script. The Miltonic void manifests itself in the calligraphy of water so faintly that only certain minds may perceive it.

The appearance and disappearance of texts is a theory about the finding and the losing of reference; it is a theory about the relationship of synchronic and diachronic systems. It is an analogue to the theory that the vertical releases the horizontal. The vertical is concrete and synchronic. The horizontal moves into the conditions of space and time. The relationship of the stone-tables to verticality conveys the impression of a meeting at the cross-roads.

The sacred being, king or god, links sky and earth, and earth and the world beneath the earth, in which live the dead and the unborn, separates out the attributes of the cosmos and places them in the four catalogues of the quarters. In death he undergoes transformation in hallucinosis. He travels through the underworld and like Hercules (and Dionysus) he must pass through madness as a stage in the journey of rebirth. In order to acquire knowledge, the initiate has to pass through the potency of minus K, and to meet with a system that reverses the model by which subject and object, mind and body, self and environment are able to communicate. Sounds and sights exist in a world in which there are neither eyes nor ears, and in which there is nothing to hear or see.

The plenitude of negation realises the fact that the kingdom of the dead has many dimensions. Music and myth arise from the grace of hallucination, misconceived of as the multi-dimensional kingdom of the dead. "Death in ancient Greece was thought to be sonorous" (Daraki, 1985, p.84). In the synchronic type of thinking of the ancient Chinese and the ancient Greeks "the perpetual movement of the universe depends on rhythm and not time, as in a dance" (Daraki, 1985, p.166).

The existence of the stone-tables mark a stage in the evolution of thought towards the world view of Kant and Freud, in which Oedipal prohibitions endorse certain legislations of space and time. The

Mosaic stone-tables petrify the dead ancestors or the enemies from whom the nomads flee. The Gorgon, who transacts with the living on the frontiers of the world of the dead, also attempts to stop the flux by petrifying the living. "Minus" loses its autonomy as the symbol of the culture of death and attaches itself to K as its negation. In place of the culture of absence, negation becomes a function of prohibition.

Fundamental to the ancient Greek belief that symbolization originates in the bringing together of two tallies is the more archaic belief that the doubling of the tallies is a way of propitiating the murdered victim.

The Problematic Nature of the Other. The Realm of Hallucination Personified as an Imaginary Twin. The Unexamined Assumption That the Other Is a "Double"

In one view, hallucinations arise from the world of the dead and the unborn. Rites and myths reverse the relationship of the living and the dead. A pressure from outside on optic and auditory pits, where eyes and ears one day may be, is no different from a pressure from within the skull or mask that indicates the seeing and the hearing of the dead. In another image, the imaginary twin and its mother personify grace, the linking of hallucination to intuition. Rites and myth reverse the relationship between the texts (nature) and the absence of texts (grace).

> A man strikes a light for himself in the night, when his sight is quenched. Living, he touches the dead in his sleep; waking, he touches the sleeper (Heraclitus, Frg. 90 [in Kahn, 1979, pp.213 ff.]).

Bion asks: Where were you in your sleep last night?

The self when awake and the self when asleep are mysterious companions. Going to sleep and waking up are dislocations. And yet the two selves live side by side, whether asleep or awake, in a relationship that inverts the mythic meaning ascribed to "incest" as a child in fusion with its mother. "A man strikes a light for himself in the night". Kahn observes a pun: *strikes a light* meaning "lighting a lantern", both kindling *and* touching, using vision to touch another, possibly to catastrophic effect. In the *Odyssey* Homer uses the same verb (*haptetai*) to describe Oedipus' act of blinding himself with a brooch that belongs to his wife–mother.

Heraclitus believes that mind in sleep knows a "private wisdom" whose value he doubts. True wisdom is a knowledge shared by minds when awake. Those who believe that "the word is common to all" will distrust the "enthusiasm of 'night-wandering sorcerers (*magoi*), Bacchoi, Lenai, mystic initiates (*mystai*)'." The Dionysus who excites the frenzy of initiates is a god who comes from the world of the dead. "Hades and Dionysus are the same. Those who celebrate the Lenaia [a Dionysian festival] rave over him" (Frg. 116, [in Kahn, 1979, p.264]). Dionysus as Hades is the invisible (*aides*) figure of Death. Kahn observes that "The identification of Dionysus and Hades [...] is mediated by verbal connections between genitals (*aidoia*), shame (*aidos*), shamelessness (*anaidestata*) and Hades (*Aides*)" (p.265).

Dionysus, rising through the root system of Hades, brings wine, joy and other benefits to the world of the living. The inside of the Ekesias cup in the Munich Antikensammlung depicts Dionysus as reclining as sole passenger on the deck of a boat (Daraki, 1985, p.31). A mast rises up close to his genitals; and a vine with huge bunches of grapes on it is tied to the mast. Neither sea nor sky is marked out; the boat might be travelling through nowhere. Dolphins beneath and beside the boat mirror the patterning of the various bunches of grapes. The boat is a form of Noah's Ark. It carries the essence of generation. It exists in the serene chaos before nature has been formed. The grapes are sky-essences. The sea is wine-coloured because Dionysus carries the vine with him as he relates depression to mania, and ascends from the kingdom of the dead through the waters of the ocean to the unattainable shining of the sky.

The carnival celebrations of Dionysus unite the kingdom of the dead with the living. During the three-day Anthesteria festival, the dead patrolled the city. Dionysus, as their psychopomp, presides over the opening of the wine jars and travels through the city in a boat on wheels.

The sleeping companion to the self that is awake knows a world in which space and time are unstable and boats travel on land or through the sky. Synchronic cultures reveal this type of experience to be recurrent. Pharaohs in dying travel by boat through the night sky. Osiris, as Dionysus's doublet, knows a double birth and a double death. Sealed alive in a coffin, he sails to Byblos as though a coffin could be a boat. Later Seth dismembers him beneath the light of the full moon and feeds his body to the fish.

Dionysus moves on a vertical line that links the depths to the heights (Daraki, 1985, p.20ff.); he relates the kingdom of the dead to the world of men. As the a-spatial and a-temporal cosmos that he represents transforms into the world of space and time, the vertical releases the horizontal into existence.

The Tiresias of the *Odyssey* is a figure of authority, the one person of flesh and blood able to survive in a world of shades. In the Oedipus legend his status as an intermediary is degraded. The horizontal of the Oedipus cross-roads, as a space–time emergence from the magical concrete thinking of the vertical, is commensurate with the significance that the legend gives to Tiresias as a shaman who rises up to link the kingdom of the dead to the world of the living. In his earlier writings Bion describes Tiresias as a degraded inhibitor of thought, but in his later writings he rehabilitates Tiresias' reputation. Similarly, he attempts to rehabilitate the reputation of hallucinatory phenomena.

9. FROM A PATERNAL TO A MATERNAL CONCEPTION OF THE TRANSFERENCE

The idolic nature of the double

The subject–object model operates on the basis that any alternative to it is accidental and phantasmal. It can represent the realm of "absence" as a type of doubling; and it can conceive of the imaginary kingdoms of the dead and the unborn as spectra that are deficient in substantiality (clones) or that have an excessive substantiality (fetishes). Clones and fetishes are conductors for the rarefaction and condensation of the beta screen. In this conception of psychic reality, doublings as mirror reflections, shadows, the absent as an extension of the present, etc., are adhesive extensions to the self; sometimes glued-on or sewn-on. Adhesion is a reciprocal for castration, and one modality is liable to turn into the other: all gain is experienced as fusion, all loss is experienced as mutilation. Doublings are the configuration of partially completed acts of separation. Siamese twins, rather than imaginary twins, personify the doublings; separation of such twins usually ends in death. Destructive narcissism, as a reversal to this situation, is liable to take over the configuration.

The ancient Greeks had powerful convictions about the double as a wide-ranging category. They classified under it three very different phenomena: the shade of a dead person; the "*kolossos*" as Vernant has described it (a material representation of the dead, often a stone stuck into the ground); *and the dream image*. They did not see the dream image as a form of thought. (The shade and the "*kolossos*" appear to be versions of the clone and the fetish.)

> It is justifiable to speak of a true psychological category [...] of the double [that] supposes a different conceptual framework from our own [...] The double is separate from the person who sees it. Its peculiar character sets it in opposition, even in appearance, to familiar objects in life's ordinary setting (Vernant, 1963 [in 1983, p.305]).

In psychic reality, the unique is a tripartite conception of the primal scene, in which an exchange between paternal and maternal understandings reflects a seminal gift between two bodies. In Milton's description of Adam's dream there are three factors. The father sacrifices the son by taking the rib out of him; the rib undergoes a multiple transfiguration; the wife/mother comes into existence as the organ of psychic perception. In Bion's terms, the conjunction of the beam of darkness and the tennis-net (the act of sacrifice) releases a glowing articulation that is like the constellations of the night sky, an emblem for the sovereignty of the organ of psychic perception. As Milton reveals, the interchange between paternal and maternal conceptions is extraordinary. Body loses any relationship it has to itself as an object of common sense; it becomes a template for the cosmos, a cosmic impress. The progression by which body, as intermediary between two domains, undergoes multiple transfigurations shows it to be the fundamental "birth" icon in thought. The insights of archaic cosmology, of which this is one, enter into body-centred psychoanalytic thinking in the same way as Leibniz thought that grace could enter nature.

Bion throws doubt on the conviction that all hallucination is subsidiary. From one point of view, the after-light is an accident of light; from Bion's point of view, it bears witness to the unknowable. It is the existence of the subject–object model that makes it appear an accident. But apart from the subject–object model it takes on the conviction of the principle of sufficient reason and as icon rather than as idol.

The Paradigm as Nipple Preconception

> The perfect city, as paradigm, is laid up in heaven for those who wish to see it (Plato, *The Republic*, 592).
> The image quality of the *logos* [is] the image quality of the entire cosmos (Ladner, 1953, p.7).

In the *Timaeus*, Plato sees the whole natural cosmos as the perfect image of the eternal paradigm (ibid., p.6). Insofar as the image is similar to the original, it is identical to it (ibid., p.7). The idea of the paradigm challenges the subject–object model postulate that all symbols are referential. The paradigm cannot be validated by the past because it has no past. It cannot be compared to anything because there is no point of comparison. It exists in relation to the indefinite. In part-object language it is a preconception of Meltzer's understanding of the nipple as a crucial link between mother and baby. Plato's "perfect city" is related, as paradigm, to an indeterminate (heaven) that mind cannot encompass. The relationship in conjecture of a clear star on the computer screen to a telescope's trawling of the night sky is a different version of the same idea. A figured and intricate intuition depends for its microcosmic beauty on some relation to an ontological mystery. The power of the thought in the infant's mouth depends on its relationship to the conception the infant has of the scope of its mother's reveries. The relationship of beta elements in the infant's mouth and the alpha elements of a mother's thinking validates both modes of thought.

But how can the indeterminate object of alpha thought authenticate so articulated an object as the elements of beta thinking; how do icons come into existence? And why should the unique have the power to transform particulars into a form of itself? Imagination, for Keats, "may be compared to Adam's dream – he awoke and found it truth" (1817 [in Forman, 1952, p.67]). The awakening takes Adam across a threshold, the nature of which implies many types of location: the threshold between Melanie Klein's paranoid-schizoid and depressive positions, between time in myth and time in history, between the state of being awake and the state of being asleep (although the physiology of sleeping states may belie this description), between life and death, between text and the absence of text. The transition is between perspectives on the same state rather than between states. Adam describes the dream:

> Mine eyes he closed, but open left the cell
> Of fancy, my internal sight, by which
> Abstract as in a trance methought I saw,
> Though sleeping, where I lay, and saw the Shape
> Still glorious before whom awake I stood;
> Who stooping opened my left side, and took
> From thence a rib, with cordial spirits warm,
> And life-blood streaming fresh; wide was the wound,
> But suddenly with flesh filled up and healed.
> The rib he formed and fashioned with his hands;
> Under his forming hands a creature grew,
> Man-like, but different sex, so lovely fair
> That what seemed fair in all the world seemed now
> Mean, or in her summed up, in her contained
> And in her looks, which from that time infused
> Sweetness into my heart, unfelt before,
> And into all things from her air inspired
> The spirit of love and amorous delight.
> She disappeared, and left me dark; I waked
> To find her, or for ever to deplore
> Her loss [...] (*Paradise Lost*, 8: 460–480).

Adam's dream sets in motion a thematic flow and counter-flow that is crucial to the grammar of this poetry.

1. The father as the "Shape" sacrifices the son. As in certain initiation rites, the male couple controls the beauty of Eve by an act of congress, in which one of the parties undergoes "death" and "re-birth". A phantasmal part-object representation of the primal scene, the wound and the rib, takes on meanings undetermined by the male couple that releases the counter-flow theme. The

infant in Adam does not so much dream as know itself to be an object in someone else's dream. To be so dreamt is to undergo the becoming of "O". A rite of passage, or threshold crossing, analogous to a surgical intervention, afflicts the dreamer. "Stooping", a term taken from falconry, relates Adam's fate to Prometheus, whose liver a bird of prey devours each night.

Virgil's Aeneas is able to travel across the boundary between the world of the living and the dead when he tears a branch of mistletoe from a host tree. In parallel to this violation of a tree, as though it were a living body, and the taking away from it of the mistletoe branch as the Golden Bough, Aeneas slaughters many animals in a holocaust. The tearing out of Adam's rib is a similar rite of passage. An unknowable code (the Shape) activates two reciprocating functions (the rib and the wound), and they become agents for meaning. The transformations of the rib "with cordial spirits warm and life-blood streaming fresh" invoke in turn the "uncaused" metamorphosis of penis, infant and mother as transformations of imaginary objects in the initiation rite. Adam's capacity for recognition depends on the espousal of the after-light in a state of perpetual transfiguration.

Freud (1927) describes the constituents of fetishism as an imaginary penis ascribed to the mother and an imagined experience of the mother's actual genitals as castrated – the wound. An ambience of surreptitious, possibly hallucinated glances gives rise to the phantasmal conceptions that Freud has observed and described. From the patrilineal point of view, women officially are without potency or threat, and men who ascribe to them the imaginary penis and the wound are deluded. But the derisory and magical "imaginary penis" of the male view, and the feared and magical "wound", have a profound depressive significance when translated into the terms of maternal reverie.

2. From Eve's viewpoint, the dream is one in which she and Adam foreshadow Mary's grieving over the mutilated body of the dead Jesus. (The puritan Milton would have thought this theme had been denied to him because his culture opposed Mariolatry.) The pivot for these conflicting viewpoints is the act of sacrifice.

Freud sees the imaginary penis and the imaginary wound as fetishes or idols. Eve sees them as iconic and as representing a fundamental truth. The wound is the suffering that a mother undergoes when she bears witness to the torture and death of a child. The imaginary penis is the optic glass, or the organ of psychic perception, a mother's capacity to reverie that comes into being as a transformation of maternal fortitude in suffering. The concept of uniqueness is forged through such suffering. Milton's intuitions concerning Eve's point of view, and his ambivalence to it, are reflected in a seemingly marginal reference in *Paradise Lost* to the "optic glass".

> [...] the moon, whose orb
> Through optic glass the Tuscan artist views
> At evening from the top of Fesole,
> Or in Valdarno, to descry new lands,
> Rivers or mountains in her spotty globe (1:283–288).

The "Tuscan artist" is Galileo. Eve is the moon who inspires the artist who is able to use the nipple–tongue telescope as a symbol for the organ of psychic perception. Eve's ability to inspire is a subtext to an extended simile in which Milton translates the moon (Eve) into Satan's shield.

3. In the patrilineal view, the mother of genius is the mother of the demonic. A reading of Adam's dream in retrogression would interpret Eve as a mother who projects obsessional murderous phantasies into her husband and children; she is not "seen" by her family because they are overwhelmed by her power to project into them; they are blind because they are possessed; and her family only know her through their guilty enactment of the Saturnalia. "Jesus", "Satan", the "reptile" might then be a damaged sibling whom the mother had wanted to murder in childhood.

The reciprocity of male and female conceptions of the sacrifice is widespread in Mediterranean environments. In between them is the transition concept of body as cosmic impress. For example, Zeus incinerates Semele who is seven months pregnant with Dionysus (this is a representation of the *pietà*). He seizes on the foetus and sews him into his thigh (the body as cosmic impress). Dionysus, reborn from Zeus's thighwomb, continues to exist in a semi-fused priestly state with Zeus in the sky (an analogue for Adam's celibate semi-fusion with God in the primal garden). In many cultures the act of sacrifice, often taking the form of the institution of divine kingship, is cyclical and unable to cross the disjunction into the dimension in which it is possible to be aware of it as the organ of psychic perception.

Milton's account of Adam's dream reveals that by the seventeenth century certain dream images had been isolated from the category of the double. Their unity relates them to grace, while the doubling that characterizes clone and fetish types of hallucination binds clone and fetish to natural contingencies. Clone and fetish are failed forms of spirituality. If Adam's dream is a prototype for the musical structuring of dream, then dreaming of certain kind, like certain kinds of myth making, is a means by which to represent ideas of grace that do not exist in nature. Dreams as agents for psychic reality function in the same way as Leibniz's principle of sufficient reason does; they validate the identity of indiscernibles "there cannot be in nature two individual things that differ in number alone" (Leibniz, circa 1686 [in Parkinson, 1973, p.88]). The theme of reference disappears as the subject–object model disappears.

A unique object has no source other than itself. It exists in the world transiently. Clones and fetishes are residuals. Fetishes are objects voided of depressive feeling, so that there is no mourning the loss that they represent; there is usually only terror. An unknowable operator has to create its own ground for being in order to be known; in this circumstance, the motive that brings about the object is the object; its entry into the world entails catastrophic change.

Melanie Klein has written that the onset of the depressive position arouses an impulse to commit murder and suicide (1935 [in 1975, p.276]). In crossing the state of dislocation/dismemberment of the depressive threshold, the traveller intuits "O" either as the paranoid-schizoid imaginary twin who is a premonition of oblivion, or as the depressive imaginary twin who is a premonition of grief. "O", when the depressive imaginary twin gives utterance to it, does not validate spatial attributes (like foreground and background), nor temporal attributes (such as future and past); it validates certain paradigms. Erroneous applications of space and time to the transference are analogous to Euclidean misconceptions concerning the grounds to being. For Bion (personal communication) the life of a good man is less an allegory than an alphabet in its combinatory powers; it is combinatory in ways that cannot be conceptualized.

The optic glass is able to contract as well as increase duration. The image of the star on the computer screen is a version of the Mosaic stone-tables. It is a cosmic contraction (the writing on the stone), in opposition to a void that the idea of magnification increases. The practical function of telescopes is secondary to their ritual meaning as sites of the holy. The magnifying powers present in a session are primarily experienced as sensations of awe. In ancient Greek thought, *logos*, as the syntax of reason, determines the cosmos (Ladner, 1953, p.7). In Mosaic thought, God translates the cosmos, the syntax of reason, into carvings on stone-tables. God, as concept, bridges the void in which the mystery of transformation occurs. Transformation operates without resort to a space–time model.

As parts of the whole, the parts are a whole that exists on the verge of spatio-temporal understanding and that is visible to a certain kind of "eye". They are fitful; they appear without apparent cause; and in the same way they disappear. But they are not accidental.

Existing between the imminent and the transcendental, the paradigm of the perfect city, situated in an indefinable space, is intrinsically without motion in its seeming to move. It is a bounded object, whose boundaries draw attention to the involuted and wrought intricacy of the structure inside, like a snowflake under magnification. The perfect city is complete in itself. It exists between the patient and the therapist. The fact that it is made up of related parts is of secondary importance. Extensions associated with space and time do not appear to be relevant to it. It projects an idea of dimensionality without itself being dimensional.

10. THE PARANOID-SCHIZOID VERSION OF THE IMAGINARY TWIN

Some months after writing this chapter, material came to light that my patient B was attempting to re-enact in the transference a relationship with his mother in which she had projected into him phantasies of having murdered in childhood a damaged sibling. B played the role of being the damaged sibling by being either the idiot brother who invites punishment for his delinquency or the false messiah who expects to be invested in so as then to go bankrupt. His mother had possibly projected the phantasy of murdering a damaged object into her husband as well as into her son: both of whom had responded in spectacularly disturbed ways.

B had reason to believe that his mother was a loving and, in many ways, a remarkable person; the split in her nurturing that allowed the murderous phantasies to operate did not make them any the less virulent. For years she appeared in the session material as an "invisible" presence, not unlike the dead mother that André Green has written about (Green, 1983, p.222 ff.).

A patrilineal conception of the organ of psychic perception would turn the meaning of the organ inside out and see it as a maternal means of projecting death into the infant. In such a transformation, Eve as the mother presides over the father's murder of her son. The telescope no longer trawls the night skies, so that a clear image can appear on the screen (the transformation of beta thinking into alpha function). It projects infinity as death into the infant. B saw "infinity" as a blood red carpet in his bedroom. In its redness he also saw menstrual blood and the battering to death of an infant – the butchery of an imbecile child who is the false messiah. He was only able to realize the existence of the carpet in the therapy at a time when he had reason to be appalled by the thought that someone might murder his son.

There is a link between imbecility and the capacity to be terrified by the eternal silence that so vexed Pascal. Blessed are the imbeciles (and the imbecile in everyone) because the imbecile is able to have some relation to "O". Prospero thinks to master nature; Caliban is possessed by it; and Caliban is able to receive the dream in a way that Prospero is not.

B is overwhelmed by the idea of his father. Evidence over the years suggests that his perception of his father as being damaged is accurate. His father and he suffer from losses in sensation: the losses add to his belief that he is a replicate of his father. His father is afflicted by numbness in various parts of his body; and he has fallen down and hurt himself quite badly. A neurologist has told his father that a certain life style is responsible for the failures in sensation. (The theme of the imaginary twin as a miscarried sibling is buried in this train of thought, but it takes a form that B finds too terrible to be able to tolerate.) He himself had been involved in an accident some years before, in which had partially lost his sense of smell. He is afflicted by a mysterious numbness in certain parts of his body; he needs to mute painful evidence. He is convinced that he and his father may have engineered their afflictions. B's failure in sensation is a psychic phenomenon as well as a physiological fact, evidence of an inhibition in the transference. He cannot be in touch with the organ of psychic perception because he insists on perceiving it as a fetish.

Adam is able to perceive the beauty of Eve because he recognizes her capacity to grieve over the death of someone other than himself. The dynamic of the situation brings him into an awareness of the unique. Without it, he would be unable to perceive Eve. She has always been there, as an essential constituent of the psychic universe. He had to change in order to perceive her. Otherwise he would have seen the animals (whom he is invited to name) and little else. Adam is able to move into a "coincidence" with the maternal transference. But B is unable to do so for any length of time. His failure marks an inability to move from the use of hallucination as a delusional system into hallucination as a factor in intuition. Failure in coincidence takes the form in the transference of informing the therapist that "we do not fit" (and one or other of us must know this) or "we fit so well that there is no problem of a fit". He is unable to coincide with the therapist in a maternal transference because he experiences the imperceptible nature of the unique aspect of the *pietà* as intolerable.

Failures in Coincidence in Terms of Clones and Fetishes

B says that he thinks of the therapist's state of mind as like a mirror reflection. "You look so happy today", he says, and then gives a list of perversions. He knows what goes on in the therapist's eyes. They are the eyes of a mother who says: "You are like your father. You are perverse. And I love you for that". He keeps out of the session a mother who mourns over the suffering and death of the imaginary twin, and perhaps this mother is inaccessible to him. He began a session by saying: "I had this wonderful feeling when we met of your warm welcome". (I was nonplussed.) He coincides with an environment that is an extension of himself. His condition is similar to an inebriate's perception of an environment possessed by euphoria or depression. He says: "I felt that I could put all my worries into you, and you would do my thinking for me". On another occasion he associated the therapist's eyes, which he experienced as rejecting, to a garden view seen through a window. He had reduced the view to a two-dimensional painting by le Douanier Rousseau, which he was unable to describe or name. He had turned eyes and landscape into clones. He had tried to activate a sado-masochistic link with the therapist.

During sleep he bangs his tongue against his teeth. He wakes in distress, with a sore mouth. In my understanding, he is trying to discover the meaning of Adam's transfiguration and failing. Discussing the way in which he uses his mouth as a womb to torture his mother's next baby is meaningful to him, but it does not modify the ritual. He hopes to project helplessness into the therapist who does not sit by his bedside while he struggles with his failure to sleep. His projection of helplessness is a stage in the formation of a sadomasochistic transference situation, a lapse back into the paternal conception of the transference.

Failure of coincidence by a cloning by which he is able to claim that there is no need for a fit.

He describes the clock by the therapist's chair as like a clock at home that his son has tampered with. He is able to think by way of metaphor; he is able to discern similarities; but a more archaic level of thought is operative. He experiences the clocks as an idea of a clock that is split into replicates. He could destroy all the clocks "in the world" without being able to destroy the idea of a clock. Conversely, nothing could put the clock straight if he could control the idea of it.

The archaic level of his thought invalidates the possibility of uniqueness in order to deny authenticity to the clocks. The first type of hallucinatory function asserts that indiscernibles exist, while the second type of hallucinatory function, which is intuition, asserts that they are phantoms; it is on this distinction that the reciprocity of hallucination and intuition depends. "The very hairs of your head are all numbered" (Matthew, 10:30; Luke, 12:7)

He denies the psychic reality of the Miltonic "Shape": the father who eats his children, the father who sacrifices his child to a god, the denominator of the many different spatial and temporal significances of emotionality, whose acts of denomination initiate catastrophic change.

The ability to move back and forwards on the threshold, to regress as well as to develop, is essential to any tolerance of the idea, let alone experience of, catastrophic change. Regression depends on the function of hallucination, while progression depends on powers of intuition that the therapist hopes will be strengthened in the patient.

Failure in coincidence, taking the form of fetishism as a misuse of psychic objects

He dreams that he is in a sleeping car on a train and that he is urinating into a small toilet. He switches his spray of urine into a rubbish container lined with a black sack, which he associates to an amniotic sac. His wife is close to term in pregnancy, and the idea of change threatens him in other ways. His dream recalls a bizarre object dream that Melanie Klein described in her 1935 paper on threshold phenomena. Melanie Klein's patient dreamt of urinating into a gas-mantel that was confused with a urinal and a frying pan.

The transformation of the imaginary penis into the organ of psychic perception cannot occur because he insists on controlling the meaning of the dream container as a version of the delusional object that Freud describes as "the wound". He cannot allow the wound to become a symbol of depressive grief.

Through an experience of metamorphosis, Adam discovers the psychic space in which Eve has being. B does not discover such a space; he uses the dream to fill a degraded representation of a woman's body with rubbish. Adam's dream reveals the grammar of intuition; B's dream reveals the grammar of an inhibited power of hallucination. In Adam's dream there are multiple metamorphoses of rib and wound as a process of substantiating the icon. In B's dream a deflection rather than a transformation occurs. (The switch in the urine flow represents the deflection.) Deflection versus refraction is a characteristic of the paternal:maternal modulation in the transference.

The transformation of toilet into womb enters into another transformation (and one that is characteristic of the archaic level in this thinking): it turns into a breast–rectum. He is eating at a table in the train with his mother and other relatives. The food on the table is in a toilet bowl. He is worried because he thinks the bowl may not be clean or adequately lined. He urinates into the object to destroy the capacity for recognition (in the same way his father puts the toxicity of the clone process into him). He dreads the possibility that the dead will murder him should he be able to sustain the capacity for recognition.

In the last two minutes of a session he says that he thinks that "this thing in my mouth moves around my body. It touches the back of my legs and gives me eczema". A tortured tongue–foetus transforms into a diseased eczema skin, which he wears as though he were a scapegoat. An object inside an orifice by contact becomes a diseased skin. The transformation makes no sense in space–time terms. A three-dimensional object, as a two-dimensional clone, projects a state of irritation into a surface. Like Adam, he is about to enter into the transfiguration of the sacrifice. A paternal conception of the transference might be about to change into a maternal one. One day he touched the abdomen of his wife, who was close to term in pregnancy, and he felt the movement of life within her; and for a moment his sense of smell returned to him.

Failure of coincidence in someone who gets the wrong end of the stick

The breast he has contact with is one with which he fuses, or confuses, in an aura of idealization. If he is separated from it, tantalizing yet meaningless hallucinated images unfold rapidly in his mind. When he escapes from states of fusion, he realises that the images are without content.

In a dream he is playing doubles at tennis and at the same time is looking down with contempt on a certain sports commentator who garbles words and phrases. The commentator has the same first name as one of the therapist's children. There is some reason for thinking the patient knows the name of the child. The garbling, associated with the commentator–therapist, is a hallucinatory re-creation of the fusion with an idealized breast that he projects into the therapist as a double figure of a father–son (or father–brother) who represent a murderous alliance (the "Shape" and Adam). If there are to be couples in his way of thinking, they are not to be an engendering mother and father: what he looks for is a fool's conception of a "cock-up".

In the tennis game he idealizes himself as John McEnroe, whom he describes as a "brat" genius. He does not allow the therapist a more amiable conception of McEnroe. He takes over characteristics of both father and brother and then dreads them as assailants. They contain a dangerous knowledge that he cannot transact with, or relate to, by coincidence. The reason why he should experience his father and brother's negation of his absolute claims over his mother as dreadful became clear when he acted out his idealized breast fusion with a partner.

It was typical of his not getting the right end of the stick, on any bodily level that he declined to use a contraceptive. He thought of his semen as a gift to his partner; this was how he thought therapists operated, and why not he? His partner did not see it this way. She said, in an unsatisfactory attempt at self-extenuation, that she had a low opinion of the father of the foetus and that she was determined to abort the pregnancy. He pleaded with his partner to spare the life of the foetus. He began to enter a psychotic enclosure, as though the impending death of the foetus were to be his death. He stopped eating. He became concerned with forms of physical deterioration – a boil on his neck, the state of the skin on the back of his legs – which related to bodily surfaces in a manner that was evocative of the quality of his hallucinations. He was concerned about one of his mother's friends, who was dying from cancer.

After the abortion, he continued the relationship with his partner. He was careful to keep any information concerning the relationship out of the therapy. It became evident that his fusion with the breast had contained within it some sado-masochistic alliance, in which sadism was projected into his partner on the model of *The Blue Angel* film perhaps, and this model in turn was based on some conception of a *pietà* as a murderous fusion. He moved to a better quality flat as a function both of hope and delusion. He talked of a pipe in the kitchen that the former owners had left uncapped and that leaks. The breast is without coincidence: it is either blocked (when it is attached to the mouth) or it leaks (when unattached to a mouth). B has similar anxieties concerning a damaged nipple.

Kingdoms of the Dead

In murdering Desdemona, Othello does not see his act as irrevocable; he would not murder her otherwise. He sees her as a figure in myth; she exists and she does not exist. If she is murdered, she will be resurrected. The imaginary twins and their mother are three narratives that can be separated or intertwined. In Othello's mind, Desdemona is one body with two souls (a hero with two mothers) or two bodies with one soul (twins with one mother). Either she arises from the death and resurrection experience that Adam undergoes in his dream (she is brought back to life from a knowledge of death), or she remains an agent for those who are unable to know metamorphosis. Separating out the self into a series of narratives is a way of maintaining a state of equivocation, in which the self is neither alive nor dead. The Shape, as Milton's surgeon, dismembers the body, but there is no transformation in hallucinosis. The reduction of experience into narratives is a way to defuse the nipple–tongue fusion.

Laura (1944) is a movie that enacts the schema of Adam's dream largely from the point of view of the paranoid-schizoid imaginary twin. Two narratives, sometimes running in parallel and sometimes in opposition to each other, modulate about a concrete equation of *almost not to exist* and *almost to exist*; and with the effect of enhancing the sense of Laura's beauty.

The First Narrative: Almost not to Exist

Waldo has two apartments. In one apartment the idea of Laura possesses him. In the other apartment, which he has given to Laura, he thinks to possess her by separating her from other men. He would have her exist in the apartment as though she were an extension of his dream life.

Waldo's narrative is founded on an error and a lie. When he describes Laura's entry into his life, and the way in which he took over her life, he believes that she is dead. She is not dead: but he is correct in thinking that in his mind he has denied her life. He thinks to have murdered her; he denies that he has murdered her; and he does not know that he has failed to murder her. In fact, he has murdered her look-alike. He controls her in fancy by acts of doubling. In the apartment in which she lives there are objects that are copies of objects in his apartment: a set of keys and an antique clock, in particular, by which in delusion he thinks to control her. Evidence of his power over Laura is that he should have her portrait placed prominently in her apartment, which establishes it as his kingdom; he keeps her as an object of worship in the kingdom of the dead. Laura is without vanity. The idea that her portrait, an icon to Persephone, should dominate her apartment is convincing so long as she is thought dead. The portrait is half-lit when the rest of the apartment is in darkness. An equation of *almost exist:almost not exist*, which is hallucinatory, is operational.

The Second Narrative: Almost to Exist

McPherson, a detective called in investigate Laura's murder, knows her only by gathering evidence about her and by investigating her intimate effects. He falls in love with her as an idea through the traces of her having once existed. In other less official circumstances, his prying and unreal relationship to her would be prurient and it would be indistinguishable in its intrusive curiosity from Waldo's interest. The two figures might be one person who has fragmented the object that concerns them (Laura) and the various means by which the object might be approached, thought about or related to. Waldo plays the role of the Miltonic "Shape" to McPherson as an inhibited Adam who fails to reach the dimensionality of Adam's type of recognition. Waldo is haunted by a certain object, but only on the condition that he can rob it of life. McPherson falls in love with an object that he knows by inference alone. He engages with Laura in a more direct fashion than Waldo, but he is sufficiently hostile to her to fail to provide her with adequate protection against Waldo's second attempt on her life. She survives in spite of his failure. The act of dreaming releases McPherson from the doubling or attention deflection that is Waldo's way of reversing dream process. He falls asleep beneath the portrait of Laura. The portrait, arranged by Waldo, represents his dream as a "fixity and definite", which is Coleridge's definition of the un-imaginative. While McPherson is asleep and possibly dreaming, Laura enters the apartment, so that on waking he finds that his dream, represented by the two-dimensional portrait, has become truth.

11. TRANSITION CONCEPTS

Adam's body is comparable to Bion's tennis-net or to the text that disappears. The body/tennis-net/text enters into a condition of transfiguration. It loses its powers of reference as the "Shape" operates on it, in the same way as the "beam of darkness" obscures the tennis-net's meaning as a signifier. The "Shape" and the "beam of darkness" have the same function. Body as "cosmic impress" is no longer comprehensible as a body. The becoming of "O" – which this is – entails loss of reference. Body/text dissolves into a "glowing reticulation", a preconceptive image of a mother able to receive an infant, as well as to grieve over its death. It shows how erroneous reference is as a type of linkage; and how much is lost when reference draws away attention from the cosmic impress as a modality of ritual thinking.

"Body as cosmic impress" is a transition concept. A positive way of thinking about failures in coincidence is to consider the nature of transition concepts. In states of transition, notions of reference disappear, or rather notions of reference indicate "nothing", if anything. A pain exists in the place where a leg had been, and mind creates an imaginary limb to locate the pain. Past and future are imaginary containers that likewise locate a pain that is otherwise inaccessible. Literate thought disguises evidence of discontinuity by use of the theory of reference. For instance, in literate thought:

> Scholars claim that swallows order their lives by the movement of the
> sun: their migrations mark periods of the equinox. Certain texts notice

that swallows move away in the autumn in order to hide in watery retreats (Granet, 1934, p.113).

But preliterate thought places the pain that arises from a severed limb in an imaginary limb; and it places discontinuity in imaginary containers. For instance, in preliterate thought:

They cease to be swallows when winter comes. By entering watery retreats, they *become* shell fish (ibid.).

Intuitions arise in states of mind in which sensations exist on the verge of spatio-temporal location. Thought is dislocated. An antagonist within the self attempts to shame the one who has the intuition by indicating this fact. The one who has the intuition destroys the intuition by seeking to locate it; that is, by seeking to "verify" or to "validate" it.

Transition concepts, as modes of intuition, belong to the cosmos rather than to the world. The cosmos is an imaginary container, an environment that is incompatible with the environment of spatio-temporal concepts. A pain inflicted on Adam as the self, an intrusive surgical operation, is transfigured into a pain inflicted on the imaginary twin, Jesus, and Adam must suffer the pain of being witness to the pain of someone other. It is not he, but an imaginary twin, who is tortured to death under the loving and helpless gaze of a mother.

Eve welcomes the reptile that enters the primal garden. The reptile is a type of pain (the monstrous, the untouchable, the unformed and un-located elements of the wilderness out of which intuition arises) that the hierarchical culture of the garden is created to defend itself against. Eve's capacity to receive the reptile is inseparable from the discovery of a new transition concept, verticality (the "fall" of man). Eve knows the joy and sorrow of the first baby. Imagination had been unable to conceive of this space, out of which new concepts emerge. In other circumstances, the baby is the murdered child of the *pietà*. A pain that is incompatible with the pains of a certain environment (the primal garden is not without pain) is liable to be transformed into Satan. The relationship of transition concepts to transformations and failures in pain transformation is central to the meaning of ritual sacrifice.

Six gods step out of the sea and meet with a group of people on land. One of the gods in touching shyness unveils his eyes and meets the glance of one of the inhabitants of the place, who is killed by the eye contact. The god who unveiled his eyes is sent back into the sea in disgrace. The catastrophe has created a space in which concepts can take on meaning. The meeting with the reptile creates a similar space: man learns from "Satan" the significance of verticality and conceptualizes unexpected dimensions in the world.

The sea and the air are environments whose types of pain are related to each other by an inversion of metaphor: they form a disjunction. The sea is a saturate of pain that concentrates itself into the eyes of the god who wishes to share his glance with one of the terrestrials. But eyes that exist in water are incompatible with eyes that exist in air. If pain is to cross from one environment to the other, there has to be a transition concept. Bion describes the negation of a pressure on a negation of organs of communication, the pits where eyes and ears may come into existence: the imaginary twin in a paranoid-schizoid form. Transition concepts bridge the gap between the pressure and the incipient organs of communication.

A woman complains about her husband's body. He is overweight. He has been physically mutilated by a succession of intrusive surgical operations. She appears to be talking about some extreme physical pain or deformation in herself that she cannot feel. She has to approach it through the body of someone else. The pain that she fails to know directly requires the linkage of a transition concept between a preconceptive "pressure" and the incipient organs of communication. "The link [...] exists before the things themselves and determines them" (Lévi-Strauss, 1968 [in 1978 p.264] quoting from Saussure's notebooks). The transition concept is possibly a deflection. Sensations arising from an oral fusion (a concrete equation between tongue and nipple) require the concept of deflection in order to transact with incipient ocular and auditory sensations. The act of sacrifice operates by similar modes of displacement.

Another woman dreams of an apartment that is identical to her own apartment, except that she is sure that it is not her apartment. The apartment arouses feelings of the uncanny; it is not her apartment and yet it is her apartment; it undermines confidence in the reality of things. In all likelihood it is her own apartment, but she has dissociated herself from it. An apartment that she had thought to steal from someone other is now an apartment that someone other has stolen from her. When placed within the model of Adam's dream, the apartment reveals itself to be a degraded form of the preconceptive link; it is a text/body that is too rigid to enter into a transformation. She intuits some unique quality in the maternal transference and retreats from it into an intermediate zone between it and the paternal transference, in which a certain type of intuition is degraded into being a delusional object, the imaginary penis.

She separates sensations that she has concerning the therapist's apartment from any understanding she might have of it as representing the therapist's mind. In place of the unique, she experiences the content of the transference as a fetish; she covets the therapist's apartment as a misunderstanding of qualities of being that she would wish to take into herself in the transference. She splits the fetish into multiple indiscernibles. She does not wake to find that her dream is truth; she awakes into a world of facsimiles. She does not meet the mother of twins, who would allow her to move from a narrative centred on her body into a narrative centred on the afflictions of the murdered twin; she loses herself in a system of mindless cloning. A pain cannot be revived in hallucination, but its insensate residue may be replicated indefinitely.

In the cosmos as imaginary container the void gives rise to forms. By way of the "rib" the Shape is able to activate transformation in hallucinosis. The woman who dreams of the cloned apartment wishes to authenticate the belief that the unexpected as recognition does not exist. She takes over the rib (or nipple–tongue) as the factor that inhibits the maternal transference from taking on dimension in the consulting room and not as the factor that enables intuition to occur in the transference. There is a sense of the uncanny in place of recognition.

Deflection

A woman in a state of psychosis has the thought that another woman, outside her apartment in the street below, is catching the light in a mirror and oscillating the mirror so that a spot of light moves back and forth on a wall inside the woman's apartment. The location of the woman outside the apartment is uncertain. Without warning, and frighteningly, she appears to be living next door. The oscillation of the mirror indicates that the transition concept of deflection is forming in the woman's mind and that the act of discovering the concept has little reference to space and time. The place of discovery is terrifying (as a form of the uncanny) because it intimates the proximity of a depressive threshold.

In order to paint on the walls of tomb corridors that cut into mountains, the artists of ancient Egypt arranged that a series of mirrors should deflect the rays of the sun down passageways and around the corners of labyrinth corridors. On one level this is textual thinking, referential, an ingenious resolution of a practical problem. On another level, the text disappears and ritual thinking occurs in its place, similar to the ritual displacement of fire in Indian sacrifice.

Deflection as a concept is essential to an identification with a creative process. It makes two out of one and one out of two; it enacts narrative doubling as a prelude to the discovery of the unique. It is a variant on the idea that the body has its phantom, a *ka*, which takes over the life of the body when the body is voided of life. But the *ka* is an aborted conception of the imaginary twin since it has no powers to metamorphose into the other; it cannot make the transition from being able to think about "my" pain to being able to think about "your" pain ("you" being the focus of a mother's love).

In the paranoid-schizoid understanding of depressive pain, deflections multiply and assume the angled corridors of the labyrinth (the corridors of the tomb). "O" is then the monster in the labyrinth. Frazer describes the monster as a masked king: the Minotaur, or the pharaoh laid out in death. In depressive understanding, however, deflections make up the prism of a mother's mind in reverie. The prism projects a spectrum or a chromatic that contains the spectres of alien pain. Cloning occurs if there is an incoherence in the discovery of deflection.[1]

> A patient says that he has no imagination, no dreams. What about that?
> (Bion, 1980, p.105)

A man says of music at a wedding "that it was so loud that he could not hear it". His retinas are damaged and he has gaps where he should be able to see. He experiences dreaming, as well as music, as functions of a human intimacy that he cannot tolerate. He has been through many therapies, and he claims that he had remained unaffected by any of them. He continues to attend sessions on the basis of wishing to spar with the therapist. ("Let's see if you can earn your fee".) He is desperate. He cannot remember his dreams. He brings laconic notes that he has made in the night concerning events that he has no recollection of.

The pressure that Bion describes as being on the eye and ear pits is an intimation, perhaps the first intimation, of depressive pain. As a preconception, as the idea of linkage itself, it takes the form of a fused sensation between tongue and nipple. Concepts of transition, by way of the tongue–nipple, activate meaning in eye and ear. The patient knows the preconceptive pressure as destroying, rather than as encouraging, the actualisation of perception because he is unable to conceptualize the nightmares that the depressive threshold activates. He seems to have no access to the imaginary containers of preliterate thought. Unable to experience nightmares, he is endangered by the inarticulate. He is unable to realize transition concepts. He exists in a void that he knows nothing of. He is close to suicide and murder, but he is unable to articulate this possibility to himself. Through a failure in linkage, he is unable to know the vocabulary of depressive change.

He dreams that he is playing tennis doubles (which in actuality he does and with some pleasure). He discovers that two-thirds of his tennis racket is unstrung. The remaining third of the tennis racket is a taut grid. He relates the state of the tennis racket to the state of his eyes. He says of his eyes that the visual field is crumbling at ten o'clock. An ophthalmologist said to him, don't jump into the Thames but you have a hereditary eye disease. What part of the image is incomplete? – wriggly? – unfocused? You will probably go blind. The dreamer thinks that not even two hundred pairs of spectacles would be of use.

The clipped manner of speaking which he ascribes to the ophthalmologist is typical of him. A discouraging presence in him tells him that his ability to experience the therapeutic intimacy is disabled. Not even two hundred sessions would be of use. The attraction of suicide, a theme often present in his thoughts, and whose existence he is inclined with decreasing conviction to deny, is present ("jump into the Thames"). He cuts out from any attempt to describe these transference possibilities. The ophthalmologist had tested his eyes by placing a grid before them, and in the dream he experienced the disabled paradigm as a damaged grid. He had attended a former therapy in another country for three times a week, until the therapist said, you are getting too dependent on me, you need a girl friend, and cut him down to two sessions. He dutifully began a relationship and found himself sexually infected. However, he relates to people, he meets with an unaccommodating object.

He attends therapy twice a week. He experiences the two sessions as destroying two-thirds of the apparatus that allows him to survive without human intimacy. He declines to take up the invitation for a third session, presumably on the grounds that a third session would leave him blind.

The idea of the well-strung tennis racket is based on the misconception that some primal articulation exists: on which grounds it is possible to classify experience so as to abort by classification any evidence of depressive pain. His belief that not even two hundred pairs of spectacles would help him implies that no means of transmission is acceptable. All systems are to him like an atonal system to which his ear cannot attune. Optic and auditory pits are under pressure, but he has no concepts to link the pressure and the incipient organs of communication. He describes his eye problem as a hereditary one. In a previous session, he had talked of hereditary disease in a different way. Walking through a part of his native city in Norway, which he associates to his mother, he saw a plaque on a house that said that a certain celebrated inventor had lived there. He had not known this and had been impressed. He heard a woman talking in a doorway to a man about his refusal to marry her, although she was pregnant.

"Marry" means realizing the link between pressure and pits as the initial stage in the search to contain a pain that is unsecured in space and time. He had visited his native city to attend a wedding, which he had almost missed because of transport difficulties. He goes to weddings quite often. He says that at some of them the Eucharist is offered, but he is unable to participate in the communion. Of the wedding in question he said, "The music was so loud that I could not hear it".

The dangerous object is a pain that cannot be tolerated, and it is faultily defused in being classified as alien. In thought space and time, past and future, come into existence as imaginary containers for an alien pain. The patient has no such deposit. The damaged tennis racket is unlike the portrait–breast into which Dorian Gray dumps the consequences of destruction. The portrait draws Dorian to it prehensively, as though a field of gravitation had become the gravitating object; the persecuting damaged object reveals itself to be in fact a depressive object that threatens development.

"Psycho-analysis is just a stripe on the coat of the tiger. Ultimately it may meet the Tiger – the Thing Itself – O" (Bion, 1975 [in 1991, p.112]). The tiger is concealed within the depressive threshold. It is always there, and premonitions of its leap can be confused with premonitions of oblivion.

He is a lapsed Roman Catholic. Before an Easter break, he dreams of throwing darts at a board close by the church where he worshiped as a boy. He refers to the importance of hitting a space associated with the number seven. I presume he is alluding to the Crucifixion and to the seven words of the Cross. He says, so what?

He would like to destroy the therapist in the same way as he would destroy his short-term women partners, who induce claustrophobia in him. He continues to hold on to the therapist, as though the fact of engaging adhesively with death was a way of postponing the onset of oblivion. He feels little passion, apart from the bitterness that he feels at being so lonely, and a love for his neutered cat. He visits a business conference centre with a colleague and is appalled to see a plaque on the wall that describes the building as a former Jesuit seminary. He later denies that he had been appalled. The shock is the shock of recognizing himself in the other. He reads the memoirs of C.G. Jung and describes Jung as "a psychotic". Through Jung (as the therapist's imaginary twin?) he is trying to discover a transition concept. He says that Jung's father was a clergyman, and that Jung believed that God had appeared to him in a dream. When he attended communion, Jung was disappointed because he recognized that the bread came from the village bakery and that the wine was of inferior quality. A failure to understand the point of things, a failure in coincidence ascribed to Jung, is characteristic of the patient. He can describe the sensations in his mouth accurately without understanding their meaning. He says that Jung, lying in bed, felt that he should meditate on a certain beautiful church: Jung imagined that God had arranged the fall of man and dreamt that a huge turd, made by Jung himself, had fallen on the church.

Over the years he returns, usually fleetingly, to the Jung memoirs. He says that Jung was terrified of the city of Rome and was delighted when a ship he was sailing in gave the city a wide berth. He dreamt that he was flying from Sicily to Milan and then took a train to Rome. He referred to Jung's caution in regard to Rome in an association to the dream. In Rome, he thought, there was a room in which the "authorities" had the apparatus to practise repression on students. He did not think the zigzag nature of this journey deserved comment. He pitched the dream like a ball into the therapist's court, saying *"that's it"*, in the same decisive voice as he says *"so what"*? Come on, earn your fee.

Sicily is the impression made on him by the dangerous object, Milan is the unthinkable core that it activates and Rome is the illumination that he cannot bear and that he relates to acts of destruction. He fears a tiger that he cannot conceptualize and that he expects will kill him. He is unable to separate acts of destructions from thoughts of destruction and he is unable to separate afflictions of destructions from thoughts about being afflicted. The church that Jung thinks of is inseparable from the turd that destroys it.

His mother bore a stillbirth when he was about three years old.

The girl foetus was her third pregnancy and died at four months; the mother had to bear the stillbirth to term. In his mother's house, he said, there was no talk of procreation and pregnancy; and he believes that his mother was cut off from the experience of loss, although he has no direct evidence for this belief. His father acknowledged the still birth, to the extent of saying that his wife had begun to stink (the church destroyed by a turd).

He is in a state of concrete equation with the cut-off mother and the unacknowledged foetus as a united couple: and he is unable to think about the equation. He confuses the tongue–nipple equation with the dead mother–foetus couple. He responds to his women partners as babies whom he cannot feed adequately and he deals with his guilt in failing them by cutting off from them. He talks of empty states of insomnia or of states in which sleep seems to drug him (so that he could avoid contact with his partner), as though he were a mother perplexed as to whether her breasts were empty or full, and who is unable to separate knowledge concerning the contents of her body from the presence of an unacknowledged dead foetus.

He referred to an uncle whose sight was impaired because he had a fragment of shrapnel in one eye. The uncle would regain his sight if the shrapnel could be moved. In the case of the dreamer, the shrapnel, as the negative hallucination or ghost of the stillbirth, an alien presence in the womb–eye, is able to invade him while condensed in matter, an equivalent for the spoon that invaded M. Unimpressed by the line of thought that would link the damaged tennis racket to an eye equated with a stillbirth womb, he was interested in the sounds that he heard from other rooms in the house, even more in the absence of familiar sounds relating to a child patient, whose therapist took a holiday of a different span from his therapist's holiday. One of his partners became pregnant and aborted the foetus; he insisted that the pregnancy had been "a figment of her imagination".

The Problem of Dislocation

"To a body of infinite size, there can be neither a centre nor boundary"
(Giordano Bruno [in Koyré, 1957, p.41]).

Infinite sounds like *indefinite*, and yet it is something other than
spatio-temporal duration; it cannot be thought about and it induces a
blankness, indiscernible from destruction, that enters into the image
on the computer screen, or the sensation in the infant's mouth,
destroying any link to the prehensile.

The image on the computer screen loses its clarity; it deteriorates;
it begins to resemble a medieval map in which a linear framework
contains blank passages. The map is unstable. A framework that
contains blank passages becomes a blank with bits of framework
moving randomly about it. It is as though the "things themselves"
had reverted to being un-located sensations. Any attempt to establish
the relationship between the image on the screen and the prehensile
power of the telescope, as in the attempt to mobilize a transference, is
experienced as a form of destruction.

Note

1. In comparison, another man has a nightmare that indicates the onset
   of depressive pain. A monster comes out of the sea and threatening to
   eat everything up. Eyes from the sea threaten to kill terrestrial eyes.
   The environment of depressive pain is inimical to the hierarchical
   environment of paranoid-schizoid culture, in the same way as the
   chromatic saturation of Serialism is inimical to the demarcations of
   tonality.

PART THREE

Transformation in Hallucinosis and the Institution of Divine Kingship

12. ANNIHILATION AND TRANSFORMATION IN HALLUCINOSIS

O gateway of the Abyss, I come to you (Wilkinson, 1992, p.139).
The greater number of telepathic intimations relate to death
(Freud, 1921, p.218).

In Bion's writings, the paranoid-schizoid and the depressive positions, as defined by Melanie Klein, enter into a state of transformation. The threshold between them (Meltzer, 1967, p.32 ff.) takes over as the field in which a premonition of an unknowable variable can occur. The two positions lose their status as positions and become essential *dimensions* of thought that reflect states of being rather than invite entry. They are perspectives, or dynamic vistas, that transform the meaning of living on the threshold, the human condition of being a fool who sails with other fools on "a ship of fools".

The "imaginary" in imaginary twins should be qualified, because the twin who embodies the paranoid-schizoid dimension is an emissary of "O" in its anti-imaginative aspect. "O" is then the tiger, an object of inspired terror. The twin who embodies the depressive dimension differs from the other twin in two ways: it exists in a meaningful relationship to a mother, so that alpha and beta thinking can enter into a marriage with each other, and it reveals how terror of the other twin is a misconception concerning the nature of psychic pain. Thinking dominated by the paranoid-schizoid twin is convinced that it *knows* reality. Intimations that arise from the other twin suggest that paranoid-schizoid thought is spectral. Thinking dominated by the paranoid-schizoid imaginary twin has mind traverse the threshold as though it were about to go over a weir and to be swallowed by the waters of oblivion. In error paranoid-schizoid thought believes that the condensation and rarefaction of threshold phenomena is delusional and does not mark a hopeful state of transformation. The extent of the difference in perception between the two twins casts doubt on the assumption that they might find some common ground in the formal and universal laws of space and time.

As the variable, "O" activates a state of *becoming* unrelated to any claim to therapeutic progress or cure. In the religious vertex, nothing progresses or is cured. There is either an evasion or a recognition of "O" by way of a *becoming*.

Bion describes a pressure in negation on incipient organs of communication. In the religious vertex, the pressure takes the institutional forms of *the sacrifice* and *prayer*.

Embedded in Freud's paper "The Theme of the Three Caskets" (1913b) are the motifs of the sacrifice and prayer. In describing the thought-provoking circumstances of a certain dream, Freud avoids the motifs, although they are implicit in his discussion. A patient dreamt of a friend who presented himself in the dream as "dumb". The dreamer learned that the friend had committed suicide at about the time of the dream and presumed that the dream had been a telepathic communication. How might one understand this presumption?

The image of the dumb man is similar to the image of the star on the computer screen, while the telepathy of a suicide is a misconception of the power of the optic glass to trawl the infinite night sky. There is a failure of beta thinking to marry into the alpha ability for reverie. If mouth as the realm of concrete thought cannot latch onto the organ of psychic perception, it is liable to enter into psychic space as vertiginous fall.

A woman had a dream about her mother as dying. She awoke from this dream in a startled state. Why startled? I asked. It took some time for the point to become clear. She was startled because she was convinced that the dream either killed her mother or in some other way was related to the activation of her mother's death. The "telepathy" of Freud's dreamer appears to be related to a destructive internal figure (the paranoid-schizoid imaginary twin?) who suggests that it can use the dreamer's dreams as instruments of destruction that attack the most loved objects in the dreamer. Perhaps a belief of this kind underlies the ancient Greek belief that dream images are doubles and not modes of thought.

In terms of the religious vertex, the suicide of the dumb friend is an act of sacrifice and the act of "telepathy" is a form of prayer. I am inclined to believe that this dream (which may have been one of the Russian patient's dreams) was a formative factor in Freud's interpretation of Shakespeare's play *King Lear*. Implicit in the structure of the dream is a link between annihilation (the sacrifice) and transformation in hallucinosis (the prayer).

In Shakespeare's *King Lear*, Edgar puts pressure on the optic pits of his blind father Gloucester; he describes in evocative detail the vertiginous sheer fall off a nonexistent cliff. He projects the image, with the power of the type of dream that implodes within the dreamer, into his father, who then is able to articulate to himself the dimension of his desire to destroy himself. He seeks to throw himself over the imaginary cliff and in so doing realises the inversion in meaning that characterizes his projection of a certain relationship of the primal scene into the beloved child, Edmund. "The dark and vicious place where he thee got/ Cost him his eyes" (V.iii.170–171). In paranoid-schizoid terms, Gloucester psychically projected abortion into his child by denying him legitimacy. In depressive terms, the blinding is one of amazement before the unknowable mystery of the holy child who contains within the act of his procreation mysteries that can only be described in terms of irrationalities. Mouths are psychically dumb for two reasons: they are lost in the gap that occurs between concrete thinking and the infinite spaces of maternal reverie; or they are struck into dumbness by the presence of a mystery. In the play Edmund represents the paranoid-schizoid imaginary twin; but embedded within his charismatic and terrible actions is the image of the depressive imaginary twin.

Bion is primarily concerned with the paranoid-schizoid aspect to intuition, *with pressures that operate from outside the subject–object model, that are inseparable from a tug into oblivion that is comparable to gravity in its power of attraction.* The pressure that Edgar puts on Gloucester translates into an incipient sense communication. It operates by way of two transition concepts: one is by way of *verticality*, the other is by way of *deflection*. Gloucester thinks to annihilate himself by falling over the cliff edge. As the double to Lear himself, he must take on the role of the victim in the sacrifice. But in place of entering the vertical as a threshold between death and life, he is deflected. He is like a fortunate patient who under the domination of the paranoid-schizoid imaginary twin survives the threshold meeting with death. *Ere Babylon was dust/ The magus Zoroaster, my dead child,/ Met his own image walking in the garden* (Shelley, 1819, 1:191–193).

A patient, who said *if I take one more step forward I shall die*, dreamt that he was looking down into a death shaft on whose walls were idealized portraits of himself and at the base of which his mother tended a fire that he associated to his father's death. He could not separate a paranoid-schizoid premonition of oblivion, the act of being sacrificed, from an intuition concerning the depressive position (the dream might have been an act of telepathy or a prayer put into him by a "dumb" friend). He could not cross the threshold in such a way as to be able to discriminate between hallucination and intuition. Some failure had occurred between a preconceptive pressure and certain incipient organs of communication.

It is possible to know the paranoid-schizoid imaginary twin as it is possible to know the spectres reflected in multiple mirrors. It is not possible to know the depressive imaginary twin, only to venerate him as the baby in the breast. By way of the depressive imaginary twin it is possible to escape from the patrilineal trap into the maternal conception and into a certain freedom in reverie. I shall focus on the important role played by the paranoid-schizoid imaginary twin in the religious vertex.

Vaughan (1977) has described the history of the controversy that has surrounded the issue of the ritual sacrifice of the divine king since the time that Frazer gave it an extended expression in *The Golden Bough*. I shall avoid the controversy and attempt a selective definition of the institution.

1. It is founded in a cosmology in which the absolute creation and destruction of the cosmos are inseparable. *Creation:destruction* is a coincidence of opposites similar to Coleridge's motto "extremes meet" or to Freud's understanding of the antithesis of primary words. Like the cross-roads in the Oedipus legend, the coincidence of opposites is not an accidental intersection, nor is it related to space and time notions of coincidence. It equates destruction and creation, microcosm and macrocosm, inside and outside, near and far. When thought enters space and time, the coincidence of opposites disappears and in its place occurs Aristotle's "excluded middle".

2. The God who creates the universe in Genesis does so by division. He articulates the dismemberment of the sacrificial victim as the grammar of the cosmos. The victim in dismemberment is the cosmos. In concrete equation thinking, the entrails of the victim are the celestial constellations. The planets revolve within the cosmic impress of the king's body as well as outside it.

3. The equation of destruction and creation has an emphasis in Africa that is different, let us say, from the emphasis in ancient China. In Africa the setting up of an act of destruction is ritually more important than the dramatization of the king's thaumaturgic powers. In ancient China, courtly etiquette centres on the king's formal and therapeutic powers as the integrator of the cosmos.

In Africa the king is the receptacle for universal pollution. He assumes the burden of cosmic destruction. His enstoolment is the final ceremony in the funeral rites of his predecessor. He exists in opposition to the clown, to the effigy and to his successor. Mockery and sadism characterize the nature of his murder. Macrocosm equals microcosm, whole equals part, and holocaust (mass murder) equals the king's death. In terms of the transference, the holocaust and the king's death are similar to the "unpremeditated blow" that Bion thought of as typifying the beta screen.

13. CATASTROPHIC FUSIONS: KINGS AND DIVINERS AMONG THE MOUNDANG OF CHAD

The first kings must have been dead kings (Hocart, 1954, p.77).

Certain African cultures revere the concept of multiple birth, of twin birth especially, and consider it a module for cosmic systems. The Dogon of Mali assert that Amma, who is God (and whose name means holding or keeping things in place), appears in the beginning as an egg made of four breast-bones. "A stomach" within the egg contains all the signs of the world. Two axial coordinates, at right angles to each other, divide the egg's "stomach" into quarters. Each of the quarters is identified with one of the elements: air, fire, water and earth. The Dogon give the point where the axial co-ordinates cross the name of umbilical cord (Griaule and Dieterlen, 1963, p.61 ff.).

The Dogon egg is a paradigm, a type of Platonic form; it is biological only by analogy. I take its likeness to a human womb as licence to describe the quarters as the sites of an air baby, a water baby, a fire baby, and an earth baby. The babies are related to each other by the axial coordinates, as well as separated by them. The axial co-ordinates function as a nurturing membrane.

The writings of Apollodorus describe a catastrophic version of the Dogon egg cosmogram. Zeus launched a thunderbolt against Semele who was seven months pregnant, incinerating the foetus and her, took the foetus from her womb and sewed it into his thigh. In time he gave birth to it (Apollodorus, c.100–200 AD, p.319). The membrane in this cosmogram is a thunderbolt and not an axial coordinate. The effect of the thunderbolt is to split the cosmogonic egg into two parts, each of which contains Dionysus split into identical twins, as though the membrane had become a mirror. One Dionysus twin is fused with the sky god Zeus as a type of ecstatic priest at one with the godhead, while the other Dionysus twin is moulded by incineration into the earth goddess Semele.[1]

Between the two images of Dionysus, one in fusion with Zeus, the other inseparable from Semele, is an unacknowledged dead sibling that carries the power to dream and to think and to read. If I put together the myth of the Dogon egg and the myth of the interrupted pregnancy, I come to the view that the axial coordinates dividing the egg, whose centre is the "umbilical cord", are membranes that keep together and separate the four babies. The babies within the segments fuse with their surroundings when some catastrophic state invades the membranes. The fusion results in an inability to think about the meaning of loss and it marks the breakdown of a system of sacrifice.

With this theme in mind, I want to look at certain data concerning Moundang culture that the French anthropologist Alfred Adler brought back from field trips made to Chad between 1967 and 1976. Among the Moundang the architecture of the diviners' circles and of the king's palace, which are similar, gives dramatic form to the catastrophe of fusion. I shall look at this data with the fusion of Dionysus + Semele and Dionysus + Zeus in mind.

At one time the Moundang were inclined to murder one newborn in any pair of twins. They put the murdered newborn into a pot, covered it with ashes and drops of water and released the pot into the river (ibid., p.232). They believed that twins took up an over-abundance of fertility, and they feared that such an abundance would exhaust the source of life itself. Giving birth to twins had the effect of closing up a mother's womb, so that if another infant were to issue from her, the infant would be a ghost. (This adds to the belief that the ghost is the unacknowledged triad member of the twinship.) The Moundang think that kings make the same excessive demand on the life source as twins, and this is why they equate kings and twins

(Adler, 1982, p.230).

Fundamental to the Moundang fear of exhaustion is their conception of the placenta. They do not say that the placenta is a twin to the newborn, as the Mbai peoples do (ibid., p.251), only that it is dangerous as a form of arrested life. Adler writes that the Moundang require the placenta to be "placed in a pot (re-integrated into the womb) and buried beneath an ant-heap (symbol of the prolific)" (ibid., p.251). Twin placentas are more dangerous than the placenta of a single child.

Turning against infanticide, the Moundang, who are inclined to be outer-directed, observed that their neighbours, the Guider, are delighted when twins are born. They took over the rites by which the Guider celebrated the birth of twins and used them in the service of placation. The following legend explains why the first of any pair of twins has come to be called *gô-comé*, which means chief-sun, or sun-king.

> One of the king's wives was hated by the other wives. When she went out into the bush with the other wives and gave birth to a baby boy, the other wives took her new-born and hid him under the leaves of the *gumelâra* tree, then returned to the village and told the king that the wife had given birth to the fruit of a *kigelia africana* tree (a branch of which is placed next to a mother, one of whose twins is a stillbirth). The mother said that this story was untrue but no one believed her. The sun saw the infant crying beneath the leaves of the *gumelâra* tree; the sun wanted to touch him but had to retreat because his touch burnt the infant. The sun told the moon, and the moon took the infant to her, fed it and nurtured it. He grew and became a shepherd boy. When guarding his flock, he would play his flute and sing, "I am the son of king Worzei. The sun found me, the moon brought me up. I lay beneath the leaves of the *gumelâra* tree". One day, one of the king's sons, a shepherd boy attending a flock nearby, heard the song.[2] Going home, the king's son asked his father: what is your name? The king said: if you want to know my name, your mother must ferment mead and kill a goat and then you will know my name. This then happened, and since the king was Worzei, he was soon united with his lost son. The king ordered

that all the wives should jump over a hole in the ground containing a fire; he wanted the wives who had lied to him to fall into the hole and burn to death. Many of the wives died in this way, but fortunately the villagers pleaded for mercy, and some of the wives were saved. The king made a sacrifice of bulls and goats to the moon. And that is why the son of Worzei was called the sun-king.

Adler indicates that while the abandoned son knows the name of his father, the other son can only come to know his father's name by way of acts of sacrifice (ibid., pp.250–251). The abandoned son appears to know his father's name by way of some relationship to the sun. In terms of the Apollodorus cosmogram, he is a version of the Dionysus twin *fused* with his father Zeus, a priest at one with the godhead, whose power is acquired through an interrupted gestation: he is someone who has died and who is thought to have been reborn. He lives in mania while his twin lives in depression, in equation with a mother who cannot give birth, whose life is the husk of a dream.

The following myth about the origins of the diviner's art supports this view. The child who is allowed to read is similar to a Dionysus fused with Zeus.

A woman gave birth to twin boys. One day God told the woman to present the twins to him. But while she presented one child to God, she hid the other, more plump one in a pot. God said to her: There should be two, why have you hidden one of them? Bring him here at once. While the mother was absent, God said to the lean child: when I tell you to cover your face, you must pretend to do so, but you may peep. The mother returned, and God ordered the children to hide their faces, which the plump child did. God began to write. The lean boy peeped through his fingers. When God had finished his writing, he ordered the boys to open their eyes. He read to them from the book (the Koran). The lean boy was able to copy out the phrases, but the plump child could not. God then said to the plump child: Since you cannot do what I order you to do, you will have to manage with the pebbles you are holding in your hand. (The boy had been playing with seven pebbles in his hand.) Line up your seven pebbles on the ground and they will speak to you my words. This will be your only source of knowledge. The thin child was a Peul [a member of a neighbouring tribe that has been converted to Islam], the plump child was a Moundang (Adler and Zempléni, 1972, p.41).

The idea of the pot recurs in Moundang thought; it is related to the getting rid of a dangerous substance. Adler claims that "the first fault" lies with the mother, because of "her wish to re-incorporate the child". In Adler's phrase, dead twins are "re-integrated into a mother's stomach" when they are buried in pots.

While the Moundang imitate the Peul manner of clothing and system of courtly entitlements, their allegiance to a certain idea of kingship provides them with the stamina to resist conversion to Islam. They say that the God of Islam sent an agent to establish God's rule over them. Their king asked one of his diviners for poison to kill the agent. The God of Islam was so incensed by this information that he sent a child to steal some of the diviner's stones. The diviner was left with only two stones. Two is a number associated with femininity: and the Moundang king is thought to be feminine; he is a bride of death. Three is a number identified with maleness; and the God of Islam is a male.

Adler and Zempléni (1972) considers how *kindani*, or the Moundang art of divination by stones, "is a weakened version of the sacred Arab script" (p.42). He indicates that divination, unlike Holy Writ, does not reveal fundamental and unchanging truths about the invisible. It is a provisional technique, a disabled mode of communication; it receives yes-and-no types of answer to specific questions (ibid., pp.212–213). The word *kindani* in actual fact signifies a "blind man's stick"; and figuratively the diviner is thought to be blind. He has little status and no professional affiliations. The story of the twins and the pebbles suggests that he is thought to be "blind" because he is the twin whose mother kept him in a pot. He is catastrophically fused with his mother, as was Dionysus with Semele.

Another more hopeful Moundang story tells of how the diviners learnt the art of reading pebbles from the monkey, an animal loved by the Guiner. The monkey instructed the Moundang in the art of divination. He initiated circumcision and invented ways to save the life of a mother in childbirth, as well as the life of the newborn (1972, p.40).

The diviners align their stones by complicated procedures: they sometimes make 5000 movements to resolve a question. The Moundang say that their tribe has stolen the land from certain sovereign powers of the earth that speak to the diviners through the stones. The sovereign powers consist of an earth goddess and a male spouse who is subordinated to her, and 48 cannibalistic "spirits of the place".

The diviners sit at the south end of a circle called a *hale* under the sacred tree *balanites aegyptica*. They imagine the axial coordinates of the cardinal points to divide the circle before them into four segments – we are back to the Dogon egg model. Adler (1978) thinks that they apportion the circle in this way to "express the elementary partition of the powers that govern the land" (p.35). In at least two different ceremonies, the diviners transpose the partition to the concentric "feminine" space of the king's palace but they make an important modification to its meaning. In the palace they partition the powers of the king's many wives and not the powers of the earth spirits. The earth spirits are the responsibility of the tribal chiefs and not of the king.

In structure the palace is a gigantic version of many houses in Lere, the principal city of the Moundang. Somewhere in between a farm and a fortress, it is concentric in shape, 200 metres in perimeter (1972, p.172). The thick earth wall that circles it bristles with turrets and towers. Built into the wall are the houses of the wives of the present king and the wives of his deceased predecessor. Adler (1982) says that "Gô-comé, the last of the pre-colonial sovereigns had nearly 200 wives, and a second circular wall had to be built around the property" (p.308). Each house has a granary and kitchen. The wives are devoted to cooking, and on feast days bring out substantial amounts of food and drink to the people in the parched lands outside.

A fortnight before the important new year ceremony of *fin-moudan* in mid-November, when the harvest has been brought in and the dry season is about to begin, the diviners set up a *hale* outside the palace walls and by way of their stones interrogate the earth spirits about the spiritual purity of the various parts of the palace and its inhabitants. The diviners think of the quarters as related in meaning to the earth's potency. The inhabitants of the palace think of the quarters as related to the rites of divine kingship, which are separated from, and even opposed to, the potency of the earth. Adler (1978) reports that the king has seized the powers of the earth by way of his fetishes and that the space that the palace fills is a violation of natural space–time (p.32).

There is a history to this conception of culture. Damba the hunter, founder of the royal dynasty, overthrew Kizéré, an impoverished king who had fed his people on beans. Damba gave his people game and other forms of meat. To this extent, Damba and his successors were violators of the earth. In this way, the king is "stranger to the earth; he is not even buried in it" (1972, p.19). More a slave to ritual than a master of it, he is too disabled by it to be a priest–king. His wives' principal function is to maintain the myth that he is someone who is not of this world – who does not eat, sleep or depend on natural bodily functions. He is not allowed to die naturally. His actual relatives (his mother and any child he might father) are banished from Lere. He is allowed no ordinary familial relationships. His enstoolment is the final stage in the funeral rites of his predecessor. From the moment of his enstoolment he is a marked man. At the moment of the enstooling, palace officials raise a straw palisade across the east–west axial of the palace grounds. The east–west axial is related to good fortune. The rain–winds blow from the east, and the king in his perambulations outside the palace always moves from east to west, possibly in identification with the sun. The north–south axial is related to misfortune.

"The king's palace is a fragment of heaven transported to earth" (Palau Marti, 1964, p.218). Its ground plan is an *imago mundi*. It represents a metaphysical conception of the king as a twin being. If the two forms of Dionysus as a mythic twinship depend for their similarity in difference on their having dismembered the idea of an unacknowledged third sibling and appropriated its qualities (like a coat–skin of many colours), then the king as two bodies, or two twins in one body, must know a reversal of this process. He must undergo rites of annihilation and dismemberment and disappear as the group hands him over to the authority of the dead. The north moiety is identified with death, and the king is a bride of death.

The south moiety is related to life, though a life that is no match for death, because it has been stolen. It contains the main entrance to the palace. The king lives in a vestibule close by it. In their investigations, the diviners begin with the king in his vestibule and they check out every aspect of his environment and his body. They then investigate the wives, whose various situations in relationship to the cardinal points indicate their status in the palace hierarchy. In the north moiety live the widows of the deceased king who must always wear the white of mourning; in the south moiety live the wives of the reigning king, who must never wear mourning, although their heads are shaved and covered in ash at the time of the enthronement.

One wife is different from the others, and she is the one person in the palace whom the diviners do not investigate, the one wife the king pays a dowry for, and she, the Queen Mother, the high priestess of the palace, is the one to whom he is most truly wedded. She lives in the north moiety and guards the regalia; and she is the custodian of the king's death. The regalia she guards are fetishes, reputedly acquired from Damba, the founder of the dynasty. They include pots, garments, ornamental walking sticks, hunting knives, a tap and a copper clock with two faces. The presence of the regalia and the wives together within the same compound underwrites the king's efficacy as a rain-bringer. On no account may he see the regalia. If he were to see the regalia, he would die.

In the north moiety, the king will be ritually murdered, usually after an eight-year reign, sometimes sooner. The manner of his murder is a state secret. He is possibly garrotted or poisoned or dies by suggestion by being shown the skull of his predecessor. As he dies, his body must be kept apart from the ground, or it will blight everything. It is disposed of in the same way as the Moundang dispose of placentas and dead twins. It is spirited out of the palace by way of a small, concealed door in the northern wall known as the anus, and kept in secrecy, far away from the palace. Eventually an uncircumcised attendant will dismember it and bury it in a pot, keeping only the skull and a bone from one of the little fingers as fetishes that are able to kill a successor at a glance.

The acts of identical twin-like doubling and impersonation that characterise the ritual life of the king – Adler has written an essay on them – become fevered at the time of his murder; it is as though the act of substitution had assumed the virulence of a terminal disease. The king's death is not announced for three months. An actor, bearing the name of a trickster hero in folktale, takes on the role of king and mimics the dead king's voice and manner. A doll lies in the dead king's resting place, and at the time of the official funeral a small boy and girl are ritually murdered and buried in the king's place, accompanied by a mannequin dressed in the king's sumptuous robes.

The king is in a state of a dual concrete equation: one equation is with the two bodies of the twins in one body; the other equation is with a confused dead mother and unacknowledged miscarriage (the *sine qua non* of all psychotic states?). The king must live a mythic eternal return of some act of abortion because the community cannot bear the dread that is entailed in acknowledging the existence of a certain ghost or hallucination, which it must do if it is to lay the dead to rest. It has to re-enact the murder of the acknowledged sibling; and it continues to be unable to lock hallucination into the process of symbol formation. Despair about the unswaying authority that disease and death has in this community (Chad was, and possibly still is, the poorest country in the world) compounds a lapse on the depressive threshold that results in a continuous group regression into psychosis.

Discussion

Moundang culture dramatizes the two opposed meanings of the concept "sacred". The king is sacred because he is both blessed and accursed. But the opposition *blessed:accursed* is less a paradigm of the Dogon egg than a paradigm of the egg in which Dionysus takes on two identical forms. *Blessed:accursed* is an opposition without mediation. It is without an axial or membrane to contain its segments. It represents the catastrophic fusions of the thunderbolt.

The split-egg model has relevance to the fusions that occur in the symbolic processes of dreaming and language. Freud (1910) was amazed to discover that in the early 1880s, and unknown to him, at the time when he had evolved the neurological concept of contact barrier and was positing fusions of opposed meanings in dream images, in which there was no mediation because there was no concept of negation, the linguist Karl Abel had published a monograph on the antithetical meaning of primal words.[3] Freud published an essay on Abel's monograph in 1910. Among other points, he said that Abel had realized that certain ancient Egyptian words that fused antithetical meanings were also reversible, as though one word could be the reflection of the other in a mirror; this is similar to the ritual twin-like doublings of the Moundang court that defend against the meaning of the miscarried third child.

Lévi-Strauss (1956) has proposed that visualizations of the microcosm as a dual system can be misleading, since visualisations may conceal a triadic structure. If oppositions do not have a triadic structure, if they do not have a mediator, which may be the presence of an un-mourned miscarriage (Bion's "caesura as transparent mirror"), they are liable to represent fusions.

The Moundang find the idea of the placenta threatening because it epitomizes the catastrophic fusion of a mother and unborn infant: the "incest" similarly that binds Tiresias to Oedipus, diviner to king, by way of blindness as a form of symbolic death.

The Gourmantché people believe that if a mother looks on her newborn before its placenta has emerged, she will go blind (Cartry, 1978). Here is a possible entry into the Oedipus legend.

The unconscious part-object meaning of the placenta is one of the sources of the incest taboo. An infant whose mother's mind is possessed by the thought of a dead child is liable to conceive of her mind as fused with the dead sibling. On occasion, the placenta can be an emblem for such a psychopathological fusion in thought. In cosmic terms it is an equivalence for absolute destruction. A mother's mind as such a placental system is not a placenta that de-toxifies but a placenta in inversion that toxifies.[4] The infant unable to find a place for itself in its mother's mind may be tempted to enter the kingdom of death and to become its unborn ghost sibling, the arrested life that the Moundang ascribe to the placenta and that is represented by the environment of the north moiety of the Moundang palace.

I recently heard of an infant whose mother had been unable to mourn a dead older sibling, a stillbirth who had been one of a pair of twins. From birth onwards, the infant had been unable to retain food, and when she was aged about one she would throw her food about as though she had no concept of stomach. She seemed to think of food that she could not retain as an alphabet that she could not understand. When I heard of her need a little later to create private spaces in which she could play, and so be enabled to think, I was put in mind of Wendy houses, which derive from J. M. Barrie's story *Peter Pan*. J.M. Barrie's mother became so fused in thought with an elder brother who had died that Barrie could only reach her by thinking to become the dead child in her mind. He stopped growing when he reached the height that his brother had reached at the time of his death. Barrie had a talent for projecting death into people. To be drawn into the mother–dead sibling fusion in reverie is to enter a Never–Never land presided over by Peter Pan as a child whom no one is able to acknowledge as dead and into whom someone or something has projected a schizoid state; he experiences the present moment as though he were buried in it. Peter is an indigestible memory. Any intrusion of reality into this psychotic milieu is greeted with terror. An instance of this terror is the celebrated crocodile with a ticking clock in its stomach that finally devours Captain Hook.

Notes

1. This line of thought suggests the following analogy. The reason why Jacob in the Bible story robs Esau of the mess of pottage, and the power to dream, is that Jacob is a *dead* twin, the depressive imaginary twin. No one knows how to mourn this loss. In paranoid-schizoid terms, Jacob is believed to steal the gist of life from his brother. Or: the dead child is an unacknowledged miscarriage that exists between Esau and Jacob. The narrative significance given to the heel of Esau's foot that Jacob grips onto at the time of birth hints at this meaning. In

Biblical thought, parts of the body are total persons: i.e. Adam's rib, the bruised heel of the serpent (I owe this example to Maria Rhode), the circumcised foreskin as the son offered up in the act of sacrifice.

2. It is part of the beauty of this story that the twinship of the two boys is only brought out indirectly, by the similarity of their work. They might be shadows of each other, or mirror reflections.

3. Emile Benveniste, among others, has raised reasonable doubts about some of Abel's conjectures; but Abel's status as an etymologist is not at issue here.

4. I am grateful to Gilead Nachmani for clarification on this point.

14. THE DREAD OF VERTICALITY THAT UNDERLIES A WORLD OF SPACE AND TIME

> Eyes and ears are false witnesses if I do not know the language
> (Heraclitus).

Whole cultures have been devoted, sometimes creatively, to mind's possession by the paranoid-schizoid version of the imaginary twin. On a visit to upper Egypt, I became aware of how the baton of a gifted guide tapped a dance over hieroglyphs carved on walls and released their meaning. The patterning created by the baton, like the computation of the geomancers of Chad, is an enactment of transformation in hallucinosis. The geomancers shift stones and by doing so speak to the ancestral and usurped spirits to whom this ground had once belonged. The ancestors determine the code. Transformation in hallucinosis is a reciprocal to the premonition of oblivion. The dead, through their agents, imbue the victim of the sacrifice with the transformatory functions of a divine king. Among the Zuñi, the act of killing turtles in the sacrifice "transforms" the turtles into ancestors who live (as once the turtles had done) beneath the waters of a lake (Mauss, 1906 [in 1968, pp. 7–8]). Transformations of this kind are basic to the syntax of myth and dream.

The history of the ancient Greek drama reveals how the acting out of transformations in hallucinosis evolved into a form of play. The cultural representation of Thanatos changes as the tomb of the divine king is transformed into an altar and then into a stage. The chorus that circles the altar is a precursor to the tragic chorus.

> Heracles [...] was honoured with fire offerings burned upon an altar instead of with a fireless *pelanos* [an offering of barley meal, honey and oil] poured into a hole in the grave. King Adrastus must have been honoured in the latter way. When the tragic chorus was transferred from him to Dionysus, the tomb around which the chorus danced became the altar of Dionysus and fire was kindled upon it, the tomb passing into a fire–altar. Thus arose the *thymele* of Dionysus [the first theatre stage] (Ridgeway, 1910, pp.38–39).

Both of the Athens theatres during the fifth century BC, when drama flourished, were dedicated to the cult of Dionysus. Dominating the proceedings at the City Dionysia (the principal theatre in Athens), and beside the acting area, stood a statue of the Dionysus himself and an altar on which a bull was dismembered in sacrifice before the performance started. The bull journeys into annihilation, while Dionysus enacts the return to life through transformation in hallucinosis.

On the stage (*skene*) stood an altar or tomb of the kind customary in streets in front of the house door; beside this altar stood a sacred table bearing cakes called *theoris* or *thyoris* (the term *thyos, thuysia*, came to be used generally of all sorts of sacrifice); in the orchestra stood the *thymele* either in the form of a platform or tomb. Before the time of Themis, a common table used for cutting up meats was used as an extemporized stage on which the poet or leader mounted and entered into dialogue with the chorus. *Thymele* derived from a term for sacrifice, it meant literally to raise smoke and to offer burnt offerings (Ridgeway, 1910, p.40).

There is an absence of span in relationships. The culture of the divine king emerges from a culture of incest and cannibalism as an attempt at differentiation. Empedocles draws a distinction between parents who cannibalize their children and children who cannibalize their parents (the oral aspect to Oedipus's acts of destroying in different ways the distinction between child and parent).

The father, having lifted up his own son in an altered form,
Slays the child, exulting greatly, and others are puzzled
As they sacrifice the pleading child. And the father, deaf to the cries,
Having slain his son, prepares an evil feast in his hall.
Similarly, the son seizes the father and children seize their mother.
And having torn from them the life-force, they eat their own flesh
(Empedocles, B 137 [in Lincoln, 1986, p.192])

A newborn separates like a phantom from a backbone that takes many forms: the altar, the cross-roads, the axial tree, the cross. From the backbone, the power of the divine king radiates like the spokes of a wheel to the quarters. The emperor of ancient China *was* the kingdom of ancient China. He existed because his kingdom had brought him into being. Similarly the king of Rwanda, who was of celestial origin and divine descent, was equated with his kingdom. His actions had a repercussive effect throughout the country. "He could not bend his knees, out of fear that if he did so, his kingdom would shrink a little" (Maquet, 1954, p.147). Also "[the stoics] believed that to move a finger modified the equilibrium of the universe" (Bouché-Leclercq, 1899, pp.28–29).

The Lenaion, the older and lesser theatre in Athens, had a programme mostly of comedies. (Aristophanes wrote *The Frogs* for it.) It had one festival, at an inclement time, the end of January, when the seas were high and few visitors came to Athens. On the other hand, the City Dionysia was a great theatre associated with the production of plays by Aeschylus, Sophocles and Euripides. It opened once a year only, and then briefly, for five or six days at the end of March, to celebrate the most splendid of the Bacchic festivals, the Dionysus Eleuthereus. Foreign delegations would arrange to come to the city at this time; their presence added to the brilliance of the procession to the theatre on the first day. It was the beginning of spring. The festival anticipates our present knowledge of the carnival as a time when death as oral sadism possesses the mind and excites an orgiastic mania. A statue of Dionysus Eleuthereus was borne from its shrine to the theatre and with it came the victims for sacrifice and the implements by which the sacrifice was to be carried out. An atmosphere of fevered excitement brought Athens to a standstill. The city gave itself over to the worship of the wine-god. "Business was abandoned; the law courts closed; distraint for debts was forbidden; even prisoners were released from goal to enable them to share in the common festivities" (Haigh, 1907, p.1). The theatre was closed for the greater part of the year; when it opened, it "possessed all the sanctity of a high temple" (ibid., p.2). The time of the festival was sacred and not one moment of it could be wasted; one play followed another from dawn to dusk. There were no other opportunities for a poet–playwright to show his work in the city itself. Few plays had more than one performance. Audiences thronged into an amphitheatre, which held up to twenty thousand people. The priests of Dionysus took the principal seats. Poets, actors, theatre managers had sacerdotal authority, and the spectators wore garlands; misdemeanours, however slight, were considered profanations, not infringements of the civil law, and were punished. "On one occasion a certain spectator was put to death for striking a personal enemy during the procession. To eject a man from a seat which he had taken wrongfully was a sacrilege punishable by death" (ibid.). The festival was given over to prize-giving, contest, acrimonious rivalry. Rich men lavished patrimony on the poets and actors. The judges, chosen from among the priests, were reputed to be discerning, although lavish spectacle could sway their judgment. Aeschylus's nephew won the prize in the year in which Sophocles' *Oedipus Tyrannus* was presented. Adjacent to the amphitheatre was a building known as the Asclepeon. Asclepius, the first physician, who had the status of a god, had worked out a dream therapy that was practised in the temple.

The Athenian drama centred on dance and the chanting of a chorus. The principal acting area of the City Dionysia was a vast circle, known as the orchestra, on which the chorus moved. The individual actor stood on a platform behind the space on which the chorus moved. The Labyrinth was the name for a type of dance associated with the name of Ariadne. The orchestra space had the meander markings of a labyrinth. In legend Ariadne (sometimes as Hera or Juno) created a space in which she could play with her infant, Dionysus Zagreus. Uncertain in form, as capable of transformation as her son could be, the mother–sister–daughter danced a celebrated "crane dance" before her child. In her hands she held a mirror, rattles and other toys, emblems for a future religion. The labyrinth made up "an arena intended for the performance of a mimetic dance [...] marked out with maze lines to aid the intricate evolutions of the dancers" (Cook, 1914, p.479.) In the *Iliad* there is an allusion to the dancing floor which Daedalus built for fair-haired Ariadne (*Illiad*, 18: 590), and in *The Odyssey* there is a hint of Ariadne's closeness to Dionysus (*Odyssey*, 11: 324). Ariadne as an analogue to Isis and Osiris is mother–sister–daughter to a god who has the power to commute between the dead and the living.

The dance evolved as a type of play out of the fundamentalist juxtaposition of creation and destruction in the sacrifice. Zeus destroys the Titans (who include Prometheus) for having murdered the child, and out of their ashes forms the cosmos or labyrinth as transition concepts. The Cretan people instituted a commemorative feast, during which they re-enacted by rite the boy's suffering and death. They would tear apart a live bull with their teeth; and then, as Firmicus states, they would penetrate "the solitude of the forest, uttering discordant cries and so feigning madness, that the crime might be set down to lunacy and not to guile. Before them was carried the basket in which the dead child's sister had concealed his heart" (Cook, 1914, p.662). With the sound of pipes and cymbals, they re-created the noise of the rattles that they believed had deluded the child, since they thought that the mother had conspired with the Titans. In legend at least, this is how the theatre emerged as a semi-independent institution from the practice of sacred rites.

Let me suppose, then, that the early Thraco–Phrygian kings, the Titans of the myth, after killing Dionysus as a kid, pitched him into their cauldron and boiled him in milk with a view to his being born again. The mystic who aspired to be at one with his god underwent, or at least claimed to have undergone, a like ordeal. He had fallen as a slain kid into the milky cauldron: henceforward he was "a god instead of a mortal" (Cook, 1914, pp.676–677).

The possessors and the possessed

Dionysus differs from other gods in undergoing the mortal experience of being born and dying. But the exigencies of rite rather than of biological fact determine his manner of birth and death.

1. His birth is twofold: birth-in-death from his mother, the earth goddess Semele, and from the thigh of his father Zeus. The ancients thought in error that the etymology of dithyramb, the rapturous birth song of the early tragic theatre, related to the double birth of Dionysus and to the double doors through which initiates had to pass in rites of rebirth (Pickard-Cambridge, 1962, pp.2–3).
2. Born from the kingdom of dead, he has to return to the kingdom of the dead when he dies, as though life were no more than an episode. He personifies the charismatic role that death plays when it activates states of enthusiasm that border on hallucination. People possessed by him no longer inhabit an environment, but must know an environment that inhabits them. In states of dismemberment they embody a cosmic impress. The mountain nurses who eat the flesh of the infant Dionysus are unable to distinguish between the power that possesses them and the tantalising edibility of the victim. The king (baby) does not personify the environment; he is an extension of the place of death.

A therapist in a session can be afflicted by mental cramp and think, if only I could get the right angle on the experience. The right angle on Tiresias and the Sphinx would reveal them to be perspicuous objects, and not bizarre ones. They are witnesses to a proto-spatial and proto-temporal world of the dead. The play does not provide the right angle.

> You have to know where to look, where the apparition will appear literally. I am not talking about a ghost; the thing that appears does appear [...] (Bion, 1980 p.65).

In a dream state, Oedipus might have imagined himself as separating from the cross-roads, as though from a mother's backbone. He is constricted. His catastrophic relationship to his parents is unresolved as a catastrophe because it is adhesive. He embodies the vertical dimension to the cross-roads concretely and he is unable to think about it.

Bion describes a patient who was a model of cooperation; he could not have hoped for a more sympathetic companion. One day Bion noticed that the patient was lying on the couch edge, frozen in terror, as though on the edge of an abyss. He was paralyzed by the onset of verticality. He seemed unaware of his situation, and Bion may have intuited it with his mind's eye rather than "seen" it. He and his patient were a perfect Kantian subject–object fit, so much so they may have precipitated the "O" model into existence as an alternative.

Someone working with the subject–object model would not have seen what Bion then "saw", or would have categorized it as a delusory perception rather than an intuition. Bion suspected that his former relationship to the patient had been a *folie à deux*. Another man complained to Bion that he was afflicted by blushing. Bion thought that he had never seen so white a face in all his life. Later the man committed suicide. The blush is like the communication of "dumbness" that Freud's patient knew in a dream. It is transformation in hallucinosis as "prayer": an inseparable adjunct to the sacrifice. The meeting with oblivion activates transformations in hallucinosis that anyone working within the Kantian subject–object model will find discreditable.

> How does a person know of blushing so invisible, noise so inaudible, pain so impalpable, that its intensity, pure intensity, is so intense that it cannot be tolerated but must be destroyed, even if it involves the murder of the "anatomical" individual? (Bion 1975 [in 1991, pp.51–52).

15. THE BODY AS COSMIC IMPRESS

The dance along the artery
The circulation of the lymph
Are figured in the drift of stars
(Eliot, 1944, p.9).

In the Northwest American understanding of the sacrifice, a quadripartite classification of the human body relates parts of the body to each other without regard to the nature of bodily joints. The nature of the cosmos determines the nature of the joints. Viviana Pâques describes the classification as: 1. Head. 2. Nape of neck *and* spinal column. 3. One arm *and* the stomach. 4. Other arm *and* the feet. In Eros, body is biological organism; in Thanatos, it is an object in rite, the substance of hallucination and intuition.

An Amerindian myth, which identifies parts of a wife's dismembered body with constellations in the night sky (Lévi-Strauss, 1978, p.27 ff.), functions as do two myths in Plato's *Timaeus*. In one of the myths the discovery of celestial coherence invites comparison with another of the myths, in which incoherence is associated to a gynaecological disease. The "disease" marks an attempt to escape from patrilineal rigidity.

A demiurge transforms vestiges or the *voided* forms of the four elements of air, water, fire and earth into an idea, which is the *logos* of the cosmos. He creates the planetary spheres and their movements, and the beauty of the movement realises the idea. A *transcendental* immunity from the afflictions of actuality saves the *logos* from an *imminent* vulnerability to destruction.

Meanwhile, a womb by magical contiguity inflames with disease organs in the body that contains it; it seems to possess parts of the body. The myth of the hysterical womb in effect describes a grammar in which the elements of the grammar repel each other as though magnetically. The grammar of hallucination more properly belongs to mouth than to womb.

In the first myth, a demiurge creates a paradigm outside any model of space–time. In the second (pre-Platonic) myth, a space within a human body is a claustrophobic minus-space that makes no sense within a space–time model, since its concept of womb creates an absence (where space might be) in which hallucinated sensation occurs.

In the myth of rationality, the demiurge translates the vestigial remains of a destroyed cosmos into an *idea* of a cosmos that is a *projection of dimensionality* rather than an object that has dimensions. One form that the idea takes, as a projection of dimensionality, is as a celestial music, the primal music of the spheres. In the myth of irrationality, the womb [Gr.: *hysterikòs*] releases itself from the ligatures that bind it inside the body and moves unpredictably and erratically about an imaginary enclosure. It transmits pain and disease to particular parts of the body by contact.

The vestigial remains of the cosmos consist of the elements: fire, water, earth and air. They are vestigial because no deity informs their presence (*Timaeus*, 53B [in Cornford, 1937, p.198]). When they are translated into planets and planetary movement, they give rise to a moving harmony of ellipses that belongs to spatiality rather than to matter, to sky rather than to earth.

Plato's planetary action has no reference outside itself. It seems spaceless and timeless, transmitting a form that is intuitive. The womb-demiurge depends on the same seven point dynamic structure in space – an axial coordinate in which the intersection is a reciprocal to the quarters of north, south, east and west. It exists on the vertical as well as the horizontal plane and it consists of three points: nadir, centre and zenith. Arguably, the womb influences four bodily parts, in parallel to the four elemental vestiges that the demiurge transforms.

The demiurge myth may have originated in a theory concerning the five elemental vestiges. The womb theory may have originated in a theory concerning the dismemberment of five organs within the body, which are associated with five senses that in turn are equated with a pentatonic conception of the cosmos.[1] A desire to classify in terms of the pentatonic in ancient China informs a classification of the cosmos in terms of the five viscera: spleen, lungs, liver, kidneys and heart. It ignores any distinction between the interior and the exterior of the body.

> There are five household sacrifices and five internal organs of the
> sacrificial victim. In the three months of spring, for instance, the
> spleen of the victim had the prominent place. In summer, this was the
> lungs; in the interposed mid-season, the heart; in autumn, the liver;
> and in winter, the kidneys. It may be further noted that these organs
> approximate in the body to the five directions. If one faces south, the
> spleen is to the left of the body and therefore east; the lungs, being to
> the front, are south; the liver, on the body's right, is west; the kidneys,
> towards the back, are north; while the heart, sacrificed at mid-season, is
> central. And these were in their turn sacrificed at the door of the house,
> the stove or hearth, the entrance gate, the path, and at the mid-season
> in the central court. All these five organs and sacrifices were associated
> with the five elements, the five creatures, the five tastes, odours and
> musical notes (Soothill, 1951, pp.32–33).

In present day Taoism, a medium possessed by the gods and carried behind a holy statue "like a baby on its mother's back" (Schipper, 1982, p.47) has thick steel needles pierce his cheeks, his arms, his calves and his tongue – "corresponding to the Centre" (ibid.).

> He is a bloodied child, wounded in his divine body by the stigmata of
> the five cardinal points [...] his blood purifies the world of any evil
> influence (ibid.).

A fifteenth-century ceremony in which death was projected into the Doge's wife (as well as into the Doge) marks a similar need to equate viscera with the cosmos. It illuminates the meaning of the office of divine king. By accepting her office, the Dogaressa became an agent for the victim in sacrifice. In the ceremony of enthronement, the Dogaressa had to accept a curse and to decline an offer of a meal. By implication, she became the food of the banquet.

> After the service in San Marco, the Dogaressa left by the door that led directly into the Palace and ascended the stairs with her attendants. When the procession entered the apartments, they passed the guilds men, waiting with their caps in their hands. During the respectful exchange of greetings, they invited the Dogaressa to sit and have a meal with them. The Dogaressa acknowledged their invitation, but answered that she did not feel like a meal. Instead she continued through the Palace, passing through hall after hall, and at last entering the Senate Hall, where she took her seat on the Doge's throne. *She heard a speech delivered by senators, in which she was reminded of her mortality and informed that on her death, her brain, eyes and intestines would be extracted and that her corpse would be displayed for three days before the funeral.* She answered that she was prepared for this, since it pleased God. Then the Dogaressa rose proceeded to the Hall of the Great Council where she took her seat on the Doge's throne, while everyone was permitted to touch her hand (Boholm, 1992, p.97; emphasis added).

The death penalty in England, as practised at one time as hanging, drawing and quartering, reflected the practice of human sacrifice. The drawing out of the victim's entrails validated the existence of the cosmic quarters as a transformation in hallucinosis.

Note

1. The Northwest American classification of the body described by Pâques exists as an intermediary between a tripartite classification and a five-part classification.

16. THE DIVINE KING AND THE MACROCOSM OF DESTRUCTION

Francis I, king of France, died in 1547. His heart, entrails and corpse were placed in three separate coffins. Officers of the court placed an effigy of the king on a bed of state and for eleven days served it sumptuous meals.[1] The effigy bore a likeness to the king that many of the mourners found disquieting. It wore majestic robes. The officers of the court took the coffin containing the corpse and the effigy first to Paris and then to the king's burial place at St. Denis. On the procession into Paris, certain mourners soberly walked by the coffin, which was covered in a black cloth, while the majority of the people in a carnival mood walked and danced around the effigy which was carried high (Schnepel, 1995, p.78 ff., quoting Giesey, 1960).

The two-tiered tomb of Archbishop Chichele in Canterbury Cathedral shows a similar coincidence of opposites between cosmic destruction and creation. On the lower tier lies a statue of the archbishop's corpse emaciated in death, while on the upper tier lies the archbishop dressed in the full splendour of office. The suffering represented by the lower statue is too convincing to allow the iconic claims of the statue above to be persuasive.

> The King has [...] two bodies, the one whereof is a Body natural [...] and in this he is subject to Passions and Death as other Men are; the other is a body Politic [...] and this Body is not subject to passions as the other is, nor to death, for as to this Body the king never dies (Kantorowicz, 1957, p.13, quoting an Elizabethan Law Report).

The functioning of the idea of the king's two bodies reverses the significance of the act by which Pollux renounces his claim to immortal life so that Castor might have a partial life. One body appropriates the essence of two lives and projects its death agony into the other. The intensity of the attraction that draws the twin bodies together is counteracted by the intensity of revulsion by which one of them takes life from the other.

When Shakespeare's Richard II dies, he "suffers death more cruelly than other mortals" (ibid., p.30). Richard is aware, as he catalogues the fate of his predecessors, that all kings are victims of the sacrifice:

> *All murdered* – for within the hollow crown
> That rounds the mortal temples of a king,
> Keeps Death his court, and there the antic sits,
> Scoffing his state and grinning at his pomp [...].

But Richard does not die at the hands of death. He dies at the hands of those who murder him. Death instigates the murderers, who operate as agents of the underworld. Death as "antic" is death as "clown" or "mountebank". The effigy as an immortal body is also "antic" in its travesty of the king's fate. A triad that is an agent for destruction afflicts the king: the clown (the king's Fool), the effigy, and the king's successor (who often usurps the throne).

Denied his rights as king, Richard no longer has two bodies: he no longer links earth and sky. The sight of his sacramental self, the celestial being that he sees in a mirror's reflection, torments him. He smashes the glass to pieces and submits himself to martyrdom. Claims that he might be a redeemer pale in consideration of the fact that the divine king is the bride to death.

> O, that I were a mockery king of snow,
> Standing before the sun of Bolingbroke,
> To melt myself away in water-drops! (IV. 1. 260 ff.)

The triad that opposes Richard is indestructible. He, on the other hand, cannot avoid destruction. His successor, in particular, represents *being* as an indestructible metaphysical essence, while he represents *non being*. His brutal and furtive murder is equated with the destruction of the cosmos as a holocaust.[2] Like verticality, or the "blush", or "dumbness", *being* and *not being* are primordial ideas that underlie the interactions of the subject–object model.

In Stoic belief, water or fire bring the cosmos into periodic destruction as flood or conflagration. Eros translates water and fire into the language of the senses. Thanatos translates fire and water into metaphysical substances, mysterious, and possibly marking the estrangement of mind from love. "Fire lives the death of air, and air lives the death of fire; water lives the death of earth, earth that of water" (Heraclitus [in Burnet, 1892, p.135]).

The gods of fire (Yogo, Seth, Jahweh) put to the sacrifice the gods of water (Nommo, Osiris, Jesus). The gods of fire are kin to the gods of air and the gods of water are kin to earth goddesses. Certain gods (Dionysus notably) complicate the rule. Fire destroys Dionysus as a water god in the womb of an earth goddess; but he is brought to life again in the thigh womb of a sky god who controls fire.

Shango

Shango is a cruel thunder-and-lightning sky god, as well as being a legendary Yoruba king. He has the same emblem as Zeus: a double-headed axe. As a child, he usurps the king's power. He has unusual powers of enchantment: he represents the indestructibility of the triad. One day he goes to the reigning king and insists that he should give up the throne to him. The king orders his men to get rid of the impudent child by throwing him into the river. The order is carried out, but within an instance the child presents himself to the king as a living being. The king orders his wives to kill the boy. They lead him into the wilderness. He jumps away from them into a tree: a moment later he swings from a branch, hanged by the neck. The wives dig a hole at the base of the tree. They sacrifice various animals. They cut the cord, so that the hanged boy should fall into the hole. But Shango springs alive once more and takes flight, saying *ko so*, meaning "not hanged". When the wives tell the king about this incident, the king wants to see the tree with his own eyes. He goes to it, but he cannot not see the boy. Returning to his palace, he finds the boy sitting on his throne. The king orders him off the throne. But Shango says that he cannot move. He says *oba ko so*, meaning "the king is not hanged", and that he has eaten the king in taking his place (Palau Marti, 1964, p.167).[3]

The "Destruction of the Cosmos" as a Function of the Transference

A "forbidden" stone object called "River-King" among the Mamprusi people of Ghana plays an important role in "making the king" in enstoolment rites.

> It is the body of an ancient Nayiiri who disobeyed his elders. He
> demanded that his palace be built in a river. His elders dissuaded him
> but he persisted. When his palace sank beneath the water, the elders
> found him transformed into stone [...]. Like the stone, [the body of
> the recently dead king] is dangerous and must be guarded by the same
> elders who serve King-River (Drucker-Brown, 1992, p.77.)

The sinking of the palace beneath water is an analogue for the destruction of the cosmos by flood. A totality (the cosmos) is condensed into a particular as a denial of any difference between the totality and the particular. In cosmic thinking, whole and part are largely undifferentiated, as in thinking by dream in which the concept of a fragment has no meaning.

Bion drew attention to the phenomenon of group suicide. At Ur of the Chaldees, the entire court in its finery walked in a procession to the communal sluice at the time of the king's death and took drugs, having arranged to have itself buried alive among the rubbish (Bion, 1973 [in 1990, p.3 ff.]). Bion considers the idea of group suicide and murder as a constant in transference representation ("to Ur is human"). He represents it in his earlier writings as the beta screen, whose effect on the therapist is like an "unpremeditated blow" (Bion, 1977a [in 1989, p.3]). Someone "withholds rather than imparts information": an imperceptible assailant murders by stealth. A culture shows itself in the consulting room that makes no sense of intimacy.

The authorities that instituted the ritual sacrifice of the Bouphonia of ancient Athens so devised it that no one would be held responsible for the violent decapitation of an ox. Violence and stealth characterized the rite.

> They chose girls to bring the water used for sharpening the axe and knife. After sharpening, one man administered the axe, another struck the ox, and a third cut its throat. The next skinned it, and everyone tasted the ox. Afterwards having sewn up the hide of the ox, they stuffed its skin with hay, sowed it up and had it stand yoked to a plough, as though it were ready for work [...].[4] They summoned all who had participated in the deed to defend themselves. The water fetchers charged that the sharpeners were more to blame than they. The sharpeners said the same about the axe administrator, and this one of the throat cutter and this one of the knife which, being without a voice, was condemned to murder [...]. They threw the knife into the sea (Porphyry, *De abstinentia* [in Vernant, 1991, English translation, pp.301–302).

In certain cosmologies concepts of damage and natural death are shunned. "The Swazi believe that no one dies a natural death" (Kuper, 1947, p.197). "The informants said that without sorcery no one died" (ibid.). The divine king *is* the contraction of total cosmic destruction, or he *is* the expansion of total cosmic creation. At one stage in the Incwala ceremonies of the Swazi, the king was placed in seclusion. The entire tribe, as well as the king, entered a state of eclipse. The king was painted black and kept in darkness; his people dwelt in darkness also. If a member of the tribe scratched himself, he would be admonished for scratching the king (Kuper, 1947, pp. 219–220).

King Angolo of Dahomey died in the mid eighteenth century. The authorities ordered the digging of a deep ditch tomb with a small entrance to it by the palace walls and had a hundred people decapitated and placed in the tomb. Blood from the decapitated bodies cemented the earth on the sides of the tomb. Twenty-five wives entered the tomb voluntarily, and the legs of fifty men in the prime of life were broken so that they could not escape from it. Food and gifts were placed in the tomb, and it was sealed for three days. During this time, the community behaved as though it were also dead. After "twenty-eight moons" the authorities opened the tomb and gave the king's skull to his successor. They ordered the decapitation of three hundred people and used the victims' blood to seal the earth-walls of an oven-like structure in which the king's skull was placed (Palau Marti, 1964, p.126).

Forty-one wives voluntarily were buried alive with King Gezo of Dahomey; and the wives who were denied this privilege were downcast. When king Oba of Benin died, his people dug a tomb beneath his palace that was so deep that many of them *drowned in subterranean water*. Members of the king's court argued in favour of which of them should have the privilege of being the king's companions in death. A stone was rolled in front of the tomb entrance after the faithful had joined the king, and guards kept watch by the entrance for a day and a night. When the entrance was opened on the following day, the inhabitants of the tomb were asked whether anyone had failed to follow the king: usually no one answered. By the fourth or fifth day all the inhabitants were dead [presumably in the first instance by suffocation] and the king's successor could enter into the rites of enstoolment.

> Certain commentators claim that headless bodies, and not living people, were entombed with the king and that the king's guards decapitated numerous people in the street and left the corpses for birds of prey (Palau Marti, 1964, p.85).

Verticality, the Breaking of the Glass and the Loss of the Sacramental Self

A legend associated with the Central Australian Achilpa, or "wild cat" aborigine tribe, concerns a sky-person and nomadic culture hero called Numbakulla, whose name signifies "always existing" or "out of nothing" (Spencer and Gillen, 1927, p.388).

At Lamburkna, where he arose "out of nothing", Numbakulla created *kurunas* or spirits and *churingas*, stone or wooden artefacts capable of transmitting psychic power. By splitting the *churingas*, he created men and women. He shaped the mountains and valleys and many other features of the landscape out of dream energy. He classified the tribes. He taught the Achilpa how to perform rituals and ceremonies. He marked out a ceremonial site, and at its centre planted a pole called *kauwa-auwa*, on which he poured blood. One day he climbed the *kauwa-auwa* and told the Achilpa headmen to follow him. But when they tried to do so, they slipped on the blood that ran down the pole. After pausing, in order to look back at the headmen, Numbakulla continued alone to climb the pole into the sky, drew the pole after him and was never seen again. Other legends – a number of them anecdotal and historical-sounding in character – are concerned with the wanderings of the Alchilpa ancestors. Some of them died from diseases, sexual and otherwise, some died when their *kauwa-auwa* broke as they tried to pull it out of the ground. Afflicted by exhaustion, this final group continued their nomadic wanderings, and carried the broken remains of the *kauwa-auwa* with them, until they could no longer combat exhaustion. They lay on the ground and died. "A large hill, covered with big stones, rose up to mark the spot" (Spencer and Gillen, 1927, p.355 ff.).

A rush of engulfing space, comparable to the breaking of Richard's mirror, takes the place of the vertical link by which the divine king joins earth and sky. In Bion's terms, the contact barrier has become a "caesura within a transparent mirror". The fact that Numbakulla's disappearance disrupts the cosmos – and yet not entirely – suggests that the cosmos is articulated like a human body. His disappearance is bound to a breakdown of the vertical axis that joins the sky to the earth's surface and the earth's surface to the earth's depths. The totem pole is a homologue for the primal axle-tree (and for the human spine), and its breaking leads to the falling apart and death of the tribesmen. It breaks at the point where it leaves its site in the earth and the tribesmen no longer have a vertical stake in earth or sky.

In the Northwest African sacrifice, as described by Viviana Pâques, neck breaking is the most significant form of dismemberment. The snapping of the totem wood as it is drawn out of the earth, as an analogue to Numbakulla's disappearance, reflects the breaking of a spine at the neck joint. In terms of cosmology, the head carries the soul of the cosmos and the body is its material embodiment. The churingas as retainers of Numbakulla's creative powers are fetish-analogues for ghosts. Some of the tribesmen are unable to separate themselves from the unconscious group object and to mourn its loss. Their thinking seems to be bound to a commitment to the vertical axis. They die because they are unable to move into a state of identification with the god who has disappeared; they are unable to experience themselves as separate from him, or as able to introject him.

Notes

1. Cf. The Mexican feast of the Dead. "Our offerings are served as daintily and as lovingly as possible, as if the dead were living guests [...].
   It is the spirit, or the essence, that the dead extract" (interview in Carmichael and Sayer, 1991, p.121). In the Eucharist, on the other hand, the living eat the "essence" of a dead and resurrected god.

2. The effigy remains in the palace throughout the interregnum, attended by sisters of the deceased king and their children. A uterine grandson is chosen as a "mock" king, or, as the Mamprusi say, a "grandson-king". From the time of the king's death, a crowd of these uterine grandchildren occupy the palace, satirising the resident court and later, the princes and chiefs who arrive to perform the king's funeral. During the interregnum the "grand-children's play", which occurs at all Mamprusi funerals, becomes a major political performance. It mocks the established court and forces a constant redistribution of gifts of cash, food and drink to the grandchildren (Drucker-Brown, 1992).

3. At his enstoolment, a Yoruba king eats the heart and tongue of his predecessor.

4. The effigy theme once more.

17. THE DIVINE KING AS MICROCOSM OF CREATION

> The communication of the dead is tongued in fire
> (Eliot, 1944, p.36).

In the cultures of Thanatos, death is the source of life. The participants in the sacrifice are agents for the dead. Destruction is creation: the dispatching of the victim is an act of birth. Osiris is twice sacrificed and posthumously he ejaculates into Isis, his mother–wife–sister, who gives birth to Horus, the first pharaoh. The icons of death project insanity, as though insanity were life. Pausanias describes small unmanned boats that travel the seas carrying *xoanan*, or painted images of Dionysus, that drive mad those who look on them.

On one level, the transformation in hallucinosis of the sacrifice parallels the transformations that cooking brings about. The dead "feed" the living; and sometimes in ways that cannot be idealised. Guests at the enstoolment of one king in Africa were obliged to eat a meat stew that they saw to be "green and slimy" and to contain "what is normally [thought to be] dangerous or disgusting" (Drucker Brown, 1992, p.83).

Shakespeare in *Macbeth* realises the link of kingship and disgusting food. The three witches, who proclaim Macbeth to be king, concoct a stew made up of bits of flesh. The motif recurs when Banquo, as a ghost, interrupts Macbeth's state banquet. Eating the imaginary twin gives Macbeth psychic indigestion and he is unable to use death to initiate a dynasty. Descending into Hecate's underworld, he sees a procession of the future kings of Scotland, among whom he has no successor. Hecate is the triple-headed goddess of the cross-roads, who as a human infant died from exposure at a cross-roads.[1] She presents portents to Macbeth that are as fearful as ghosts. The witches' cauldron resembles the *bothos* through which the Greeks poured libations into the tombs of the dead; the cauldron shafts down into Hecate's kingdom.

The ancient capital

The site of the capital city in ancient China lay at the centre of the universe. An identical panorama opened out on each of the four sides of the city. In the beginning there was no shadow and no echo. The wonderful tree that grew at the centre of the world united the nine sources of the nine heavens and bound the extremities of the world to it. No object near the tree at midday threw a shadow, nor had an echo. "By a perfect synthesis (the result of a hierogamy or sacred marriage) the central unity absorbed into itself all contrasts and alternatives, attributes and insignias" (Granet, 1934, p.268).[2]

Ancient Chinese thought observes an affinity between two systems. One is a five-part system that consists of a code in relation to four reciprocals. The five-part system translates into a paradigm of the axial intersection: a centre that is linked to the cardinal points. The other (a tripartite) system consists of an imperceptible code, the *Tao*, and two reciprocals, *yin* and *yang*. The systems that Saussure and Bion have separately formulated are similar in function. An unknowable code activates functions without content into generating meanings through reciprocation. Yin and yang are the functions. The two systems and the classifications of the ancient Greeks are similar (cf. Needham, 1956, pp.245 ff.).

The yang of an outward radiant progression of the sun across the sky is reflected in a circumspect yin, the pool where transformations occur, sacred pools "where every morning the mother of suns bathes the rising sun [...]" (Granet, 1934, p.107). Each month throughout the year the emperor proceeds from room to room in his circular palace as though round the compass, performing an appropriate sacrifice for each season. By his progression he unites the quarters and the seasons. He makes a "sacred circle", as though weaving the space in which a sacrifice might occur. He has the authority to determine the schedule of the calendar and to regulate all astronomical investigation; he is the agent for all time and space.

> When the ruler of men came forth to direct and arrange the world, his throne was called heaven's throne and his people were called heaven's people. The important point in ordering their movement was that these should correspond to the signs of heaven and accord with the heavenly seasons [...]. To manifest his potency, the ruler of men should change the rooms of his abode, and of his position, in accord with the seasons; the direction of the ruler's throne had be placed correctly in relation to the "central star" (Soothill, 1951, p.25, quoting the *Ta tao Lu*).

The emperor linked sky and earth and reconciled states of being and non being, light and shadow, voice and echo. As pivot to the quarters of the imperial city, he embodied the sacrality of the cosmic axial co-ordinates. "The true sovereign provides the beat of the dance, and everything under the heaven follows" (*I Ching* [in Lynn, 1994, p.41]).

The surveyors of sites for new cities, who wished to lay out the ground plans for a new city, had first to describe its axial co-ordinates as though they were shadowing forth the vertical centre and its relationship to the four orients.[3] By pondering over the play of shadow and light (one form of the yin and the yang), they were able to came to an opinion as to the best place to lay down a gnomon as an axial centre around which the city might be built.

> Mystical Chinese politics has always maintained that at midday in mid summer in the capital city of the perfect emperor the gnomon must throw no shadow (Granet, 1934, p.267).

The gnomon is a bamboo-pole type of sundial. It marks the authority of the emperor as a pivot. Like Numbakulla's totem-pole, it is a cosmic spine. The concept of *gnosis*, or knowledge, possibly derives from it. Needham (1956, p.245) raises a truly startling possibility when he points out that *stoicheia*, Plato's term for an element, in origin is a term for the gnomon. He allows for the inference that the gnomon is a psychic fact about the depressive threshold. The becoming of "O" manifests itself on the depressive threshold by states of annihilation that activate states of transformation in hallucinosis. Annihilation and transformation in hallucinosis together induce catastrophic change. The ritual of the sacrifice, which combines these factors, is an attempt to find a depressive basis for measure.

The patient knows the narrative of his or her body as an object submitted to the sacrifice. The narrative of the patient's body sometimes has not as yet been extricated from the narrative of a mother's body. The body text, in disappearing, is replaced by a body-text that bears the impress of the cosmos, an order of imaginary metamorphoses. The patient may experience the metamorphoses in terms of bizarre objects, like the patient who dreamt of a urinal–gas mantle.

In the tenth book of Plato's *Republic*, Er the Pamphylian in death enters a cosmos in which whorls circle a shaft of light. The shaft of light is of indefinite length. A patient on the depressive threshold might dream of this shaft. In considering "the revolutions of a well-made globe" (*Laws*, X. 898), Plato describes rotation about a centre as an indicator of intelligence at work. If Er's vision were a dream, it might be a dream about how intelligence conducts itself. In the cultures of Thanatos, the dead reduce the living to mirror reflections of themselves. The world of the dead determines the rites of the living; the dead endow the victim of the sacrifice with a sacrality that radiates throughout the cosmos of the living and determines the rhythm of its dance.

In the culture of the depressive threshold the living pass through a state of ritual death in which they realize that figures that they had thought dead and persecutory are in psychic terms alive and able to endow them with measure. The depressive imaginary twin does not control the living; he is an emissary who conducts them towards life.

Notes

1. "Hecate, as a newly born infant, was exposed at a cross-way".
   (*Hastings' Encyclopaedia*, "Cross-roads").

2. The school of *yin* and *yang*, or the doctrine of the "interrelation of
   heaven and man [...] was not linked to the vision of any single
   individual or to any single text and the question of its beginnings
   remains a matter of great dispute. It is in fact considered by some to
   be a primordial and quintessential expression of the "Chinese mind".
   Any reader of Marcel Granet might indeed regard it as the central
   stream of the entire Chinese "structure of thought" (Schwartz, 1985,
   pp.350–351).

3. "This fourfold or fivefold division probably represents an ancient clan-
   ordering [...] now lost in the mists of time. The fifth element, that
   of kingship, represents [...] a "third" element, harmonizing the two
   social antithesis into a "higher unity', relating them to the immutable
   cosmos" (Van der Kroef, 1954, p.855).

18. THE DOUBLE LABYRINTH

Work with autistic children has revealed how the criss-cross of pencils, or an interest in a window-frame intersection, can establish a move from understanding the world of meaning two-dimensionally, as consisting of surfaces, into a three-dimensional world, in which individuation occurs, and in which there are concepts of inside and outside and of containment (Meltzer et al., 1975, p.223 ff.; Tustin, 1981, pp.156–158).

The intersection can take the form of a labyrinth; and the labyrinth can mark a rite of passage. In northern India at one time midwives would show an image of the labyrinth as a "mimetic charm" to women exhausted by a protracted birth labour (*Hastings'* *Encyclopaedia*, "Charms and Amulets [Indian]"). The labyrinth, as icon, signifies the necessity in existence of acts of sacrifice as the fundamental cosmic coincidence of opposites. The icon of the caesura as transparent mirror does not arise from acts of birth, rather the existence of the icon determines the meaning of acts of birth.

On a steatite plaque discovered a century ago at Memphis in Egypt, there are two maze patterns, so related that they constituted a double labyrinth (Deedes). In the top labyrinth a meander transforms into two silhouettes that face each other. The silhouette on the right wears a pharaoh's crown. The silhouette on the left has a crenulated line in place of an abdomen. The crenulated line has spikes or teeth that stick out of it at right angles and it resembles the Egyptian hieroglyph for a gate.

At the time of his dying, the pharaoh crossed the threshold that exists between life and death, saying "O Gateway of the Abyss, I have come to you, let this gate be opened to me" (Wilkinson, 1994, p.139). At the same time he came into contact with his double or *ka*, who carried his immortality. "To go to one's *ka* meant to die" (ibid., p.49). The figure with an abdomen drawn as though it were the hieroglyph for a gate is presumably the pharaoh's *ka* or double.

The steatite plaque describes a doubling of the pharaoh and his *ka*. The environment of the labyrinth is tied to the bodies of the two figures, as though viscera existed in some disembodied state as prototypes of a timeless and spaceless world. The threshold gate is the intersection between the pharaoh and his *ka*.

To personify a life or death as an invisible *ka* who on occasion can be encountered as a double depends on the proposition that life and death can be known, whereas in fact life for the most part, and death wholly, can only be undergone. In Bion's thought, the depressive threshold is the ground for all activity. Bion removes the turbulence from object relations by defining it in terms of the becoming of "O". Human beings can live out "O", or it can live out them. They cannot know it. Hallucinations imply a knowledge of "O" (whereas intuitions as maturations of hallucination admit to ignorance of "O"). The doctrine of the sacrifice institutionalises mind's estrangement in death from its object. The act of sacrifice enacts the meaning of intuition as a function opposed to epistemological procedures.

In hallucination there is a retreat from intuition into an equivocation concerning being and not being. The pharaoh may think to enter *non being*, but his state of *non being* keeps him tied to the *being* of the *ka*, as though he were the shadow to a state of *non being*. He exists in *being* and *non being* as two environments. He does not know Richard II's anguish when faced by the separation of his terrestrial self from his celestial reflection in the mirror.

Being is the "abode" that takes forms that defy the propriety of nature: the ship of death that the pharaoh sails is the ship that Dionysus sails, or the coffin by which Osiris crosses the sea to Byblos; it is dislocated and a-temporal. *Non being* is the environment of the labyrinth. The pharaoh realises that *being* has moved into his *ka* as a geometric reflection of himself. The labyrinth as *ka* is an emanation of the pharaoh's nature as the victim in the sacrifice, and an emblem of his perplexity.

Scholars have proposed that the double labyrinth represents the unification of upper and lower Egypt, as well as the sexually charged presence of a *labrys*, the double-headed axe of the thunder god. A world arises out of the mirroring by which the branches of the tree of life reflect the structure of its labyrinthine roots, as though seen in a pool.

One of the names of the Minotaur who dwelt at the centre of the Cretan labyrinth was Asterios; his tail or his body contained all the stars (*Hastings' Encyclopaedia*, "Minotaur"). In ancient Egyptian mythology the body of the goddess Nut, like the Minotaur's tail/ body, contains the night sky. The sun passes through her body in a nightly act of sexual congress and procreation. Nut is the mother of Osiris, Seth, Isis and Nephysis whose ritual enactments of dismemberment and unification are more securely bound to space and time than hers might be.

19. THE DURATION OF THE BODY AND THE REVERBERATION OF THE IMAGE

> Something strange and terrible is happening here. Question: why
> is this happening here? Answer: because it is terrible. The terrible,
> impressive, horrible, tragic, etc. – not the trivial and insignificant –
> gave birth to these events (Wittgenstein, 1930 [in 1979, p.3]).

The Vedas abstract an idea of the five senses from a conception of
five types of breath (Onians, 1951, pp.70–73). Certain Greek authors
describe the senses as translations of breath. Theognis: "In men of
understanding the eyes and tongue and ears, and mind are rooted
in their breasts" [i.e., their lungs]. Homer: "seeing delights the lungs
and is the work of breath". Aristotle: "deafness is a congestion of
the lungs" (ibid., pp.70–73). The relationship of breathing to sense
communication has an affinity to the relationship that Bion describes
between a pressure and the incipient sense organ. In order for a
linkage to occur between pressure and the incipient sense organ,
mind must intuit certain concepts concerning transition. Intersection,
conceived of as the axial co-ordinates, a coincidence of destruction
and creation, is one such concept.

Bion considers the existence of links that are psychic equivalents
to screams that no one utters and that no one hears and yet that
can have a devastating effect (1980, p.120). Freud realised that such
links existed. "[Freud] had to entertain the idea that events which
had never taken place could have serious consequences" (Bion,
1975 [in 1991 p.176]). Links of this kind are, in Bion's words, "pure

transference" and exist in an empty consulting room, where there is neither patient nor therapist, merely a communication without communicants. The axial co-ordinates are links of this kind. When centred on body, they are prototypes for an experience of duration in space and time; they extend into mind–space as the spine and musculature of thought. Two of the three narratives that make up Adam's dream represent them. The axial co-ordinates, as a system "in which two axes intersect at a point 'O'" (Bion, 1965, p.77), are agents for turbulence. Disembodied, as forms of intuition, they reverberate.

The body of Adam, as spread-eagled giant, is transfigured into a cosmic impress. The mysterious rib moves from sensory modulation into a respiratory mode; the axial co-ordinates realize the third (maternal) narrative, and Adam's body becomes the body of the depressive imaginary twin. The axial co-ordinates are then organs of psychic perception, a "primal articulation" (to use Claude Lévi-Strauss's phrase) that tempers sense information.

A certain woman patient enjoys and respects the otherness of nature, but she is unable to tolerate the impression of otherness in psychic reality. She avoids any encounter with the impression. She reverses the possibility of being dependent on an internal mother by various uses of concrete equation thinking. In dreams the child within her assumes the role of a controlling mother. If she glimpses an otherness indicative of an internal mother, she glimpses it in the allusive form of a warm-hearted daughter, or of a pair of empty baby-shoes beneath a hedge. She observes the world about her, but she fails to "see" psychic truth, because the existence of psychic truth is autonomous as well as invasive and cannot be directly arrived at through an observation of the world. Physically slight, she would at one time sit on the end of the couch, lower her back onto the couch and slide up it in a way that put her therapist in mind of a piece of airmail onion-paper sliding into an envelope. Her way of relating to the couch changed, but the therapist recalled her former way of securing herself to it one morning when she reported a dream. She said that she had slept badly the night before. She had not felt comfortable in bed, and it was only on the way to the session that she had remembered the dream. She was lying on a straw mattress in a hut with four other people. When she turned over, she found that the face of the partner on either side to her was too close, and she was conscious of how she and her partners were breathing into each others' faces in a way that she found distressing. She related this experience to memories of people who came too close at parties or on crowded trains and to fears of failures in breathing and of suffocation while swimming, to birth anxieties, to mothers whose breasts impede the breathing of the feeding baby, to cramped states in sessions, and to husbands who invade her sleeping space in bed. (She deals with this difficulty by climbing out of bed and creeping into the empty space vacated by her husband.)

An internal mother insists on transforming herself from a two-dimensional into a three-dimensional being. The patient has a persecutory reaction to intimations of growth. The four points that she holds to herself are a quadripartite image of herself, as though she and it were fused twins. The self fragments the mirror into which it looks. The totality that does not fractionalize determines the reality of the totality that can be fractionalized. A mind about to undergo an experience in which it loses its capacity to think about the experience projects a fragmented conception of the experience as transformation in hallucinosis into the quarters, as idealized trajectories of a premonition of oblivion.

In ancient Chinese thought, emperor and his people faced each other like a face and its reflection in a mirror. The emperor's life determines the changing nature of fractions. His birth date and death date were pivots to the calendar. In such a system (Granet, 1934) numbers described arrangements and not quantities or durations; they had the meaning of numbers on playing-cards. The quarters then are four suits that define court protocol.

Certain Amerindian myths (Lévi-Strauss, 1964 [in 1970, p.53]) postulate parallel continua that reflect each other, like face and image in the mirror (but without the conviction that one of the two is "real"). The disruption of a parallel between the sacred and the profane releases an un-annotated link, similar to the scream that no one utters and that no one hears. "[...] discontinuity is achieved by the radical elimination of certain fractions of the continuum. Once the latter has been reduced, a smaller number of elements are free to spread out in the same space" (ibid., p.53).

The Dogon talk of the fundamental twin nature of the universe (Griaule, 1966, p.168). Similarly, the Bambara people of Mali have a myth concerning *gla*, or void – and the impulse to move, dream, awake, resurrect. Speaking with the voice of the void, *gla* replicates itself as another *gla*, revealing the underlying cosmological principle of twinship (Dieterlen, 1950 [in 1988, pp.28–30]). There is a vibration or turbulence, out of which appears a contrary sense of both fusion/implosion and separation/explosion. The *gla* fuse and separate more than once: in their second fusion and separation, they are four points, or quarters.

The dreamer releases four points that extend from her into a no-where and no-space, the "blind mouth" of infinity. The extending lines are at right angles to one another. The four points, insofar as they exist in space–time, coincide with North, South, East and West. Out of them arises a vertical axial co-ordinate that joins up to a sixth point that is coincidental to an imaginary zenith in the sky and to a seventh point that is coincidental to an imaginary nadir beneath the earth's surface.

Underlying the imaginary fusions of mirror reflections without duration is the possibility of a violation by expanding air. The dreamer may be oppressed by the proximity of the four points, but if she were separated from them, she would be obliged to enter an environment of dismemberment, in which she might not survive.

The horizontal axial co-ordinates realise the concepts of duration and of distance, the emergence of otherness in nature, though not in psychic reality. The intersection is a variable, Lévi-Strauss's floating signifier, Bion's contact barrier. By being embodied, it communicates the error that it is a "centre".

Misusing the Concept of Centrality

"In Ireland one may still be confronted with the riddle: 'Where is the middle of the world?' The correct answer is 'Here' or 'Where you are standing'" (A. and B. Rees, 1961, p.187).

Axial co-ordinates as architectural forms exist in megalithic sites; in the remains of ancient cities such as Ur of the Chaldees, Mohenjo Daro in the valley of the Indus, in the temples of Angkor and Babylon, the Egyptian pyramids, the palaces and cities of ancient China; and in sacrificial sites in pre-Colombian Mexico and in Phoenicia. They underlie a system of classification that is widespread among the Amerindians. They are tokens of an astro-biological kind of thought (Berthelot, 1949).

> The individual and the group thinks three-dimensionally in terms of six directions and six poles (often orientated cosmologically) or rather seven poles, for one has to count the centre (the ego, or me) as a point in space of unusual quality, from which extend the symmetrical relationships of above and below, before and behind, and then of right and left (Mauss, 1933 [in Karady, 1974, p.145]).

Adam's thinking is of this kind before he enters the physical metamorphoses of his dream.

> The splitting of experience into left-hand experience and right-hand experience is bound up with other intuitions of bodily dimensions, such as above and below and before and behind [the body]. The reasoning of a greater part of mankind has depended on a feeling for these various dimensions. [...] The centre is sometimes equated with the cosmic centre and sometimes separated from it. The cosmic centre may be the camp, the sanctuary, the omphalos (the navel of the world), the Etrusco-Roman *mundus* (ibid., p.145).

Adam discovers through the transformations of his dream that the centre exists as an everywhere and nowhere in every time and no time as an imperceptible code that precipitates action without determination. A late mediaeval theologian found use for this idea.

> Cusanus found the metaphor [of God as an infinite sphere] in the writings of Meister Eckhart, who in turn refers us to the pseudo-Hermetic *Liber XXIV philosophorum*, dating back to the twelfth century.

> Here we find for the first time the formulation, "God is an infinite
> sphere, whose centre is everywhere, whose circumference [is]
> nowhere" (Harnes, 1975, pp.7–8).

Mirrors that reflect each other create an imaginary space. The breaking
of the glass transforms the imaginary space into separate images; and
the fragments of broken glass become the faces of various gods. In
early Buddhist art the four faces of a deity represented the quarters,
each face being painted a different colour.

> The four cardinal points play an important role in the representation
> of Buddhist deities. [...] Avalokitesvara is surrounded by four divinities
> placed at the four cardinal points, each with his own appropriate colour
> (Berthelot, 1949, p.58).

Hecate and Hermes, as gods of the cross-roads, had three or four faces,
and each face looked in different compass directions. The different
quarters reflected back a face.

In Yorubaland, Frobenius found little clay cult objects that
consisted of a central cone, representing the god of world order, with
four smaller cones around it representing the gods of the cardinal
points. [...] A pillarstone at Keimaneigh (South of Cork) is said to be
a petrified woman and in it are five cavities with five oval stones in
them. That, according to this definition, constitutes a cairn (A. and
B. Rees, pp.187–188).[1] In Merioneth, a "houseful of children" was
defined as five, one in each corner and one in the middle (ibid., p.
396).

The deities that arise out of fragments of the broken object may
take on aural as well as visual forms. The *Aitareya Upanishad* describes
the *creation: destruction* of the first man Purusa as a dismemberment,
in which parts of his body were transfigured into parts of the cosmos.
When Purusa's ears broke off from his body, "there was hearing, and
from the hearing (came) the four quarters" (cited in Lincoln, 1986,
p.32). Purusa's dismemberment recalls how Adam's rib assumes the
properties of metamorphosis when it is separated from Adam. Mind
disintegrates in the face of the pressure imposed on it by beauty when

beauty is experienced as a conflict that cannot be resolved (Meltzer and Williams, 1988). On the threshold, there is murder and suicide.

The quarters contain the bits of the fragmented object. They are supports as well as inventories for the attributes of the world. The Indian king Yayàti falls from the sky (and grace) because of a transient spiritual flaw. The differing virtues of his four grandsons, who represent four kingdoms, or the quarters, are efficacious enough to restore him to grace, and he returns to his place in the sky (Dumézil, 1971 [in 1973, p.28 ff.]). The grandsons' raising of the fallen king realises the principle of verticality as an ascension rather than as a descent into oblivion. It has a cradling oscillatory quality about it that is intrinsic to the mirroring conception of a *microcosm: macrocosm*.

Twins face each other as a water baby and an air baby in a new version of the Narcissus myth. The air baby cannot tolerate being apart from its twin (as though bodily they had once been the same organism), or apart from the primordial element of water in which the other twin lives. The existence of eyes that emerge from a watery environment eradicates terrestrial eyes.

Shakespeare's Richard II smashes the glass that reflects an image of himself as an agent of sacrality and he is bereft of office. Separated from his former personification as an agent of creationism, he must suffer the fate of being identified with an isolated conception of cosmic destruction. He must know, through his body, the meaning of the breaking of the glass. The scream that no one utters and that no one has heard finds a way to communicate itself through him.

A womb, whether full or empty, carries a preconception of a gaze that activates reverberation if it should engage with a foetus. As the anointed king Richard II carries the reverberation. In the Wilton diptych, he kneels in prayer on one side of the diptych, and various saintly royal figures stand beside him. On the other side of the diptych, as though in mirror reflection, are the virgin mother and her baby, who extends a hand to Richard. The mother and baby are separate from Richard; but by the act of prayer, they are in a state of proto-identification/equation reverie with him. Behind the mother and child are angels with many-plumed wings that resemble luminescent mirror fragments. The four points, the four faces, as fragments of broken glass provide the ground out of which arises the principle of reverberation.

> For we have at our disposal, above all in mythology, examples of
> what I call mental reverberation, in which the image multiplies itself
> without seeming end. A fundamental fact of social life, as well as of the
> individual mind, is that the symbol – a summoned-up genie – has a life
> of its own. As with the many arms of Vishnu, each of which represents
> an attribute, as with the many plumes on the headgear of the Aztec
> priest–god, each of which reflects a different aspect of god, the symbol
> acts and reproduces itself without end (Mauss, 1924 [in 1950, p.300]).

If some of the forms into which the image translates – Vishnu's many arms, the plumes of the headgear of the Aztec priest–god, "each of which reflects a different aspect of god" – should enact the reverberatory nature of the image itself, they do so because they function in the same way as the fragments of Richard's mirror. The image that reverberates exists in a suspension that is no-where and in no-time. It is an idealization that arises out of a premonition of oblivion (the scream that no one utters and that no one hears).

The Exploding Star

Cosmic thinking does not separate psychology from natural philosophy. Plato uses a term, *stoicheia* or gnomon, which discovers the elements in some conception of a pivot to the axial co-ordinates. Aristotle extricates the discipline of natural philosophy from the general field of cosmology when he describes the four elements as qualities.

The Dogon conceive of a primal egg in which the axial co-ordinates hold together a womb-like environment of air fire earth and water that contain separate personalities. Eyes and ears in one compartment may enter into conflict with eyes and ears in another compartment if the system breaks down.

Children in North West Africa master a certain creationist paradigm by the age of seven (Pâques, 1964). A double helix, made up of two cone-like whirlwinds, one upturned on the other and that spiral in contrary directions, emanates the spectral presence of a cosmic tree that binds sky to earth – and earth to its quarters. The parts of the star-helix are either separated or united without conflict. The star reflects the double function of the axial co-ordinates: both as the four points that are unified with the self and the four points that separate from the self as extensions. The star when exploding operates on various levels of meaning. In one concrete equation it is the first sky. On either side of it are secondary stars. It is egg-shaped and contains all creation. Part of it is coloured red; and red equals woman, pregnant womb and birth (more concrete equations). It is first thing created, first ancestor, human head. Part of it is coloured white (and white equals man). It is three in one and one in three. It is "one equated with man"; it is "three equated with man and a breast on either side of him". The breasts on either side are wives. The man's arms, when star equals his body, are secondary stars. The arms when outstretched equal the first creation and equal an erect penis with testicles on either side of it.

From its beginnings, the star-as-head is composed of three elements: an upper half that is white and dry and a lower half that is red and humid. A black spiralling type of germ, drawn as a serpent, divides the two halves (Pâques, p.47). On another level of meaning, the star is fragmented. Its white half is an egg to the east that equals white sign, sky, fire as a primordial element, stone, meteor, mountain, while its red half is an egg to the west that equals red sign, the primordial element of earth (in one of its aspects), water as a primordial element, iron, grotto, a lake confined in the mountain.

The black spiralling germ (a version of Bion's contact barrier as a variable) is a trident to the north and an up-turned spiralling cone to the south. Without its central line, it is an up-turned cone that spirals in space. Trident equals black sign, the opposition of attachment and separation, fecundity, the primordial element of earth (in its second aspect), the triple serpent, the cosmic tree. The up-turned spiralling cone to the south is the primordial element of air and the whirlwind.

The four signs that indicate the four primordial elements and the quarters are man when they are united. East equals head, north equals nape to neck and possibly the spinal column, west is both arm and stomach, south is both arm and feet. Man consists of four primordial elements and seven parts.

Thinking of this type is evocative of the correspondences in French symbolist poetry of the mid- and late nineteenth century.

1. Following Freud, the therapist hopes to register un-annotated mental links, i.e. the scream that no one utters and no one hears. Consciousness of existence begins with the logic of hallucination or non interruption: a state in which surfaces exist without context. The nature of the surface contains the coincidence of opposites: it is membrane (creationism) and it is gap (destruction).
2. Knowledge concerning the transmitter and receptor of the communication arises later. Bishop Berkeley was perplexed by the epistemological status of the tree that falls in the seclusion of the forest and thought it necessary to suppose the existence of a God, the quality of whose perception is able to underwrite the tree's existence. Un-annotated links become meaningful communications.

The Nature of the Intersection Point

The intersection of the axial co-ordinates is a variable that represents a "form of things unknown".

A patient brings two dreams that enact the problematic nature of the depressive threshold crossing. In the first dream a black tent fills a fifth of a room. Overwhelmed by dread, he is unable to approach it: he thinks that the tent contains an abyss. In the second dream he is in the doorway to an operating theatre in which surgeons and doctors are investigating a man's body, perhaps with a view to operating on it. In his youth he had played the role of Thomas Beckett in a play in which four knights murder Thomas. The tent filled a fifth of the room. The cardinal points of the axial co-ordinates (the four knights) dismember the king at the no-where no-time intersection. The two dreams represent a religious vertex reading and a medical vertex reading of a depressive threshold experience.

He is exercised by the problematic relationship of personality and body. He feels projected into by his mother. The conflict in environment in which one type of eye is set against another type of eye is one in which a mother as separated environments in the mind splits sense communication as though they were factors in some argument that the mother has with herself. The patient is perturbed by the elusive nature of symptoms (factors in a mother's argument with herself), in a way that is evocative of Sydenham's attempt in the seventeenth century to distinguish the relationship between demonology and hysteria. The tormenting symptomatology of the body (epitomized by the idea of referred pain) parallels the "O" turbulence contained by the tent.

The patient refers, in an association, to a woman with a melanoma of the left eye and relates her condition to an "itchy mole" on another woman's thigh, and his anxiety that the mole might be cancerous. Beauty, dirt, evil and depressive anxiety lie in the eye of the beholder and can lead to the insight that "if she dies, I die also". Depressive understanding differs from states of fusion, since it implies a recognition that psychic otherness differs from otherness in nature. The patient describes the melanomic eye as "the common site", unconsciously "the common sight".

In a celebrated aside, Freud wrote of the ego as a body ego (Freud, 1923, p.27]). "The ego is ultimately derived from bodily sensations [...]. It may thus be regarded as a mental projection of the body [...]" (ibid., p.26, note 1). Bodily sensations determine the ego to the same extent as a mother, as the body, uses her infant (the ego) as a container for her projections. Breaking out of the condition of having been projected into activates the infant into states of catastrophic change.[2]

Coleridge writes in *The Friend*: "I can recall no event of human history that impresses the Imagination more deeply than the moment when Columbus, on an unknown ocean, first perceived the change of the magnetic needle." One of those "phenomena as startling as they are mysterious, (that) have forced on us a presentiment of (their) intimate connection with all the great agencies of nature; of a revelation, in cipher, the key to which is still wanting".

To lose sight of the axial coordinates as a system that describes duration is a stage on the retrogression that discovers them as an image in reverberation.

Notes

1. The five children measure out the space of the room in a beautiful if controlling enactment of the mystery of the primal scene; to which, at this stage of writing, the book is moving. In indicating "O", the axial co-ordinates evoke the primal scene.
2. Arguably "body ego" is the precipitate of maternal projections into the foetus or the infant.

20. THE FETISH AS SUBSTITUTE FOR THE ORGAN OF PSYCHIC PERCEPTION

An infant without a mother, or unable to internalise a mother, may construct a ritual surrogate for her, so that it has some means to know its own thoughts. It may even believe itself to be projected into by the ritual surrogate. It seeks to isolate itself from premonitions of dying. Shakespeare's Richard II enacts a premonition of death when he breaks a mirror and separates himself, as terrestrial twin, from the fragmented image of his celestial twin. The slivers of glass, as a failure in coincidence, realize as a pattern the existence of a third twin that personifies the fact that it can bring together or separate two aspects of the self. The mirror is a ritual surrogate.

In a veiled way, the central character of *The Tempest*, Prospero, is a divine king like Richard II; he thinks to preside over his own dying. Prospero has two types of mirror: *water*, whose mysterious powers the sea that surrounds his isle represents, and *an audience's mind* that is denied an object by which it can think for itself. Prospero transliterates the audience's mind into myriad reflections of his own face.

Bion alludes to the perceptions of a spectator who stands on the further side of a piece of glass on which Picasso paints. Picasso, like Prospero, takes over the transforming power that otherwise would belong to the glass as mediator between two reciprocals. Trapped in the glass two-dimensionally, the spectator might be the substance out of which the painting is made, rather than a mind that is able to think about the painting.

Coleridge recognised that in some way Shakespeare's *The Tempest* could not be thought about. He sought to resolve its elusive nature by describing it as "dream-like" in its equivocations, although it is not dream-like. He grappled with its perplexity by referring to failures in audience understanding. Some people suspend disbelief and "choose to be deceived" (Coleridge, 1818–1819 [in 1960, p.116]). Conceivably, the characters in *The Tempest* are dead: or they exist in some interim state between life and death that protects them from a fear of a threshold identified with annihilation. The audience is involved in this defensive process: hence the blankness in definition that Coleridge was able to observe. Someone in dying – let us say Prospero – and loses the ability to think about the experience (in the first instance associated with an ability to share in a mother's ability to reverie) and then erroneously may presume that not it but the world is dying. Christine Henry has written a book about the Bijogo under the title *Les îles où dansent les enfants défunts*. The title might apply to the people on Prospero's isle, whose status as living or dead beings is problematic. Near the end of the play, Prospero's evocation of a "dissolving globe" that leaves not a rack behind pins to an actual place metaphysical concerns about events in which the ability to think about the events is unsure.

The Contraction of Tripartite Space

As relevant to the drama as to myth and rite, the coincidence of *creation: destruction* has a triadic structure in which a variable, "coincidence", is personified as an intermediary/intercessor between twins (the "opposites" of creation and destruction, or depressive and paranoid-schizoid). Shakespeare collapses the triadic structure in *The Tempest* by postulating the idea that the twins as two spaces – audience space and acting space – are replicates of each other and not alternatives with a variable placed between them. The result inhibits any ability that the audience might have to discriminate between the perception of hallucination and intuition.

A theatre interior consists of three spaces: stage, auditorium and in between, in the proscenium theatre, a zero space in which the curtain rises and falls. The zero space is the counterpart to the altar in the theatre of Dionysus on which the sacrificial bull is slaughtered. Certain Indonesian temples are "divided into three parts [...]. This triad corresponds to the three divisions of the cosmos: the antithesis of upper and under world, united by the heavenly element" (Van der Kroef, 1954, p.856).

> The whole community is divided into two parts which are mutually antagonistic yet complementary; the total community can only exist if both occur and if both actively come into contact with each other. A marriage is the occasion for them to do just that (ibid., p.853 [quoting by de Jong]).

> "The sacred opposites of heaven and earth, male and female, whose fusion is the essence of the cosmos" (ibid., p.853).[1]

In Shakespeare's earlier plays, language extends like a sculpture into three-dimensional space. In *The Tempest* there is a conflict between the three-dimensional resonance of imagery often associated with music and water and a scenic presentation that foreshadows the court-centred two-dimensional scenery of a Caroline masque, painterly in its communication of a possible flatness in surface.[2] The two-dimensional effect is reflective of hierarchic art in general, as in the profiled art of the pharaohs' tombs.

In the opening scene of the play the resources of stage, space and time, and the audience's expectations, are swallowed up in the experience of a galleon sinking in a storm at sea: there are no witnesses left to the destruction. In the next scene the audience learns that it, as well as the travellers on the galleon, has been misled; no one has drowned, nothing has been lost. Or so it seems. Shakespeare describes the clothes of the drowned courtiers as "glistening". The effect is eerie and imaginative in its power to evoke the unimaginative.

A foreboding, concerning the loss of a Ptolemaic world-centred cosmos, united with a possible premonition concerning the future execution of an English king denied his authority, underlies the play's difficulties in coincidence. Shakespeare conceives of opposition as between the absolute power of a king's court when on land and its absolute loss when the king's galleon sinks at sea. It is as though a palace (Nonesuch?) containing the king and his entire court had sunk beneath the surface of the waters. Shakespeare projects the idea of death into the audience in the same way as Prospero projects an idea of death into the courtiers. The audience, as well as the courtiers who had thought to die, is denied any sustained space in which to think about the existential possibility of having to undergo drowning.

The Total Court Is Drowned: The Total Court Survives

The environment of the sacred king replicates his dual representation as *not being* and *being*. The coincidence of cosmos as destruction and creation persists in spite of human ignorance concerning its nature. In unselfconscious worldliness, the courtiers are somnambulists, or they are (to use a modern and problematic term) trauma victims, new-borns who have "mislaid" the schema of the primal scene, as well as the experience of their own birth.

The audience may begin to wonder if anything is real; a doubt echoed in the play by the enactment of states of delusion and inebriation. For the duration of the action after the sinking of the galleon, the audience is arrested by an image of *terra firma*, Prospero's isle, a bounded space that Prospero is able to dominate by magic but not to control. Music and love move through and about the isle, as water flows through a river harp, in spite of Prospero's wishes.

Coming to the isle, or leaving it, most of the characters associate the crossing of water to rite-of-passage fears concerning birth or death, or more fundamentally to states of becoming or of not being. Undergoing a "drowning", whose status in reality is problematic, adds to the condition of ontological doubt. Even Prospero thinks of his departure from the isle as a stage in a journey towards death, but in an unreal way. Nobody undergoes depressive intuitions of annihilation.

Coleridge rebukes critics who wish to describe form in art as a kind of formula. He projects his own inclination to naturalism –

evident in his descriptions of *The Tempest* – onto the French critics of a century earlier, who had insisted that plays should observe the three unities: by which they had meant that audiences and characters on stage should think to live in the same space–time continuum, and to undergo an action that is an audience–actor continuum, so far as setting in space, time and action is concerned. Audiences with such expectations, thinks Coleridge, are unlikely to grasp the nature of *The Tempest*. They will think of it, as the French do, as "a miraculous monster, in whom many heterogeneous components [are] thrown together [...] producing an irregular and ill-assorted structure".

Coleridge scapegoats the French critics for a point of view that many people maintain. The "French critics" have an experience similar to the one Bion had with his "On Arrogance" patient. They come into contact with the Oedipal sphinx and they are faced by incomprehension and a breakdown in expectation. The contact barrier is voided of definition (which is one meaning of the monstrous). Audience, or therapist and patient, find themselves in an identical space–time continuum, with a loss of any presence of the imaginative in the room.

A "transcendental" element in a session – some gesture or phrase by a patient – may convey a meaning so condensed that it takes a considerable span in space and time before the therapist discovers that it has been translated into an imminent meaning. Birth and death are no more than evocations of some fundamental rite of passage that logically precedes embodiment and through which the therapist hopes to travel.

Exceptional among Shakespeare's plays, *The Tempest* observes the three unities. Audience and characters on stage, in an adhesive identification with each other, are reflecting symmetries. The play resembles an imperial Chinese city in which every aspect of the cosmos is reflected in a mirroring presence at the centre. The contact barrier has lost its function as a transforming mediator and staves off any evidence of splitting in the unconscious group object that the actors, the parts they play and the audience share.

Hallucination and Imagination

Nietzsche (1873) saw a positive in water. He described Occidental philosophy as beginning with Thales' realization that everything is one and that water is the unity to being (Nietzsche [in 1911, p.86 ff.]); water to this extent is a pivot between not being and being, the living and the dead; a coincidence out of which musical forms may arise. The Chinese emperor moves through the rooms of a circular "hall of light" creating the calendar and planetary movement, the "mystic dance" of the "starry sphere" – "mazes intricate, eccentric, intervolved, yet regular" (*Paradise Lost*, Book 5).

Nietzsche was impressed by Thales' ability to juxtapose a sensible world, realized through sensation, with a metaphysical world, realized through the imagination. Thales was not thinking about water in an analogical way; he was not alluding to amniotic fluid, or to the poetic significance of womb or myth water. The water Thales was thinking of was *real*, but his insight concerning its nature was metaphysical.

However water, like fire, as a coincidence between the opposites of creation and destruction, is liable to be overwhelmed by one or other of them. It is like Richard II's broken mirror.

> Psycho-Analyst: [...] I do not like looking-glasses, sheets of water, novels, psycho-analysis.
> Robin: "Sheets of water" you say. Would you include sheets of amniotic fluid?
> Psycho-Analyst: Certainly – any liquid. I would go further and suggest that sheets of reflective fluid of any kind become objects of dislike.
> Alice: You mean the fluid does not have to be liquid but can, as at birth, be changed to a gaseous fluid?
> Psycho-Analyst: Quite so. But liquid or gaseous, the fluid can be constantly changing from [a] calm reflecting state to a turbulence (Bion, 1979, pp.56–57)].

The reticulations of music, like the "rising world of waters dark and deep" that John Milton thinks of as won from the void and formless infinite, are an agent for the imagination and for dreaming. But they can be also an agent for the anti-imaginative: drownings of truth, submersions that destroy belief in the institution of baptism, hallucination in the sense of a blanking out.

Prospero's use of water to simulate the drowning of his enemies is akin to an envy that works its transformations without leaving a mark. Prospero has water in a spectral guise deny his enemies their right to being. He projects the terror of death into them, and then removes the experience from their minds. His misuse of water diminishes his capacity for wonder, so that he knows water as being at most a margin to his kingdom. The error of the courtiers, and in part of Prospero himself, is to think that sanity is comparable to dry land and that creative turbulence can be kept to the margins, as something to be used. But misused water is the anti-imaginative itself; it equivocates issues of being and not being; and anyone enveloped by it enters the never-never land of the living dead.[3]

The King above Water

Prospero is an analogue for the two beings on whose united power as a pivot the structure of the play depends. His shift from being an analogue for one split aspect of the pivot to the other split aspect is unheralded by the action of the play and it is pointed up by the radical difference of his relationship to the audience at the beginning of the play and his relationship to it at the play's end. "The great globe itself [...] shall dissolve" (*The Tempest*, IV.i.145) and cf. his concluding speech in octosyllabics in which he pleads for the audience's indulgence.

The first pivotal being is Alonso, king of Naples, a king above water, who reconciles being and non being, but in such a way as to equivocate the concepts of being and non being, so that they arouse the type of doubt that Descartes described when faced by a hallucination. Alonso's presence on Prospero's isle has an uncanny quality about it. He is the king above water, assured of his courtly status, and yet he might be the ghost of someone who has actually drowned. His authority as divine king is disabled. He is so immersed in courtly intrigue that he is unable to perceive any spirituality in the culture of the isle. Prospero submits him to a phantom drowning and then removes the experience from his mind, perhaps entirely, in a negation of the meaning of baptism. It may have less changed the king than confirmed the fact that his mind was without the capacity to think imaginatively. He is drowned into worldliness, as though he were unable to learn from the experience of being psychically born.

Alonso, as a king–priest who has lost his vocation, reflects the predicament of Prospero, a king–priest estranged from vocation who has lost any sacramental image of himself. It is as though Richard II, in realizing the separation of his two bodies as terrestrial and celestial selves, had avoided the meaning of his predicament as the victim of the sacrifice by losing himself in the fragments of the broken mirror.

The King Beneath Water

The second pivotal being is an aspect of Alonso that Alonso himself denies, the site of imaginative thinking, the king beneath water, who exists in the mind of Alonso's son Ferdinand alone and in the mind of the spirit Ariel, who helps Ferdinand to understand the relationship of mourning and the imagination. (Someone largely in a state of adhesive identification may yet have a split-off part of the self that undergoes the experience of depressive threshold transformation.) This is Alonso as the imagined drowned king, who undergoes the transfiguration of baptism, and who does not exist in actuality. Ferdinand mourns an idea: he does not know that his actual father is still alive; which is just as well, for the idea is an inspiration, and his actual father is unable to represent inspiration. Alonso as the non-existent drowned king is the principle of imagination, the transforming mediator of the contact barrier. He is able to submit himself to the creative powers of water and music.

> Full fathom five thy father lies; /Of his bones are coral made;/ Those are pearls that were his eyes:/ Nothing of him that doth fade, But doth suffer a sea-change/ Into something rich and strange (I.ii.397–402).

Bion has described the awe he felt when reading the passage in Virgil's *Aeneid* in which the god Somnus "hurls Palinurus into the sea with such violence that part of the ship is torn away at the same time" (1973 [in 1990, p.17]). Prospero undergoes a similarly disturbing transition in relation to his objects, which may have taken the form of a disquieting "birth" experience, when he is sent into exile by way of a failing vessel, a negative version of his idealized picture of the world as a "baseless fabric". "A rotten carcass of a butt, not rigg'd,/ Nor tackle, sail nor mast; the very rats/ Instinctively have quit it" (I.ii.146–148). The Boatswain echoes Prospero when he says that "we were dead of sleep [...] beneath the hatches [...] horrible awakening" (V.i.229). In pre-Oedipal terms, Prospero splits the maternal object into Miranda, aged three, as the good breast (she was a cherubim "that did preserve me") and into a placenta in a state of deterioration at the time of birth – the rotten carcass invaded, rather than rejected, by persecutory siblings (the "rats"), a paranoid-schizoid misconception of the couple in *pietà*.

At the end of the play, Prospero must reconcile himself with a lost image of his sacramental self. He is estranged from any thought of himself as a thought that exists within a benevolent environment, the potential space in a mother's mind in which she is able to think about an infant when she is absent from it. As a prototype of modern man, alienated from spirituality, he has to resort to creating an environment that is hallucinatory in order to survive. It is characteristic of his modernity that he should seek out the powers of life among "primitive people", as though he had to be born into an alien world. Like Robinson Crusoe, he has complicated feelings about his Man Friday. He describes Caliban as his "dark alternative": "this thing of darkness I/ acknowledge mine" (V.i.275).

Caliban shadows forth Prospero's lost dream self, in the same way as the watery reflection of the imaginary Alonso carries Alonso's potential to exist in three-dimensional psychic space. He links earth and sky like a divine king. "[...] in dreaming/ The clouds methought would *open*, and show riches/ Ready to drop upon me; that, when I wak'd,/ I cried to dream again" (III.ii.138–141). Caliban's use of the verb "open" is comparable in its difference to the use that Prospero makes of the same verb. "[...] graves at my command! Have wak'd their sleepers, op'd, and let them forth/ By my so potent art" (V.i.48–51).

Caliban receives dreams *from the skies* as a gift, while Prospero expects to raise the dead *from inside the earth*. Denied turbulence, Prospero knows embodiment and hallucination, not intuition. He describes the world as an "insubstantial pageant" (IV.i.155), although the world itself – short-lived in individual experience – is not insubstantial. By way of his earthiness, Caliban is put in touch with air and water, the elements by which reverie is engendered. The enslaved isle continues to speak through a music of air and water that Prospero cannot hear. Ferdinand asks: "Where should this music be? i' th' air or th' earth?/ It sounds no more: and, sure, it waits upon/ Some *god o 'th' island*. Sitting on a bank,/ Weeping again the King my father's wrack,/ This music crept by me upon the waters [...]" (I.ii.390–396).

In hallucination the infant thinks to hold an absent object in thrall to itself as a fetish. Pushed as a thought out of the benevolent environment in which imaginative transformations occur, mind undergoes an absence or blankness where space might be. The courtiers, Antonio and Sebastian, enter into an intrigue while "asleep with eyes open". People who sleep with their eyes open are corpse-confused because they are without some variable to transform fact into dream. If a mediator were to transform facts into dream, they would have to experience the painful dissolving of an unthinkable thought that they see as an obdurate monster. "The original question", claims Bion (1963), "is posed by a monster" (p.47). How can mind "dissolve" or resolve such a monster? As a failure in definition, as a failure in coincidence, the monster is an alternative to an idea of the self as a thought in the benevolent environment of someone else's mind.

A Cosmos That Consists of Hallucinations

In W. W. Jacob's short story *The Monkey's Paw* an elderly couple are granted three wishes. Their first wish results in their son being inadvertently crushed and killed by some machinery. They bring their son back to life with their second wish. As the son approaches the door of their house, they imagine him in his mutilated state, and they devote their third wish to returning him to the dead. W.W. Jacob's story puts into reverse the process of transformation that occurs in

Adam's dream.

Bringing the dead back to life by manic reparation, which is what Prospero claims to do, is to retrieve the environment of the imagination as an environment of hallucination. The dead witch Sycorax, a degraded analogue to the mother who dies in childbirth in *A Midsummer Night's Dream* and to Hermione in *A Winter's Tale* (Hermione and her new-born, Perdita, are presumed dead), personifies the fused object that excludes Prospero's double, *Prospero as a thought*, from an environment of the imagination. Prospero recalls that Sycorax confined Ariel "into a cloven pine; within which rift/ Imprison'd thou didst painfully remain/ A dozen years; within which space she died,/ And left thee there. It was mine Art" says Prospero, "[...] that made gape/ The pine and let thee out" (I.ii.274). Rarefying a condensed state (the cloven pine) is a beta element transformation in hallucinosis that travesties the idea of a depressive threshold transformation.

Ariel and Caliban are split aspects of a self that has "died", an aborted foetus that is unavailable to the living self. In the cosmos of hallucination, Ariel functions as an angelic aspect of projection, while Caliban carries the power of fetishism. The two figures counterpoint the worldliness of the king above water. Hallucination and fetishism are ways of dealing with the fact that the dreaming self has been lost in a mind that cannot think because it is fused with a dead person as a substitute for an internal object. In their elemental relationship to air and earth, Ariel and Caliban, more than any of the other characters, bring out the cosmological import of the play. Both of them are in contact with powers of music and dream that Prospero is exiled from. Ariel personifies the link between air and water; Caliban personifies the link between earth and sky. Both of them have a relationship to Miranda and Ferdinand that is expressive of a tenderness towards the primal scene (the axial intersection) that Prospero knows only fitfully.[4]

Notes

1. On the other hand, gender confusion and cross-dressing at one time characterised the Indonesian theatre.

2. Nicolas Poussin, in paintings of this time, foreshortens the depth of perspective space into an effect reminiscent of low-relief carving.

3. Did Shakespeare see the courtiers at King James's court and wonder: are these people devoid of any knowledge of death; or are they so fearful of death that they cannot dream, or enter into reverie, apart from the type of reverie that motivates deathly intrigue?

4. Prospero depicts one of the meanings of his own death when he arranges the magical sinking of the king's galleon. In ancient Africa, kings were either buried in boats or close by boats that were presumably intended to carry them through the celestial overworld. Alonso and Prospero must know the painful meaning of "losing" a daughter to the life cycle. The marriage of Alonso's daughter in Tunis/Carthage in North Africa activates the preoccupation with oblivion.

PART FOUR

The Play Shakespeare Did Not Write

21. THE GIFTS OF THE SATURNALIAN KING

> The *kachina* dances are perhaps the most beautiful of Zuñi
> ceremonies. Instituted according to tradition solely as a means of
> enjoyment, they became the most potent of rain-making rites, for
> since the divine ones no longer come in the flesh, they come in
> their other bodies, that is as rain. (Bunzel, 1932, p.517)

The depressive and the paranoid-schizoid twins appear in Zuñi
mythology in relation to water as a maternal element. Gods who
embody the rain represent the depressive twin, while the murdered
kachina children who live beneath the surface of a lake represent the
paranoid-schizoid type of twin, who has the power to abduct living
children and even to become them.

Lévi-Strauss (1952) makes this point in *"Le Père Noël supplicié"*,
a paper that does not appear in the collections of his papers. On 2
December 1951 the ecclesiastical authorities of Dijon burnt Father
Christmas in effigy; they had hoped to end a growing "Père Noël" cult
in France. Lévi-Strauss saw the authorities as re-enacting the divine-
king sacrifice of the king of the Saturnalia, but without any awareness
of what they were up to. He indicated a structural analogy between
the masked Pueblo Indians who enact the *kachina* ceremonies and
Father Christmas as a deteriorated representative of divine kingship.

Pueblo Indian villagers disguised in costumes and masks dance
out a representation of the gods and ancestors, in which they hand
out rewards and punishments to the village children. One of the
conventions of the ceremony is that the children *have to pretend not*

to recognise the disguised villagers, in the same way as children in other cultures pretend not to recognise "Father Christmas". The *kachina* ceremony reverses the meaning of the link in the Oedipus legend between reward and punishment and *a failure to see through a disguise.*

The act of deception, whether persuasive or not, is placatory. The disguised *kachina* adults enact the role of children who have drowned, possibly in some rite-of-passage sacrifice, at the time of the first migrations. The dead children live in a village beneath the surface of a lake. At one time the dead children took revenge on the living by coming to the villages and stealing the living children. The villagers attempted to save their children from abduction by promising the dead children that they would be remembered in masked dances and ceremonies, in which the adults would represent them. The condition for this promise was that the dead children would not leave their underwater village. Lévi-Strauss proposes that the adults in the village deceive their children because they believe that the living children are the dead children in disguise. Initiates create a fictional space and practise rites to describe a reality that the uninitiated embody unthinkingly. The elite seek to metabolise the meaning of events that occur outside its walled kingdom: an unstable way of thinking about the unthinkable that breaks down at any sign of discontinuity, as at the year's end or at the witching hour of midnight, when reversal in perspective (*une réciprocité de perspectives*) intensifies.

During the Saturnalia the uninitiated (children, slaves, the dead) determine the categories of social and gender distinction.

The Breakdown of Reciprocals

A mirror in an Arcadian sanctuary devoted to Despoina shows the reflection of huge statues of gods situated behind the one who looks into the mirror. "On the right, as you leave the temple, there is a mirror fitted into the wall. Anyone who looks into this mirror will see himself either very dimly or not at all, but the images of the god and the throne are clearly visible" (Pausanias [in Frazer, 1898, p.422]). A therapist might be startled when looking into the mirror of a session to discover that selfhood has disappeared to be replaced by an image of the gods in effigy. Conceivably Freud, as he worked with his Russian patient, looked into the mirror of the session and saw a reflection of an absence where the gods might have been and was impelled to formulate the concept of the primal scene as a description of the reflection. But he then felt drawn to secure the primal scene to space and time. A French commentator (Duparc) has described Freud as latching onto the primal scene as a fetish, so to avoid an experience of it as the uncanny.

Descartes observed that when a limb is severed, mind "hallucinates" an imaginary limb so as to contain an unsecured pain. When one of the reciprocal functions on which the unknowable variable depends to create meanings breaks down, a similar transformation occurs. An imaginary limb appears and obscures the presence of the severed limb, so that the idea of a severed limb seems to disappear. The severing of the limb, the loss of the organ for psychic perception, marks the therapist's relation to a mirror that either reflects body alone or blurs out body and reveals agents for the imperceptible code that cannot be related to. Is there then a different type of reflector available that allows for imaginative conjecture? Conceivably Freud, in working with the Russian patient, found such a mirror in the text of Shakespeare's *King Lear*.

His paper "The Occurrence in Dreams of Material from Fairy Tales", which is about a mythic aspect to the celebrated dream his Russian patient had about wolves, and his paper "The Theme of the Three Caskets", which includes a reading of *King Lear*, were published at the time that he was working with the Russian patient. I conjecture that the interplay of the Russian patient's experience and the Shakespeare text had Freud discover a play that Shakespeare did not write and that is a reciprocal to the play that Shakespeare did write.

King Lear is a mirror that reflects *an absence* of the gods. A painful severance occurs when religious apprehensions exist without the presence of religious objects. The pain increases the rack of sexual feelings in their hunger for objects that satisfy. (The tormented sexual struggle of Goneril and Regan over Edmund as an object of un-consummated desire results in their death.) A negation of "O" comes into contact with a negation of sensory equipment and realises a becoming in negation, a culture of non being. The paranoid-schizoid imaginary twin communicates terror. Its optic and auditory pits, negations of eyes and ears, are places of the skull and of the holocaust.

22. THE OPENING AND CLOSING OF SHUTTERS ON A WINDOW

The noticeable effects of working in a maternal transference with a man whose mother died in pregnancy when he was less than two years old were threefold.

1. He began to seek out people who had once known his mother and to construct an image of her. He had no way of knowing whether the information was true, and he was inclined to accept it uncritically. He seemed to have no awareness that he might find an image of his mother within himself. If he had intuitions of an organ of psychic perception, they were of a concrete kind.
2. He became aware of the extent to which he had to side-step intimacy in his relationship with his partner. He responded to his partner's feelings as though they were incomprehensible and dangerous. The relationship broke down.
3. His initial projection into the therapist – of a sensation – was narrow and intense. The opening paragraph to chapter one of this book gave an account of this projected state. The therapist found himself moving along a deteriorating surface, as though the patient's words were mosaic pieces whose edges had disappeared.

The claustrophobic situation switched into one of agoraphobia when the therapist thought about the experience after the session. Agoraphobic sensations took the form of a dismembering and falling apart through indefinite space. It was not clear why the theme of the victim in sacrifice should have occurred at this point. Less directly and more slowly, another phantasy came into focus. The agoraphobic space was unmonitored: the science of astronomy and the night sky could not be related. In order to be in contact with the power of maternal reverie, the infant has to pass though a stage of attempting concrete definitions of this intuitive link. One such concrete definition is the optic glass. But in the case of this patient, evidence of the optic glass as an organ of psychic perception was minimal. There was no way to think about the space or the objects that it might contain.

Monitoring of intuition in the room was fitful. Scannings in thought failed to meet up with any mind to correspond to it. Intuitions came into being without context, and obvious links disappeared. A dream provided an iconography for these sensations and an implicit analogue for the therapist's hunch that a link existed between the celebrated dream of the wolves and Freud's understanding of Shakespeare's *King Lear*. The therapist was unable to understand these events at the time when they occurred.

In the dream *he was inside a large barn. He was aware of watching and of being watched. A man outside the barn drove a flock of birds into the barn. One bird escaped and entered into a cavity space in one of the barn walls. Someone was opening and closing shutters.*

The cavity wall has the same meaning to the patient as the effigy has to the divine king. It is a concretisation of the "gaze in the womb", the idea of maternal reverie in fusion with the imaginary twin in the form of a foetus. In Bion's early thought, this is the point at which alpha and beta thinking separate from each other. The optic glass is a concretisation that belongs to the same series.[1] The cavity wall marks an inversion in meaning of the optic glass and the process by which the paranoid-schizoid imaginary twin moderates into the depressive imaginary twin. It probably belongs to the theory of the imaginary twin in negation.

The patient's projection of claustrophobia and projection in the absence of agoraphobia formalise into the cavity wall as an icon of negative space. In place of "twin" functions on either side of a floating signifier that is the organ of psychic perception as a mediator between paranoid-schizoid and depressive twins and a moderator of depressive threshold pain, there is lability between states of rarefaction and condensation. The cavity and the thickness on either side of it are alternately representations of a claustrophobia and an agoraphobia that are unstable and rigid.

In the act of conception the bird as a communication of the father's eloquence enters the cavity as the imaginary twin: its presence can be experienced as a positive or negative space. As negative space, it is "the optic pit", Gloucester's blindness as a condition of Everyman, the caesura in the transparent mirror. The belief that nature abhors a vacuum is a way of expressing fear of the negative conception of the imaginary twin. The cavity wall is a reification (a fossilization perhaps) of the idea that "O" in negation puts pressure on negations of the sense organs.

It is tempting to follow Freud (1918) in his understanding of the opening of the window in the Russian patient's dream in terms of scopophilia, especially so since the motif of the opening and closing of the shutters in the barn dream is close to the motif of watching and being watched. But in regard to the later patient's associations to the dream – they indicated a break-through in feeling – it is more convincing to think of the opening and closing of the shutters as a concrete realization of the organ of psychic perception and an attempt to convert the negative space of the paranoid-schizoid twin into the positive space of the depressive twin, a transformation by means of which the function of maternal reverie might enter dream thought.

Freud conceives of negative space in two ways: as a casket made of lead and as Cordelia, the beautiful queen of France, a Joan of Arc figure who holds her child to the task of honouring its role as the divine king and victim of the sacrifice. Cordelia is the indicator of the path through annihilation that occurs on the depressive threshold.

> Why, he was met even now
> As mad as the vexed sea, singing aloud,
> Crowned with rank fumiter and furrow-weeds,
> With hardocks, hemlock, nettles, cuckoo-flowers,
> Darnel, and all the idle weeds that grow

> In our sustaining corn.
> (*King Lear*, IV.iv.2–5)

Cordelia keeps her father to his role as the divine king. He is a corn-god who sustains the harvest by drawing the destructive power of the weeds onto himself. He cannot escape from the obligations of his task by acts of self-degradation or by loss of faith or by loss of mind. Whatever the king might wish, he has to be the victim in the sacrifice, if Albion is to be saved from corruption.

The "mother" in the consulting room was not the familiar and positive figure of the "absent mother", with her well-delineated atmospheres and dimensions; she was a mother related to cataclysm. Although incompatible with the patient's experience of an actual mother loss, the mother related to cataclysm was compatible, as an objective correlative (or ritual surrogate), for the therapist's own childhood memories of France just before and after the Second World War and for the ravaged psychic landscape that Shakespeare describes in *King Lear*.

The therapist had to find a "supervisor" within or without the self who could embody the landscape of cataclysm as well as locate it. Reconstructing the landscape was not enough; it had to be directly known, in the same way as Gloucester had to know the negative landscape of a fall from a cliff through his contact with Edgar. Prospero's wish to bring alive the dead, to reconstruct circumstances, and Caliban's need to receive dreams as gifts that descend from opened clouds are different ways of responding to "O". Reconstruction, Prospero's way, depends on the false postulate that the objective correlative can be created as a means of holding together a symbolization in feeling, when in fact the objective correlative is meaningful only as an optic glass used in the service of intuition. The optic glass is a concretization of an understanding of intimacy in which the other partner in the intimacy operates in dimensions that are beyond the understanding of the self as the mouth at the nipple. "Reconstructing" the landscape is not adequate to the task; it has to exist as a multi-dimensional and prior imaginative conjecture before it can be responded to.

The patient's communications could not have been more cut

off from the depth of musical dimensionality that characterises *King Lear*. But in one particular he had an affinity to the play. There is no mention, and no indication, of a mother in the twining of the fates of the Lear and Gloucester dynasties. Acute to the quality of this absence, Freud reverses it into a positive negation in his paper on the three caskets. He describes Lear's daughters as standing for three aspects of a mother. One aspect of the mother is linked to an unacceptable conception of death. Cordelia's "no" to her father (as son) is in effect a mother's assertion that the son must travel by way of the *via negativa* as a precondition to having life.[2]

Freud says little about the Russian patient's mother; he lays emphasis on the theme of a father's use and misuse of potency. His interpretation of *King Lear* is informative about the mother's absence. In place of the Cordelia mother who says "no", the Russian patient has an attractive, even seductive sister who terrifies him by pointing to a picture of a striding wolf in a book of fairy tales. The wolf is a representation of the paranoid-schizoid imaginary twin. The sister later committed suicide. The Russian patient attempted to dissociate himself from any feeling concerning her death by displacing his feelings of grief onto a charismatic figure, the long dead poet Pushkin. The suicide of the sister is an outcome of one version of the primal scene. The Russian patient is presumed to have witnessed a sexual act in infancy, in which his father anally raped his sister.

Placing together King Lear and the Russian patient case history elicits certain concrete equations. Cordelia and her "no" become a mother who contains a dead foetus, who in turn become the attractive sister with the book illustration of the wolf, who in turn become the sister with Pushkin as the charismatic dead baby, who in turn become Cordelia and Edmund (the name of Shakespeare's actual brother, or so I understand from a plaque in Southwark cathedral). Edmund is "illegitimate" because he is agent for an unacceptable pain. He is the charismatic and beloved child who has died, Jacob to Edgar's Esau. Edgar is the author's mouthpiece (I think), who feigns or knows a psychotic breakdown in his journey across the wilderness.

Poor Tom, that eats the swimming frog, the toad, the tadpole, the wall newt and the water; that in the fury of his heart, when the foul fiend rages, eats cow-dung for salads, swallows the old rat and the ditch-dog, drinks the green mantle of the standing pool [...] (*King Lear*, III. iv.134–127).

The Russian patient's overt identification with Jesus as his imaginary twin, on the grounds that he and Jesus were born on Christmas day, completes the series of equations by which Cordelia's "no" becomes the mother of the *pietà* in vigil over the murder and death of her son. The Russian patient achieves an identification with Jesus by confusing the nature of time in myth and the nature of time in history. In myth, time is always eternal recurrence, a theme from Nietzsche whose source Freud (1919) was aware of when he described the uncanny as "constant recurrence" (p.234). The fact that the same day in the calendar commemorates the Russian patient's birth and the birthday of Jesus is allowed to override the fact that the birthday did not occur in the same year.

But why three mothers? Triple-faced Hecate stands at the intersections of a cross-road and looks in each direction. Her glance, like light refracted through a prism, deflects pain. The patient had a cavity wall (exo-skeleton) as a ritual surrogate for the maternal reverie function. He was full of noise; or rather he was without the composure of silence. He rustled, he puffed, he creaked when he moved. He might have been made of stiff canvas, like a tent. He could have been a child brought up in an institution (claustrophobia), or he could have been a nomad (agoraphobia). He dreamt schematically of taking a tent and going on a camping holiday, or of living out in a London park and of being indifferent to the fact that it was raining. The failure in sensation in regard to the rain reflected the existence of dreams in deposit and unavailable to him, concerning the reality in sensation of rain. He dreamt of high cliffs that overlooked the sea. He was convinced that no one would fall over the cliffs. He was dissociated from any realization that he might drown in some agoraphobic idea of sea or sky or reality itself.

The idea of living "out in the open" and the linking of cliffs and cliff-falls momentarily brought King Lear into focus; but again the analogy lay in the therapist's response to the transference. It was incoherent and there was no point in mentioning it, and indeed the therapist found no occasion to mention to the patient the possible resonance between his experiences and Shakespeare's play. In regard to the barn dream, the patient had a powerful association, but more powerful than either dream or association was the therapist's sense of an absence in meaning between them. It was no longer possible to feel secure in what Rilke has called an "interpreted world".

The patient described how he had been watching a television "soap" in which a father tells his daughter about the mother's death in a car crash. He was filled with grief, perhaps for the first time in his life, concerning his mother's death; and the movement into grief is enacted by the opening and closing of the shutters as representations of acts of interpretation. He realized that transference factors were playing some part in his grieving. He was brusque when his partner tried to console him. He wept as he reported watching the "soap", and he recalled two occasions when he had felt pressure on his lungs and thought that his ribcage (or possibly his heart) was about to burst.[3]

When his mother had died, his father had held him all night and walked up and down the room. He refers bitterly to his step-mother and then wants to censure the criticism.[4] In time, his step-mother had separated from his father and had prohibited the patient from visiting his father's sister and daughter, whom he compares to the daughter in the television "soap". The alleged cruelty of his step mother, which was of mythic proportions, is inseparable from the cruelty of a concrete representation of the organ of psychic perception that in remaining concrete separates him from psychic growth: He wants to hear good about his actual mother, but he also wants to hear bad about her, and this takes the form of listening to gossip about his step-mother (of which there is no shortage). His mother and his step-mother are at one in being constructions largely unrelated to direct experience. The formation of the concrete representation of the organ of psychic perception is bound up with his need to find a mother by any means, even if it is only a mother by hearsay.

The unacceptable pain contained in Cordelia's "no" gets in the way of moving from the negative space of concrete conceptions of the meaning of reverie into positive space. Freud intuited this difficulty when he wrote in his *King Lear* paper about a patient who believed that a certain dream was a telepathic communication from a "dumb" man, the subject of the dream who was reputed to have committed suicide at the time that the dream occurred. Cordelia's "no" is similar to the "blush" that another man who committed suicide complained about to Bion and that Bion thought of as imperceptible. The scream that no one utters and that no one hears is the act of sacrifice as a message that no one transmits and that no one receives and that has to be destroyed in order to be found meaningful.[5] The imaginary twin in negation turns the becoming of "O" into a journey into terror.

Freud relates *King Lear* to the dumb man dream (surely the gist of the *King Lear* paper); Melanie Klein relates hallucination to absence; Bion relates hallucination to modulatory powers that are evocative of a mathematician's thinking: intuitions that mark the evolution of a Shakespearean dimension in psychoanalysis.

The prism cannot regulate the boundaries of the spectrum that it creates when light shines through it. The dead one disappears, and in the act of entering oblivion undergoes a transformation in hallucinosis. The dead one returns through the act of disappearance as evidence of a refraction of light through the prism of a mother's eyes. Shakespeare looks into the 'vexed sea' and perceives a cornfield with alien flowers in it and at the same time personifies through the movement of the waters an image of the rain god as scapegoat. Similarly the lake-eyes of a mother lost in death cannot keep the dead *kachina* children within the water; they return like gods whose gaze is one that the terrestrial children cannot tolerate.

To be installed as divine king is to be set up as the victim who will be sacrificed; it is to be classified under the heading of total destruction as well as of total creation; it is to enter a class under which nothing falls.

The idea of the imaginary twin as a mode of unacceptable suffering in a mother's mind cannot be kept in perspective. It overrules intuitions concerning concepts of magnitude and duration. Insecurity of duration in space and time fuels the cloning effects of the uncanny in states of retreat from pain. The idea disappears or it appears; it recedes without reason or it comes too close.

The Russian patient experiences the myth of being born on the same day as Christ, never mind the year or the century, as a source of persecution, as well as a spur to feelings of grandiosity. He wants to enter Christ and acquire his status, but he fears that Christ will reverse this perverse intrusion and enter him, leaving him with the agony and death of the crucifixion. His nurse suggested to him that "Since Christ had made wine out of nothing, he could also have made food into nothing, and in this way avoided defecating" (Freud, 1918, p.63). His outrage at this lie resonates during his first meeting with Freud (Gay, 1988, p.287), when he accuses Freud of being a "Jewish swindler" and suggests that they should practise anal intercourse together (as though Freud were Jesus, the imaginary twin in negation). Christ swindles the Russian patient by projecting his mouth and anus into the Russian patient, so that the Russian patient thinks that he has twice as many problems with these orifices as anyone else might have.

Lear suffers the same fate as the Russian patient. The Russian patient wants Jesus' status as a divine king without having to undergo the act of sacrifice. Lear wants to continue as the divine king without taking on the "victim" clause in the contract. He hopes, as did Macbeth, to negotiate a deal with triple-faced Hecate and to placate dead ancestors by making a legacy to his daughters; he is like the masked dancers who attempt to placate murdered children by enacting the *kachina* ceremonies.

Notes

1. And so is the phantasy by which Freud recognized his kinship with the Russian patient: that of being a new-born in a caul.

2. Ella Freeman Sharpe (1950, p.225) takes the argument one stage further. She points to a concrete equation between Gloucester's agony in being blinded and Goneril's possible pregnancy – an inference supported only as an "unconscious" reading of the text. A negation of "O" (the other foetus as the imaginary twin in negation) presses in on a negation of optic pits. Sharpe's account of the play anticipates future conceptualizations. She appears to see Lear and the Fool as versions of the paranoid-schizoid and the depressive imaginary twins.

3. The cavity wall begins to transform into the contact barrier with twins on either side of it. The near bursting of his heart is reminiscent of Lear's belief in a likeness between dying and falling in love.

4. His father's helpful arms turn into the step-mother as a cruel restrictive cage.

5. "Suicide is the one authentic act of sacrifice" (Lévi, 1898, p.133).

23. THE HIDDEN GOD

> A boy calls out, asking his aunt to speak to him, because he is
> frightened of the dark. His aunt says, "what good would that do?
> You can't see me". The boy answers, "that does not matter. If
> anyone speaks, it gets light" (Freud, 1905, p.224 n.)

Years before in childhood the Russian patient had dreamt recurrently
of a window opening at the end of his bed. In the garden outside
the window he would see five or seven wolves seated in uncanny
stillness on the branches of a walnut tree. Facing him, as he lay on
Freud's couch, was a grandfather clock.

> In the room in which the first sessions were held there was a large
> grandfather clock opposite the patient, who lay on a sofa facing away
> from me. I was struck by the fact that from time to time he turned his
> face towards me, looking at me in a very friendly way as though to
> propitiate me, and then turned his look away from me to the clock. I
> thought at the time that he was in this way showing me his eagerness
> for the end of the hour. A long time afterwards the patient reminded
> me of this piece of *dumb show* (my italics) and gave me an explanation
> of it; for he recalled that the youngest of the seven little goats hid
> himself in the case of the grandfather clock while his six brothers were
> eaten up by the wolf (Freud, 1918, p.40).

The enquiring looking back at Freud expresses some need in the
patient to integrate an experience of the clock into the transference.

Freud thinks that the patient wants to escape from a devouring wolf psychoanalyst through the open door of the session's end.

When linked to the idea of repetition, the opening of the window belongs to the same series as the opening and closing of the shutters in the barn dream. The Russian patient fears to be trapped in an object that has pulse. The pulse in the dream landscape that faced him as he lay in bed and the ticking of the actual grandfather clock that faced him later as he lay on the couch is a reciprocation of functions without content. Steady breathing appears to be an entrapping. The unacceptable pain associated with the imaginary twin converts him into a paranoid-schizoid presence, a negation that exists in a negative space. Choking and gasping and swallowing replace steady breathing. Terror informs the reciprocity by which the oceanic spatiality of a landscape, on which a window opens and closes, translates into an idea of time. The Russian patient knows the space before him as either claustrophobic or agoraphobic. The mouths of wolves are paranoid-schizoid deteriorations of a depressive experience of the stigmata.

The Monads of Ignorance

The dreamer of the barn dream and the Russian patient intuit an unconscious affinity between their capacity to breathe and the functions of the maternal breast. In the barn dream the image of the cavity wall is a representation of negative space. Its counterpart in positive space is the relation of the lungs and the thorax.

Lungs and the thorax evoke the expansion and contraction of space in archaic cosmology (the alternation of microcosm and macrocosm). The axial co-ordinates derive from sensations about the bone cage. Certain thinkers in ancient Greece believed that the lungs were the seat of the mind and that breathing was a form of proto-thinking (Onians, 1951, p.60, ft. 2). In reverie, mother and infant breathe through a lung–mind that is sometimes a shared object and sometimes two objects that are able to communicate by a single means. The organ for psychic perception, the optic glass or psychic telescope, is the psychic source for the idea of a shared ground in reciprocation. The ancients located the organ for psychic perception in the thorax, and in bone structures allied to the thorax, as well as in the lungs. The closeness of Pelops' shoulder-blade to his lungs accounted for its sacrality. The sacrality of Adam's rib derives from its proximity to the lungs–breast as the organ of psychic perception.[1] In acts of divination the lungs "showed the state of mind of the god, who at the moment of sacrifice was believed to have been identified with the victim [...] The lungs were the soul, and the breast was the seat of thought. It is still for us the 'wish-bone'"(Onians, ibid.). The Dogon peoples of Mali believe that breastbones contain the spiritual principles of man, since the power of "the word" is inside them in the form of a granary, in which there are the eight symbolic seeds of the eight primal ancestors. Water within the breastbone germinates the seeds. A process of ebullition activates speech (Calame-Griaule, 1965, pp.59–60).

Breastbones alternate between being organs of psychic perception and penile fetishes, as when they are called "wish bones" or "merry thoughts", objects that arouse consternation, as well as excitement.

Plato describes the thorax as a bird-cage.[2] As the axial coordinates, it is the tree of life as well. The birds that enter Plato's bird-cage (breath as an analogue for semen or milk) are monads of ignorance as well as monads of knowledge. In breathing the infant can learn of an aestheticism that is not related to knowledge, in feeding on milk it can know the engendering of its curiosity. Bion gave thought to the question as to what the basic psychoanalytic constituent might be. He asked the question: what is a psychoanalytic fact? Plato's conception of a breath of air as a monad of ignorance is one answer.

The clock experience is not set in clock time. Freud picks up a mythological resonance to it that he thinks is characteristic of his patient – the story of the goats and the wolves as a lateral extension into folktale – and that in effect takes psychoanalytic thought away from the diachronic considerations of history.

The grandfather clock case in myth is the place in which the goat has a one in seven chance of surviving death, or in which it has a seven in one chance of being killed. The lung-like place that may save the goat from death is likely to be the place where it is aborted.

Time is a rudimentary concept in mythology; it is no more than an adjunct to the idea of eternal return. In the paper on "The Three Caskets" Freud (1913b) provides mythological information of a kind that supports this train of thought: by a series of free associations, he relates the dream of the dumb man and the meaning of Cordelia's "no" to two stories from folklore, *The Twelve Brothers* by the brothers Grimm and *Cinderella*.

The fundamental motif of the Grimm story is that the birth of a thirteenth child, a girl, will lead to the destruction of twelve brothers. Either there are twelve births and one abortion, or twelve abortions and one birth. Myth is baffled by the concept of linear time and postulates that the clock cycle of twelve hours reverses at great speed within the space of one hour from twelve o'clock into one o'clock (effectively zero); in a similar fashion, the steady cyclical progression of the months of the year reverse into a nothing within the instance of the midnight of New Year. Conceivably Bion was thinking of the sudden loss of augmented time when he referred to the "ghosts of departed increments" (1977b, pp.315ff.]).[3]

Time in reverse, spelling abortion, summons up the idea of the imaginary twin in negation and the idea of negative space. It summons up the presence of Saturn as the father who eats his children, the time of the Saturnalia, the mouth of the wolf as a primitive recoil from the meaning of the stigmata. Who is to be cast in the role of the victim to the sacrifice? Cinderella, like the goat in the clock case (and Freud thinks her relevant to the matter in hand), thinks that the movement into the abortion span, the witching hour of midnight, will result in her being saved (everything will "fit" – shoes, lover, breast) and that "others" will have to bear the brunt of annihilation. In the confusion of time's reversal, a cruelty in judgment appears, and splitting is resorted to as an expedient to fend off a destabilised system of perspectival reversal, the mechanism of genocide, in which no one can be sure about who is the victim and who is allowed temporarily to survive.

The Russian patient's dream displaces the oscillatory effect of the opening of the window onto the view seen through the window, in which a configuration of Christ alternates with the light and shade of the tree form. In Bion's description, light and its absence, a tennis-net and a glowing reticulation, similarly alternate. The tree changes in meaning like the veiling and unveiling of light, the caul as veil, the mystery of the imaginary baby located in the nipple. It may be one tree, or many trees, and it may represent knowledge, ignorance, life or death. The axial coordinates un-focus into what Mauss has called a reverberation.

The capacity to reciprocate is at the basis of aesthetic experience. An alternation of light and dark as a manner of breathing can create a remarkable moment, as in the theatre. The lights in the auditorium fade and the stage area is filled by light, perhaps from behind a glowing scrim. The audience becomes the world of the ancestral dead, the drowned children, while the actors step into the orbit of life, as though they were the awakening dead. They carry the idea of a veiling, when the imaginary twin is experienced as an agent for the depressive position, and an idea of a mask when the imaginary twin is experienced as an agent for the paranoid-schizoid position.

A Benin musician wrote to a friend in America about a visit to the Paris opera. "I thought I had gone raving mad [...]. I found myself bang in the middle of a possession ceremony!" The experience reminded him of Africa and the moment before the *vodun* possession ceremonies began, a moment that he loved, when the musicians tuned their instruments and a "certain vibration" filled the air.

> As I sat at the Opera, I experienced the same impression of music awakening. The musicians took their places in the pit and began to warm up, one playing a few notes of the scale, the other a brief arpeggio. The music took possession of the place, just as it does at home (Rouget, 1980, p.245).

In the transference, the "few notes of a scale" and the "brief arpeggio", like the scintilla or after-effects of light that Bion describes as witnesses to the presence of "O", are tokens of the emerging of an archaic language. But the positive experience contains its own negation. A pressure on optic and auditory pits evokes imperceptibles – stigmata, blushes, states of dumbness – that "swallow" the field.

Pulse, a token of the primal scene, underlies the intuitive insight of the boy who could experience the sound of his aunt's voice as light. The musicality of speech is as linked to the capacity to breathe as luminosity is linked to the friendly contact of an aunt's voice. The fact that a pulse informs transformation and the emergence of meaning illuminates Freud's need to turn to Shakespeare as a consultant on the Russian patient case. Shakespeare's musicality, an auditory equivalent for the optic glass, depends on the generation of a pulse out of which a world of the imagination is able to arise.

Notes

1. When this icon is degraded into being an idol, it becomes the imaginary penis, which is one of the two forms of Freudian fetish.

2. The thorax as *mind*, that is. "Every mind contains a kind of aviary stocked with birds of every sort [...]. When we are babies we must suppose this receptacle is empty and take the birds to stand for pieces of knowledge [...] (*Theaetetus*, 197d ff.).

3. John Donne links this notion of annihilation to the "deep midnight" of St. Lucy's day, in his time the shortest day of the year. The poet, resolutely archaic in his cosmology, and like a divine king equated with the calendar, is "ruined" by love and then is "re-begot/ Of absence, darkness, death; things which are not". The king in the Swazi Incwala ceremonies knows a similar equation with darkness and loss of dimensionality as a stage in the process of rebirth.

24. THE RELATIONSHIP OF SWALLOWING AND THE PREHENSIVE OBJECT

> An iron filing prehends the magnetic field in which it lies; that is, it converts that field into a mode of its own behaviour (Collingwood, 1945, pp.173–174).

Two series of myths associated with Minoan Crete are informative about the nature of the organ of psychic perception. In the first series of myths, Rhea saves the infant Zeus from the swallowing mouth of Chronos, the infant's father, by bringing him up in the Diktean cave. She is guarded by the *kouretes*, who move around her, creating an impenetrable circular wall by their ritual dance. The infant Zeus grows with astonishing speed, as though he were able to put into reverse the act of swallowing. He destroys Chronos.

> A divine baby who grew up with phenomenal speed and seeks a divine consort, a murderous attack made upon him by others who would occupy his place and win his bride, a miraculous restoration of the dead to a new life are evidence of various cults that have in common the annual birth, death and resurrection of Dionysus, the son of the sky-father by the earthmother (Cook, 1914, p.695).

The nature of this evidence is equivocal. Aratos describes the nurturers of the child as having "reared him for a year" (ibid., p.647), which implies that he grew up in a year (in which his growth is similar to vegetable growth), or that he was fostered after that time. The motif of rapid growth reverses the motif of greedy cannibalistic swallowing that occurs in relation to the dismembered victim of the sacrifice. In certain legends the kouretes (Cretans?) are the Titans (earthly kings) who dismember and eat the child. In other legends they are agents for Hecate (Jones, 1944, p.113).

Vibrant and disturbing presences of a similar kind turn up at the end of the 19th century in rural carnival pantomimes in Thrace, one of the regions associated with the cult of Dionysus. Gypsy actors burlesque the primal scene and act the motif of the child's rapid growth. Two of the actors, strangers to the place, "sat on the ground facing each other" and one of them "pounded on the ground with a stone" while the other (man or woman) "lifted her skirts up and down [...]"

> a pantomimic representation of the forging of the plough-share, the man hammering like a blacksmith, whilst the fanning with the skirts represents the action of a pair of bellows. At this point the child [*fostered by a comedy nurse*] begins to get too big for its cradle and demands meat, drink and a wife (Ridgeway, 1910, p.19).

The child's swift growth is a reversal of the contraction of the increment in twelve hours that occurs as the clock moves through the witching hour of twelve to one. In Bion's earlier writings, as in his account of the weir dream, contraction demonstrates the condensatory and aborting powers of the beta screen. In his later writings, disturbances of this kind indicate the onset of a becoming of "O". Pain requires a principle of sufficient reason if it is to be received as an icon rather than as an idol. Otherwise it is experienced as stemming from an alien environment. If it is to be tolerable, it requires some principle of mediation in its new environment.

A member of an infant observation group reported that while watching a two-month-old boy as he awoke in his cot, she had taken pleasure in his state of well being and had made the observation, which had the quality of a phantasy, that the boy was swelling up, as though growing too big for his cot. She had thought: this is ridiculous, and she had attempted to dismiss the observation from her mind. She was talking about what she thought she saw when she looked at the boy. She was also talking about a growth in her own mind, through the experience of having made contact with the child. She could not accept an intuition of this type and projected it onto the child in a way that allowed her to reject her perception of amazing growth as ridiculous. It can be hard to tolerate the possibility that anyone (even oneself) should be nourished by the presence of a new-born.

Another observer made contact with a West African mother and newborn son in a room where the new-born was sleeping in a cot some distance away from her. She could not see the new-born, but she could hear its breathing and in a kind of ecstasy she thought of its breathing as filling the room. It took almost a year of observation to realize that the observer's phantasies were in part the result of a projection of the child's mother, who felt the need to enact a rivalry over a loved object with the observer. The first time the observer saw the boy, he was wrapped in a yellow robe and she described him as though he were some legendary prince. His mother held him up against her shoulder, and he seemed so strong that the observer thought that he did not need neck support. Her idealisation of the infant continued for about four months, until one day she heard the mother in conversation on the telephone with a so-called "friend", who was talking about unfaithful husbands. The mother was perturbed by some element of projection in this conversation: and for the first time the observer was aware of the infant not as an object of desire in the primal scene but as a frail and helpless baby.

A student had a once a week therapy with a mute 8-year-old child for a period of two years. The child's mother, a single parent, told the student that the child was benefiting from the therapy and making progress at school. The child was generous also. In her silence she communicated by communicating visual hallucinations. Sitting in front of the student, she would look at him impassively. Sometimes her glance had a hint of the sardonic about it. Nothing happened; and yet she appeared to grow to a great size. The student could not believe his eyes.[1] She became, seemingly, a giant Japanese doll. The experience had no relationship to the categorizations of recollection, reconstruction or verification. It was an intuition that could be described as icon or idol. The muteness, the sense of sense disablement, of annihilation, activated a covert transformation in hallucinosis.

Outside the cave a divine king, who wears a sun mask and who projects destruction into others, is at the centre of the labyrinth. In relation to the cave, the labyrinth disappears. In fact, the actual existence of the Cretan labyrinth is suspect. Sir Arthur Evans among others has attested to the similarities between Cretan and Egyptian culture; and the Cretan labyrinth exists, if only as an after-light, to the labyrinth sites in which the first Egyptian pharaohs were buried. The pharaoh is the paranoid-schizoid imaginary twin. The division of his corpse into perishable and imperishable bits endorses the myth that divine kings have two bodies. The division of the body distinguishes between the clinging to surfaces in states of claustrophobia (his body is reduced to being an exoskeleton) and an agoraphobic release into space, in which there is an equation of entrails and cosmos.

His perishable entrails were placed in four jars that represented the quarters (among other meanings); they were known as Canopic jars. The outside of his body was mummified. The placing of an actual mask over the corpse's face emphasized the mask-like qualities of the face. The paranoid-schizoid imaginary twin is an intermediary between icon and idol. It fails to realize the idea of rebirth and of mythic circularity.

A Mother's Emanation

An infant sometimes knows before anyone else that a woman is pregnant. Is its intuition like a dog's sense of smell or hearing? Or does it experience the mother's body as giving out an emanation, comparable to the radiance that it might see in her glance when she feeds it?[2] In terms of sight, the emanation has the form of a pattern: a precursor of calligraphy perhaps. A carved wooden prow of an Asmat canoe at the Paris *Musée de quai Branly* has a man give birth to a woman out of his head, and she in turn gives birth to an infant, out of whose navel emerges a triangular shape, resembling a bird's beak, containing a filigree pattern. The umbilical cord, as part of the sign system of unconscious thought, tapers into a representation of a bird, whose ground is a sky associated with futurity. The umbilical rope unfolds into a sky kingdom. It evokes fibre-like premonitions about pregnancy: as when mothers bend forward to brush their loosened hair, or weave tapestries, or knit, or tie and untie knots – acts that choreograph pregnancies in thought. If a newborn is able to "see" an imagined future, it does so because, for a while at least, it is in harmony with some relationship between the idea of being pregnant and an idea of hopefulness. Clouds, if they appear in the sky of futurity, are patterns associated with meaning. They spread out and fill space.

The emanation, as filigree pattern, is benign; but it can be perceived as a persecutory phantasmagoria.[3] A thorny shrubbery extends around Sleeping Beauty, who sleeps because she has been "pricked". She has the inwardness of a woman who communes with a foetus within her: the prickly spirals of thorns that surround her may prick the suitors into a similar withdrawal from consciousness.[4] Her suitors face the prospect of psychic death. If they can travel through death into life, they may realize that the shrubbery, as an emanation of a pregnancy, generates reverie. The new life, out of which the emanation arises, cannot be directly known, but it can be inferred by way of particulars, such as the thorns in the hedge.

A certain patient brought a dream, which put us both separately in mind of the legend of Sleeping Beauty. On this day, unusually, she was late – by about six minutes. She said that a train carriage had been derailed (at Layton), and the theme of lateness and latency was elaborated on when she said that she had been held up for ten minutes in a tunnel. She had been irritated by the delay; and she conveyed a distanced sense of busyness, of a havoc and confusion occurring outside the tunnel and not really related to her.

In her dream, which appeared to be about a birth situation, but experienced from outside a mother's body, she found herself in a garden faced by a dense undergrowth, which she thought of as shrubbery. She was cutting through it with her secateurs, and she came across a pair of small child shoes, indeterminate of sex, on the ground. There was no child. She asked, almost plaintively, whether the idea of the shrubbery related to her thoughts and feelings. A fortnight before she had brought a dream in which she had found a baby rabbit beneath a hedge. She alluded to the legend of Sleeping Beauty, and said that Sleeping Beauty had been "pricked" and lay behind an undergrowth of prickly thorns or rose bushes. Her way of thinking suggested that for her Sleeping Beauty was an emblem for a pregnant mother, whose emanation was experienced as a deterrent to those who might be hostile to the foetus inside her.

The patient's response, when I communicated this thought to her, was to transform the tangible thorny shrubbery into swirls of blue tobacco smoke: the shrubbery that pricked and scratched turned into a configuration associated with choking.[5] Her partner, she said, smoked his pipe all over the house; she feared to die from passive smoking. He would stand before her, when she was seated, and before her very nose he would pack his pipe with tobacco from a rank pouch. Or he would appear in doorways, going puff–puff. Blue clouds of smoke swirled around him; she choked. A psychotic conception of choking, and perhaps its enactment, exist before the experience of breathing.

Bion (1963) compares beta elements to particles in an "uncertainty cloud" that agglomerate as an aborting type of container (pp.40 ff.). He compares them to the minus K making of fetishes, amulets and riddles as a magical procreation that controls or destroys the procreative capacity of others. A calligraphy that points like an arrow into the future undergoes a reversal in direction; and in place of an opening out of celestial space, and the emergence of meaning, there is a constriction that results in annihilation.

The change in the way in which the patient symbolized the emanation from shrubbery to tobacco smoke was marked by a corresponding shift in the therapist's thought. What was the link, if any, between a mother's emanation and the charisma of the pharaoh? The first pharaohs were placed in a labyrinth inside a pyramid. The patient's dream suggested that the labyrinth and the fetishes were attempts to evoke pregnancy as an emanation. Cogently it has been argued that

[...] in the case of the early royal tombs [...] there was apparently no reason in social conditions for concealment [...]. There was peace in the land, and from all accounts the pharaohs reigned as gods and were buried as gods, with the most elaborate ceremonies; no hint appears of molestation from any human agency (Deedes, 1935, p.12).

The labyrinth reified the charisma of the dead king. The prism, Bion's diamond, is the "domain" of the depressive imaginary twin. The labyrinth is the "domain" of the paranoid-schizoid imaginary twin. It is a faulty conception of "O". "We shall show them that by admitting the infinity of the fixed stars they become involved in inextricable labyrinths" (Kepler [in Koyré, 1957, p.60]).

Notes

1. He thought that something in her communication of the visual made him distrust his capacity for perception; he could not see that the optic glass phenomena that were occurring in the room had only a marginal connection to visual sensation.

2. The labyrinth is a faulty representation of the emanation.

3. I now see, years later, that this comparison is an attempt to differentiate between two types of hallucination.

4. Annihilation activates transformation in hallucinosis: this is *pietà* material.

5. Cf. Bion's patient, who "saw" a blue haze and two "probability clouds" (1967, pp.96–97). The capacity for benign hallucination, challenged by the depressive power of a mother who contains the imaginary twin changed into a paranoid-schizoid hallucination founded in respiratory failure.

25. ABSENCE OF BREATH AND CORDELIA'S MIRROR

> A centre or point, in itself perfectly simple, [in which] is found an infinity of angles formed by the lines that meet there (Leibniz, 1714, *Principles of Nature and Grace* [in Parkinson, 1973, p.195]).

In describing the nature of alpha function, Donald Meltzer (1986, p.116 ff.) was struck by a similarity between transformations in regard to a patient's dream image and an association he had to certain transformations in drawings of fishes and skulls in D'Arcy Wentworth Thompson's *On Growth and Form* (1917). A grid of Cartesian co-ordinates placed behind the drawings brings out the similarity in difference between the different fish and skulls. The Cartesian co-ordinates represent a varying field of force that modifies the various types of fish and skulls. Stretched or released like India rubber, the co-ordinates change the configuration of the fish and the skulls. The co-ordinates as a constant restrict the idea of variability to a form of torture that Donald Meltzer relates to Bion's concept of "reversal in alpha function". The ways in which the changing angles of the axial co-ordinates deform space reveal beta screen rarefaction and condensation under a new guise. The fact that the process of deformation creates images of fish and skulls that once existed suggests that this simulation of a field of force is analogous to certain conceptions of evolution.

At the end of the chapter on comparative transformation, Donald Meltzer refers to a communication from Bion, in which Bion describes the diamond as an image for transference exchange. "A ray of light entering the stone is reflected back by the same path in such a way that the light is augmented" (Meltzer, 1986, p.121). Bion describes a model that is a reversal of the idea of the Cartesian co-ordinates; it releases rather than restricts. It opens up a spectrum in which spectra can have habitation, as opposed to the spectrum as a Procrustean place of torture.

The existence of a wilderness that surrounds a cultivated space is a potent idea in many African mythologies, as well as in many of the mythologies of the ancient world. The wilderness outside the village space is a place for ghosts, monsters and unformed bits of being (the untouchables). The floating signifier in Lévi-Strauss's Amerindian model of triadic space, which allows moieties to perceive the topography of the village differently, is separated from the indeterminate wilderness outside the culture of the village. Bion's contact barrier similarly does not function as more than a means of contact between the two imaginary twins; it does not acknowledge the existence of a reality outside this triadic conception. The contact barrier as prism, though, extends beyond the reciprocation of the twins into a reciprocation with the indeterminate and the feared. The model of the village and the wilderness outside occurs in Lévi-Strauss's understanding of the *kachina* ceremonies.

Newton's experiments with the prism, through which he refracted light to reveal the spectrum, while working within the Kantian model, opens up an alternative to the Kantian model. The prism, as an image for a mother's capacity for reverie, is a resonant representation for the becoming of 'O'. It contains and releases imperceptibles.It depressively draws into the centre the fragmented and disordered world of the periphery. It is the missing construct between the axial co-ordinates as an idea for a three-dimensional intersection and the experience that Mauss has described as a reverberation. The prism enacts the tripartite fracture of light implied by Freud's intuition of three mothers. In art, an introjection of the prism occurs in the technique evolved by Cézanne known as *pentimento*. The technique is a crucial device in modernism. Originally the term, meaning *repentance* in Italian, described modifications in composition of a painting that has become visible with the thinning of the paint surface over a passage of time. The painter had made an error, which he had then corrected; hence the concept of repentance. Cézanne and his followers (notably Matisse) include the device of 'correction' in the final effect as a fact about the object that they describe. It is no longer a consequence of the painter's psychology; it is the attribute of a motif realized through the substance of art: "repentance" is a function of an unknowable variable and not of the subject–object relationship. Cézanne returns art to an iconicism that recalls the program of Byzantine art. There is an "increasing preoccupation with the relationship of the image to its prototype (rather than to the beholder) and an increasingly strong belief in the potentialities of the image as a vehicle of divine power" (Kitzinger, 1954, p.149 – writing about Byzantine art before iconoclasm). In Bion's view, an after-image acquires meaning through its relation to an unknowable prototype; its relationship to the beholder does not endow it with any significance. A mirror held to Cordelia's mouth is devoid of breath: yet it speaks of Cordelia as an after-effect, an undying charismatic presence of the inner world, Lear's daughter as everyone's "soul in bliss".

Art of a certain kind is concerned with images of the mother as the depressive imaginary twin might see them. *Pentimento*, like Mauss' reverberation is identical to the function by which Picasso – whom Bion has described on one occasion as the imaginary twin – is able to describe an image of the head in three aspects. In a momentary intuitive identification with the depressive imaginary twin, Freud sees Lear's mother as three beings. In so doing, he uncovers the meaning of the relationship of the three witches in *Macbeth* to Hecate of the triple glance.

But who would take the aesthetic possibilities of triple-headed Hecate seriously if Picasso had not realized a radiant sculpture of Jacqueline as three profiles in right angles to each other, flat surfaces alternating light and dark, as though the faces were versions of the sky at day and night? The three profiles of Jacqueline by their angle to each other indicate the possibilities of three dimensions, each repenting the existence of the other, while maintaining the tensions of a flat surface. If Picasso's forms evolve, or have some organic relationship to one another, they do so in ways that are unlike the post Darwinian evolutionary morphology of D'Arcy Wentworth Thompson.

The paranoid-schizoid imaginary twin might believe that Picasso, haunted by Jacqueline, had thought to escape from a tormenting introjection by caricature. The depressive imaginary twin perceives embodiment differently. It sees "perceptual errors" as the realization of a psychic object. The gaze contains many gazes that evolve through space as pulses in breathing. The boy that Freud referred to who modulated the sound of his aunt's voice into an experience of light was identified with the depressive imaginary twin that could translate a hallucination into an intuition.

All art entails a struggle with the paranoid-schizoid spectra. Picasso works in paranoid-schizoid sympathy with the Afro–Mediterranean ideology of the sacrifice as a communication from the dead that speaks to the living by means that are disguised. A pressure intensifies deformation and dislocation. The deformations and dislocations in his art (and in the art of black Africa) are functions of the dislocated nature of the divine king, who is the subject of the Russian patient's dream. Disguise, a function of liminality, is the manner by which the gods of non-existence make contact between incompatible "domains" (by metaphor or juxtaposition). The divine king needs disguise to bridge states of dislocation, or rather he must know the nothing and nowhere states of the inhabitants of the wilderness. Oedipus crosses the liminal spaces of two births and of two escapes from death. His act of self-blinding realises a paranoid-schizoid fact; that everyone is disguised to the other; and that disguise is a mode of survival at a time of dislocation.

The masks worn by the *kachina* actors function as intermediaries between the living and the dead. Strangers wear a mask representing the disembodiment of the drowned children; hence they are to be feared. The dead of ancient Rome, strangers from another place, people afflicted by dislocation, appear as *larvae*: that is, as spectres that are masked. (In Latin and early English *larva* is a ghost, spectre, hobgoblin and mask, as well as an insect in a grub state.) The *larvae* are the living about to be born, as well as the dead masquerading as newborns.

Gardens are cultivated places, wolves are creatures of the wild. The two can be separated in part, but only in part. Even the unpolluted Garden of Eden contained one or more trees of a problematic nature, and a reptile that was a free-thinker. The opening of the window in the Russian patient's dream indicates that the wolves entered the garden because a depressive imaginary twin had invited them in through the prism of a mother's eyes. The mother's eyes reflect the depth of the lake in which the children have drowned and out of which children will be born. Her unmasked sight is a prism that reflects the light of the spectrum, of love for the father sky; she brings the spectres into life; the marginal and the profane enter the sacral centre. The depressive imaginary twin is the point of light deflection in the prism; he is the divine king.

> The king represents the indissoluble binding together of myth and
> history. As a god, the king lives in myth; as a man, he lives in history: a
> duality that resolves into the unity that is the king (Palau Marti, 1964,
> p.29).

History, when isolated from myth, re-enters it as an unwelcomed wilderness, in the same way as myth, when isolated from history, is inclined to invade history as the uncanny.

26. THE WORLD'S DEEP MIDNIGHT

Hallucination is an imaginative or anti-imaginative function. Imaginary twins personify it. In Judeo-Christian parlance, the imaginary twins are angels, emissaries of the unknown, who modulate depressive pain if they are unfallen, or who transmit paranoid-schizoid anxieties when they are fallen. The angels "see" and "hear" without eyes and ears. Bion's "beam of darkness" presses on sites of incipient communication. In paranoid-schizoid states the sites are places of death. In depressive states they communicate the symbolism that grace is able to discover in nature. The depressive angel transforms imaginative hallucination into intuition.

The beam of darkness flows between the primal couple and anticipates the act of insemination. It contracts the self into nothingness, as does John Donne's "world of deep midnight". The mirroring of the tennis-net no longer reflects the one who looks into the mirror, the terrestrial and celestial conjunction of the self. In its place, an Arcadian mirror reflects only the primal objects.

At one end of the beam of darkness, the paternal "Shape" dismembers Adam. In removing one of Adam's ribs, the "Shape" releases Adam from the patrilineal inheritance. A rib enters a process of multiple transfiguration. The "imaginary penis" transfigures into an angelic presence and then into the organ of psychic perception.

Intuition discovers the forms of culture through the beam of darkness. The pharaoh's boat sails across the night sky, as though the night sky were the beam of darkness. The human body belongs as much to the world of the glowing reticulation as to the world of the tennis-net. It has the power to be a cosmic impress with the charismatic power of a fetish, or a work of art. Insofar as it involves multiple transformations of part objects in condensation, it is evocative of Freud's conception of the uncanny.

The primal scene as an actuality is an instance of the primal scene as an idea that exists outside space and time. The phantasies of the generative couple interact on various levels of meaning, in which the significance of the tennis game and of the glowing reticulation are two meanings among many. The body as cosmic impress originates as a thought that the interacting couple may share. Or fail to share: the seed then falls into the abyss.

Hallucination and intuition are forms of representations. Paranoid-schizoid hallucination represents the form of idols. Depressive hallucination is the means by which the unknowable assumes embodiment. The transformation of depressive hallucination into intuition indicates that "O" is present as a psychic becoming.

The self can survive the existence of an intolerable and denied depressive pain by sense misuse. It allows itself to be blinded and deafened by its capacity to see and hear. The imaginary twins are blind and deaf in ways that the self is not because they receive a certain pressure on incipient organs for communication and either modify or pervert it. Without the intercession of the imaginary twins, the self would be unable to discover intuition, whose structure lies in the transaction between the primal objects and the image of the self as nothing as reflected by the Arcadian mirror.

References

Adler, A. (1978). Le pouvoir et l'interdit. In J. Rouch et al. (Eds.), *Systèmes de signes. Textes réunis en hommage à Germaine Dieterlen.* Paris: Hermann.

Adler, A. (1982). *La Mort est le masque du roi.* Paris: Payot.

Adler, A., and Zempléni, A. (1972). *Le baton de l'aveugle.* Paris: Hermann.

Alexander, H.G. (Ed.) (1956). *The Leibniz–Clarke Correspondence.* Manchester: Manchester University Press.

Anon. (800 BC). *I Ching*, translated by Richard John Lynn. New York: Columbia University Press.

Apollodorus (c.100–200 AD). *The Library*, translated by J.G. Frazer, in two volumes. Loeb edition. London: Heinemann, 1921.

Aristotle (c.340 BC). *Metaphysics.* In J. Barnes (Ed.), *The Complete Works of Aristotle, Vol. 2.* Princeton, NJ: Princeton University Press, 1984.

Barnes, J. (Ed.) (1984). *The Complete Works of Aristotle, Vol. 2.* Princeton, NJ: Princeton University Press.

Bastide R. (1962). La nature humaine. In *Bastidiana*, 1994, 7–8.

Benveniste, E. (1939). Nature du signe linguistique. *Acta Linguistica*, 1 (Copenhagen). In *Problèmes de linguistique générale.* Paris: Gallimard, 1966.

Benveniste, E. (1952). Communication animale et langage humain. *Diogène*, 1. In *Problèmes de linguistique générale.* Paris: Gallimard, 1966.

Berthelot, R. (1949). *La pensée de l'Asie et l'astrobiologie.* Paris: Payot.

Bick, E. (1968). The experience of skin in early object relations. *Int. J. Psycho-Anal.*, 49: 484–486.

Bion, W.R. (1953). Notes on the theory of schizophrenia. *Int. J. Psycho-Anal.*, 1954, 35: 113–118. Also in *Second Thoughts*, London: Heinemann, 1967, pp. 23–35.

Bion, W.R. (1957). On arrogance. *Int. J. Psycho-Anal.*, 1958, 39: 144–146. Also in *Second Thoughts*, London: Heinemann, 1967, pp. 86–92.

Bion, W.R. (1959). Attacks on linking. *Int. J. Psycho-Anal.*, 40: 308–315. Also in *Second Thoughts*, London: Heinemann, 1967, pp. 93–109.

Bion, W.R. (1962). *Learning from Experience.* London: Heinemann.

Bion, W.R. (1963). *Elements of Psycho-Analysis.* London: Heinemann.

Bion, W.R. (1965). *Transformations.* Heinemann: London.

Bion, W.R. (1967). *Second Thoughts.* London: Heinemann.

Bion, W.R. (1970). *Attention and Interpretation.* London: Tavistock.

Bion, W.R. (1973). *Brazilian Lectures 1.* Rio de Janeiro: Imago Editora; London: Karnac: 1990.

Bion, W.R. (1975). *A Memoir of the Future, Book One: The Dream.* Rio de Janeiro, Brazil: Imago Editora; London: Karnac, 1991.

Bion, W.R. (1977a). *Two Papers: The Grid and Caesura.* Rio de Janiero, Brazil: Imago Editora; London: Karnac, 1989.

Bion, W.R. (1977b). *A Memoir of the Future. Book Two: The Past Presented.* Rio de Janiero, Brazil: Imago Editora; London: Karnac, 1991

Bion, W.R. (1979). *A Memoir of the Future, Book Three: The Dawn of Oblivion.* Strath Tay: Clunie Press; London: Karnac, 1991

Bion, W.R. (1980). *Bion in New York and São Paolo.* Strath Tay: Clunie Press.

Bion, W.R. (1987). *Clinical Seminars and Four Papers.* Oxford: Fleetwood Press; reprinted as *Clinical Seminars and Other Works*, London: Karnac, 1994.

Blake, W. (1794). *Infant Sorrow.* In G. Keynes (Ed.), *Songs of Experience.* Paris: Trianon Press, 1967.

Boholm, A. (1992). The coronation of female death: The Dogaressa of Venice. *Man,* 27 (1): 91–104.

Borges, J.L. (1954). *Historia universal de la infamia,* translated by N.T. de Giovanni as *A Universal History of Infamy.* London: Allen Lane, 1973.

Bouché-Leclercq, A. (1899). *L'Astrologie Grecque.* Paris: Leroux.

Bumbacher, S.P. (1994). Cosmic scripts and heavenly scriptures: The holy nature of Daoist texts. Paper presented at the conference "Scripts and Cosmograms", Edinburgh.

Bunzel, R.L. (1932). *Introduction to Zuñi ceremonialism.* 47th Annual Report. Bureau of American Ethnology: Washington, DC.

Burkert, W. (1983). *Homo Necans: The Anthropology of Ancient Greeek Sacrificial Ritual and Myth.* Berkeley, CA: University of California Press.

Burnet, J. (1892). *Early Greek Philosophy.* London and Edinburgh: A. and C. Black.

Calame-Griaule, G. (1965). *Ethnologie et langage. La parole chez les Dogon.* Paris: Institut d'Ethnologie, 1987.

Carmichael, E., and Sayer, S. (1991). *The Skeleton at the Feast: The Day of the Dead in Mexico.* London: British Museum Press.

Cartry, M. (1978). Les yeux captifs. In J. Rouch et al. (Eds.), *Systèmes de signes.* Paris: Hermann.

Codrington, R.H. (1891). *The Melanesians.* Oxford: Oxford University Press.

Coe, R.T. (1976). *Sacred Circles: Two Thousand Years of North American Indian Art.* London: Arts Council of Great Britain.

Coleridge, S.T. (1817). *Biographia Literaria.* In G. Watson (Ed.), *Coleridge's Biographia Literaria.* London: J.M. Dent and Sons, 1965.

Coleridge, S.T. (1818). On the principles of method. Essay VII. *The Friend.* In B.E. Rooke (Ed.), *Coleridge's The Friend, Vol. 3.* Bollingen Series. Princeton, NJ: Princeton University Press, 1969.

Coleridge, S.T. (1818–1819). *Lecture Notes.* In T.M. Raysor (Ed.), *Samuel Taylor Coleridge's Shakespearean Criticism, Vol. 1.* London: Edward Dent and Sons, 1960.

Collingwood, R.G. (1945). *The Idea of Nature.* Oxford: Oxford University Press.

Cook, A.B. (1914). *Zeus: A Study in Ancient Religion, Vol. 1.* Cambridge: Cambridge University Press.

Cornford, F.M. (1937). *Plato's Cosmology.* London: Kegan Paul.

Daraki, M. (1985). *Dionysos et la déesse terre.* Paris: Les Editions Arthaud; Paris: Flammarion, 1994.

Deedes, C. N. (1935). The Labyrinth. In S.H. Hooke (Ed.), *The Labyrinth.* London: Macmillan.

Dieterlen, G. (1950). *Essai sur la religion barbara.* Paris: Presses Universitaires de France; Brussels: Editions de l'Universite de Bruxelles, 1988.

Donne, J. (c.1617). A nocturnall upon S. Lucie's Day, being the shortest day. In H. Grierson (Ed.), *The Poems of J. Donne.* Oxford: Oxford University Press, 1933, reprinted 1951.

Drucker-Brown, S. (1992). Horse, dog, and donkey: The making of a Mamprusi king. *Man,* 1 (1): 71–89.

Dumézil, G. (1971). *Mythe et épopée, Vol. 2,* translated by Alf Hiltebeitel as *The Destiny of a King.* Chicago, IL: University of Chicago Press, 1973.

Duparc, F. (1992). Nouveaux développements sur l'hallucination négative et la représentation. *Rev. Franç. Psychanal.*, 56 (1).

Durkheim, É., and Mauss, M. (1903). De quelques formes primitives de classification. Contribution a l'étude des représentations collectives. *Année*, 6: 1–72. In V. Karady (Ed.), *Marcel Mauss. Oeuvres*, 2: *Représentations collectives et diversité des civilisations*. Paris: Les Editions de Minuit, 1974, pp. 13–89.

Eliot, T.S. (1921). The metaphysical poets. In *Selected Essays*. London: Faber & Faber, 1953.

Eliot, T.S. (1932). *Selected Essays* [revised edition]. London: Faber & Faber, 1951.

Eliot, T.S. (1941). *The Dry Salvages*. In *Four Quartets*, London: Faber & Faber, 1944.

Eliot, T.S. (1944). *Four Quartets*. London: Faber & Faber.

Empson, W. (1961). *Milton's God*. London: Chatto and Windus.

Esquirol, J.-D. (1838). *Des maladies mentales*. Brussels: Meline, Cans et Compaguri.

Fletcher, A.C. (1904). *The Hako: A Pawnee Ceremony. Twenty-Second Annual Report. Part Two*. Washington, DC: Bureau of American Ethnology.

Forman, M.B. (Ed.) (1952). *The Letters of John Keats*. Oxford: Oxford University Press.

Frazer, J.G. (Ed. and Trans.) (1898). *Pausanias' Description of Greece*. London: Macmillan and Co.

Freud, S. (1905). *Three Essays on the Theory of Sexuality. SE*, 7: 130–245. In J. Strachey (Ed.), *Standard Edition of the Complete Psychological Works of Sigmund Freud*, 24 volumes. London: Hogarth Press and The Institute of Psycho-Analysis, 1953–1974.

Freud, S. (1910). The antithetical meaning of primal words. *SE*, 11: 153–161.

Freud, S. (1911). Formulations on the two principles of mental functioning. *SE*, 12: 218–226.

Freud, S. (1913a): The occurrence in dreams of material from fairy tales. *SE*, 12: 281–287.

Freud, S. (1913b). The theme of the three caskets. *SE*, 12: 291–301.

Freud, S. (1915). *The Unconscious. SE*, 14: 161–209.

Freud, S. (1918). From the history of an infantile neurosis. *SE*, 17: 7–122.

Freud, S. (1919). The uncanny, *SE*, 17: 219–252.

Freud, S. (1921). Psycho-analysis and telepathy. *SE*, 18: 177–193.

Freud, S. (1923). *The Ego and the Id. SE*, 19: 12–66.

Freud, S. (1927). Fetishism. *SE*, 21: 152–157.

Freud, S. (1941). Findings, ideas, problems. *SE*, 23: 299–300.

Gay, P. (1988). *Freud: A Life for Our Time*. New York: W.W. Norton.

Giesey, R.E. (1960). The royal funeral ceremony in Renaissance France. In B. Schnepel, *Twinned Beings: Kings and Effigies in Southern Sudan, East India and Renaissance France*. Göteborg: IASSA, 1995.

Granet, M. (1934). *La pensée chinoise*. Paris: Éditions Albin Michel, 1968.

Green, A. (1983). *Narcissisme de vie, Narcissisme de mort*. Paris: Les Éditions de Minuit.

Griaule, M. (1966). *Dieu d'eau*. Paris: Fayard,1975.

Griaule, M., and Dieterlen, G. (1963). *Le renard pâle*. Paris: Institute d'Ethnologie, 1991.

Grierson, H. (1933). *The Poems of John Donne*. Oxford: Oxford University Press, 1951.

Haigh, A.E. (1907). *The Attic Theatre*. Oxford: Oxford University Press.

Hamilton, E., and Cairns, H. (Eds.) (1961). *The Collected Dialogues of Plato*. Princeton, NJ: Princeton University Press.

Harnes, K. (1975). The infinite sphere: Comments on the history of a metaphor. *J. Hist. Philosophy*, 13: 5–15.

Hastings J. (Ed.) (1908–1926). *Encyclopaedia of Religion and Ethics*. Edinburgh: Clark.

Heraclitus fl. (504 BC). *The Art and Thought of* Heraclitus, edited by C. H. Kahn. Cambridge: Cambridge Unversity Press, 1979.

Hocart, A.M. (1954). *Social Origins*. London: Watts.

Hofstader, D. (1980). *Godel, Escher, Bach: An Eternal Golden Braid*. London: Penguin.

Hubert, H., and Mauss, M. (1899). Essai sur la nature et la fonction du sacrifice. *L'Année sociologique*, 2. In V. Karady (Ed.), *Marcel Mauss. Oeuvres*, 1: *Les fonctions sociales du sacré*. Paris: Les Éditions de Minuit, 1974, pp. 193–307.

Hubert, H., and Mauss, M. (1909). *Collected Papers on Religion*. Paris: Alcan.

Hume, R.E. (1931). *The Thirteen Principal Upanishads Translated from the Sanskrit*. Oxford: Oxford University Press.

Hutchinson, T. (Ed.) (1905). *The Complete Poetical Works of Percy Bysshe Shelley*. Oxford: Oxford University Press.

Jaques, E. (1959). Disturbances in the capacity to work. In *Creativity and Work*. Madison, CT: International Universities Press, 1990.

Jones, H.L. (Ed.) (1944). *The Geography of Strabo, Vol. 8*. London: Heinemann.

Kahn, C.H. (Ed.) (1979). *The Art and Thought of Heraclitus*. Cambridge: Cambridge University Press.

Kant, I. (1787). *Kritik der reinen Vernunft*, translated by N. K. Smith as *Critique of Pure Reason*. London: Macmillan, 1929, reprinted 1950.

Kantorowicz, E.H. (1957). *The King's Two Bodies*. Princeton, NJ: Princeton University Press, 1981.

Karady, V. (Ed.) (1974). *Marcel Mauss. Oeuvres*, 2: *Représentations collectives et diversité des civilisations*. Paris: Les Éditions de Minuit.

Karp, I., and Bird, C. (Eds.) (1980). *Explorations in African Systems of Thought*. Bloomington, IN: Indiana University Press.

Keats, J. (1817). Letter to Benjamin Bailey, 22 November. In M.B. Forman (Ed.), *The Letters of John Keats*. Oxford: Oxford University Press, 1952.

Kitzinger, E. (1954). The cult of images in the age before iconoclasm. *Dumbarton Oaks Papers*, 8. Cambridge, MA: Harvard University Press, pp. 85–150.

Klein, M. (1935). A contribution to the psychogenesis of manic-depressive states. In R.E. Money-Kyrle, B. Joseph, E. O'Shaughnessy, and H. Segal (Eds.), *The Writings of Melanie Klein, Vol. 1*. London: Hogarth Press, 1975, pp. 262–289.

Koyré, A. (1957). *From the Closed World to the Infinite Universe*. Baltimore, MD: Johns Hopkins University Press.

Kubler, G. (1962). *The Shape of Time*. New Haven, CT: Yale University Press.

Kuper, H. (1947). *An African Aristocracy: Rank among the Swazi*. New York: Africana Publishing Company, 1980.

Ladner, G.B. (1953). The concept of the image in the Greek Fathers and the Byzantine iconoclastic controversy. *Dumbarton Oaks Papers*, 7, pp. 2–34.

Ladner, G.B. (1979). Medieval and modern understanding of symbolism. *Speculum*, 54. In G.B. Ladner, *Images and Ideas in the Middle Ages: Selected Studies in History and Art, Vol. 1* (pp.239–282). Roma: Edizioni di Storia e Letteratura, 1983.

Ladner, G.B. (1983). *Images and Ideas in the Middle Ages. Selected Studies in History and Art*. Roma: Edizioni di Storia e Letteratura.

Leibnitz, G.W. (1714). *Principles of Nature and Grace*. In G.H.R. Parkinson (Ed.), *Leibniz: Philosophical Writings*. London: J.M. Dent and Sons, 1973.

Lévi, S. (1898). *La Doctrine du sacrifice dans les Brâhmanas*. Paris: Leroux.

Lévi-Strauss, C. (1949). *Les structures élementaires de la parenté*, translated by R. Needham as *Elementary Structures of Kinship*. Boston, MA: Beacon Press, 1969.

Lévi-Strauss, C. (1950). Introduction à l'oeuvre de Marcel Mauss. In *Marcel Mauss. Sociologie et Anthropologie*. Paris: Quadrige, pp. ix–lii.

Lévi-Strauss, C. (1952). Le Père Noël supplicié. *Les Temps Modernes*, 77: 1572–1590.

Lévi-Strauss, C. (1955). The structural study of myth. Translated by C. Jacobson and B. Grundfest Schoepf. In *Structural Anthropology*, Vol. 1. London: Peregrine: 1977, pp. 206–231.

Lévi-Strauss, C. (1956). Les Organisations dualistes existent-elles? English edition, "Do dual organisations exist?" In *Structural Anthropology*, Vol. 1. London: Peregrine, 1977, pp. 132–163.

Lévi-Strauss, C. (1957). Le symbolisme cosmique dans la structure sociale et l'organisation ceremonielle de plusieurs populations Nord et Sud-Americaines. In *Le Symbolisme cosmique des monuments religieux*, Serie Orientale. Roma, Is. M.E.O., 1957, pp. 47–56.

Lévi-Strauss, C. (1962a). *Le totémisme aujourd'hui*. Paris: Presses Universitaires de France. Translated by Rodney Needham as *Totemism*. London: Merlin Press, 1964.

Lévi-Strauss, C. (1962b). Jean-Jacques Rousseau, fondateur des sciences de l'homme. Translated by Monique Layton. In *Structural Anthropology*, Vol. 2, 1976, pp. 33–43.

Lévi-Strauss, C. (1962c). *La pensée sauvage*. English edition, *The Savage Mind*. London: Weidenfeld and Nicolson, 1972.

Lévi-Strauss, C. (1964). *Le cru et le cuit*. Paris: Plon. Translated by Doreen and John Weightman as *The Raw and the Cooked*. London: Cape, 1970.

Lévi-Strauss, C. (1966). *Du Miel aux cendres*. Paris: Plon. Translated by Doreen and John Weightman as *From Honey to Ashes*. London: Cape, 1973.

Lévi-Strauss, C. (1968). *L'origine des manières de table*. Paris: Plon. Translated by Doreen and John Weightman as *The Origin of Table Manners*. London: Cape, 1978.

Lévi-Strauss, C. (1978). *The 1977 Massey Lectures*. Toronto: University of Toronto Press.

Lévi-Strauss, C. (1979). *La voie des masques*. Paris: Plon.

Lincoln, B. (1986). *Myth, Cosmos and Society. Indo-European Themes of Creation and Destruction*. Cambridge, MA: Harvard University Press.

Lovejoy, A.O. (1936). *The Great Chain of Being*. Cambridge, MA: Harvard University Press.

Lynn, R.J. (Tr.) (1994). *I Ching*. New York: Columbia University Press.

Maquet. J.A. (1954). *Le système des relations socials dans le Ruanda ancien*. Tervuren: Musée Royal de Congo Belge.

Marshak, A. (1972). *The Roots of Civilization*. London: Weidenfeld and Nicolson.

Mauss, M. (1906). Essai sur les variations saisonnières des sociétés eskimos. Essai de morphologie sociale, *L'Année sociologique, 9:* 39–132. In V. Karady (Ed.), *Marcel Mauss. Oeuvres*, 1: *La fonction sociale du sacré*. Paris: Les Editions de Minuit, 1968.

Mauss, M. (1924). Rapports réels et practiques de la psychologie et de la sociologie. *J. Psychol. Norm. Pathol*. In *Sociologie et anthropologie*. Paris: Quadrige, 1950.

Mauss, M. (1933). Intervention à la suite d'une communication de M. Granet: "La droite et la gauche en Chine". *Bul. Inst. Franç. Sociol.*, 3. In V. Karady (Ed.), *Marcel Mauss. Oeuvres*, 2: *Représentations collectives et diversité des civilisations*. Paris: Les Editions de Minuit, 1974.

Meltzer, D. (1967). *The Psychoanalytical Process*. London: Heinemann.

Meltzer, D. (1973). *Sexual States of Mind*. Strath Tay: Clunie Press.

Meltzer, D. (1984). *Dream-Life*. Strath Tay: Clunie Press.

Meltzer, D. (1986). *Studies in Extended Metapsychology*. Strath Tay: Clunie Press.

Meltzer, D. (1992). *The Claustrum*. Strath Tay: Clunie Press.

Meltzer, D. (1994). *Sincerity and Other Works*, edited by A. Hahn. London: Karnac.

Meltzer, D., Brenner, J., Hoxter, S., Wedell, D., and Wittenberg, I. (1975). *Explorations in Autism*. Strath Tay: Clunie Press.

Meltzer, D., and Williams, M. H. (1988). *The Apprehension of Beauty*. Strath Tay: Clunie Press.

Merchant, W.M. (Ed.) (1955). *Wordsworth Poetry and Prose*. London: Rupert Hart-Davis.

Milton, J. (1667). *Paradise Lost*. In D. Bush, *The Portable Milton*. New York: Viking Press, 1949.

Needham, J. (1956). *Science and Civilisation in China. Vol. 2: History of Scientific Thought*. Cambridge: Cambridge University Press.

Nietzsche, F. (1873). Philosophy in the tragic age of the Greeks. In *Early Greek Philosophy*, translated by M.A. Mugge. London and Edinburgh: T.N. Foulis, 1911.

Nietzsche, F. (1911). *Early Greek Philosophy*, translated by M.A. Mugge. London and Edinburgh: T.N. Foulis.

Nilsson, M.P. (1927). *The Minoan-Mycenean Religion and Its Survival in Greek Religion*. London and Edinburgh: T.N. Foulis, 1950.

Nilsson, M.P. (1949). *A History of Greek Religion*. Oxford: Oxford University Press.

Onians, R.B. (1951). *Origins of European Thought*. Cambridge: Cambridge University Press.

Palau Marti, M. (1964). *Le roi-dieu au Bénin*. Paris: Éditions Berger-Levrault.

Pâques, V. (1964). *L'Arbre cosmique dans la pensée populaire et dans la vie quotidienne du nord-ouest africain*. Institut d'Ethnologie. Paris: L'Harmattan, 1955.

Parkinson, G.H.R. (Ed.) (1973). *Leibniz: Philosophical Writings*. London: J.M. Dent and Sons.

Parkinson, G.H.R. (Ed.) (1989). *Spinoza's Ethics*. London: J.M. Dent and Sons.

Pausanias (c.200 AD). *Description of Greece*. In J.G. Frazer (Ed. and Trans.), *Pausanias's Description of Greece*. London: Macmillan and Co., 1898.

Pétrement, S. (1984). *Le Dieu séparé. Les origines du gnosticisme*. Paris: Les Éditions du Cerf.

Pickard-Cambridge. A. (1962). *Dithyramb, Tragedy and Comedy* (2nd edition). Cambridge: Cambridge University Press.

Plato (385 BC). *The Republic, The Laws, The Timaeus*. In E. Hamilton and C. Huntingdon (Eds.), *The Collected Dialogues of Plato*. Princeton, NJ: Princeton University Press, 1961.

Porphyry (c. AD 234–305). *De abstinentia*. In J.-P. Vernant, *Mythe et pensée chez les Grecs: études de psychologie historique (Les textes à l'appui, 13)*. Paris: F. Maspero, 1963. English translation, *Myth and Thought among the Greeks*. London: Routledge and Kegan Paul, 1983.

Radin, P. (1923). *The Winnebago Tribe*. 37th Annual Report 1915–1916. Washington, DC: Bureau of American Ethnology.

Raysor, T.M. (1960). *Samuel Taylor Coleridge's Shakespearean Criticism in Two Volumes, Volume 1*. London: J.M. Dent and Sons.

Rees, A., and Rees, B. (1961). *Celtic Heritage. Ancient Tradition in Ireland and Wales*. London: Thames and Hudson.

Ridgeway, W. (1910). *The Origin of Tragedy*. Cambridge: Cambridge University Press.

Rooke, B.E. (1969). *Coleridge's "The Friend"*. Bollingen Series. Princeton, NJ: Princeton University Press.

Rosen, C. (1975). *Schoenberg*. London: Fontana Modern Masters.

Rouget, G. (1980). *La musique et la transe: Esquisse d'une théorie générale des relations de la musique et de la possession*, translated by Brunhilde Biebuck as *Music and Trance*. Chicago, IL: University of Chicago Press, 1985.

Saussure, F. de (1916). *Cours de linguistique générale*, edited by T. de Mauro. Paris: Éditions Payot, 1972.

Schipper, K. (1982). *The Taoist Body*. Berkeley, CA: University of California Press, 1993.

Schnepel, B. (1995). *Twinned Beings: Kings and Effigies in Southern Sudan, East India and Renaissance France*. Göteborg: IASSA.

Schwartz, B. (1985). *The World of Thought in Ancient China*. Cambridge, MA: Belknap Press of Harvard University Press.

Segal, H. (1957). Notes on symbol formation. *Int. J. Psycho-Anal.*, 38: 391–397.

Shakespeare, W. (1597). *Richard II*. Folio Edition. Oxford: Oxford University Press, 1968.

Shakespeare, W. (1605). *King Lear*. Harmondsworth: Penguin, 1972.

Shakespeare, W. (1611). *The Tempest*. Harmondsworth: Penguin, 1968.

Sharpe, E.F. (1950). *Collected Papers on Psycho-Analysis*. London: Hogarth Press.

Shelley, P.B. (1819). *Prometheus Unbound*. In T. Hutchinson (Ed.), *The Complete Poetical Works of Percy Bysshe Shelley*. Oxford: Oxford University Press, 1905.

Soothill, W.E. (1951). *The Hall of Light: A Study of Early Chinese Kingship*. London: Lutterworth Press.

Spencer, B., and Gillen, F.J. (1927). *The Arunta*. London: Macmillan.

Spinoza, B. (1677). *Ethics*. In G.H.R. Parkinson (Ed.), *Spinoza's Ethics*. London: J.M. Dent and Sons, 1989.

Tausk, V. (1919). On the origin of the "influencing machine" in schizophrenia. *Psychoanal. Q.*, 1933, 2 (3–4): 519–556.

Thompson, D.W. (1917). *On Growth and Form*. Cambridge: Cambridge University Press.

Turner, V. (1967). *The Forest of Symbols*. Ithaca, NY: Cornell University Press.

Tustin, F. (1981). *Autistic States in Children*. London: Routledge and Kegan Paul.

Van der Kroef, J.M. (1954). Dualism and symbolic antithesis in Indonesian society. *Amer. Anthropol.*, 56: 847–862.

Vaughan, J.A. (1977). A reconsideration of divine kingship. In I. Karp and C. Bird (Eds.), *Exploration in African Systems of Thought*. Bloomington, IN: Indiana University Press, 1980.

Vernant, J.-P. (1963). *Mythe et pensée chez les Grecs*. English translation, *Myth and Thought among the Greeks*. London: Routledge and Kegan Paul, 1983.

Vernant, J.-P. (1991). *Mortals and Immortals. Collected Essays*, edited by Froma I. Zeitlin. Princeton, NJ: Princeton University Press.

Watson, G. (Ed.) (1965). *Coleridge's Biographia Literaria*. London: J.M. Dent and Sons.

Wheatley, P. (1971). *The Pivot of the Four Quarters*. Edinburgh: Edinburgh University Press.

Wilkinson, R.H. (1992). *Reading Egyptian Art: A Hieroglyphic Guide to Ancient Egyptian Painting and Sculpture*. London: Thames and Hudson.

Wilkinson, R.H. (1994). *Symbol and Magic in Egyptian Art*. London: Thames and Hudson.

Williams, M.H. (1982). *Inspiration in Milton and Keats*. London: Macmillan.

Wittgenstein, L. (1930). *Remarks on Frazer's "Golden Bough"*. Doncaster: Brynmill Press, 1979.

Wordsworth, W. (1802–1804). *Ode. Intimations of Immortality from Recollections of Early Childhood*. In W.M. Merchant (Ed.), *Wordsworth Poetry and Prose*. London: Rupert Hart-Davis, 1955.

Zahan, D. (1995). *Le feu en Afrique*. Paris: L'Harmattan.

INDEX

Abel, K., 135, 137
abortion, 71, 85, 105, 123, 134, 208
absence of text, 9, 82, 94
Achilpa tribe, 154–155
acoustical figure, 39
acoustical image, 37
Adam, 101, 107–109, 169
    body of, 108, 166
    dream of, 92–94, 96–97, 103, 106,
        111, 166, 187
    rib of, 95, 137, 170, 207
    transfiguration, 92, 95, 101, 104, 108,
        184, 223
adhesive identification, 5, 181, 184
Adler, A., 127–132, 134
Aeschylus, 140–141
Africa, 125, 157, 172, 209, 221
    ancient, 188
    North, 188
African fetish sculptures, 44
African myth(s)/mythologies, 78–79, 219
Afro–Mediterranean ideology, 221
agoraphobia, 195–197, 200
Alexander, H.G., 73
alpha elements, 27
alpha function, 46, 99, 218
alpha thought, indeterminate object of,
    93
Amerindian, 56, 62, 77
Amerindian model of triadic space, 219
Amerindian myth(s), 48–49, 73, 145,
    167
Amma, 126
ancient Chinese capital, 158–160
Angolo, King of Dahomey, 153
annihilation and transformation in
    hallucinosis, 59, 121–125
anxiety, depressive, 175
Apollodorus, 126–127, 129
Aristophanes, 140
Aristotle, 56, 58, 125, 165, 172
Athena, 44
Athens, 139–141, 153
atomisation, 61–63
aural space, 48
Aztec sculpture, 15

baby:
    air, 126, 171
    medical-vertex, 19, 71
    water, 126, 171
Bach, J.S., 61
baptism, transfiguration of, 184
Barnes, J., 56
Barrie, J.M., 136
Bastide, R., 50
Beckett, T., 174
being and not being, 180
Benin, 15, 154, 209
Benin sculpture, 15
Benveniste, E., 38, 40, 137
Berkeley, Bishop, 174
Berthelot, R., 169–170
beta element(s), 27, 69, 216
    agglomerates, 57
    impacted feelings as, 45
    in infant's mouth and alpha elements
        of mother's thinking, 93
beta element evacuations, 80
beta element transformation in
    hallucinosis, 187
beta screen, 23, 28, 30, 58, 76, 91, 125,
    152, 212, 218
    and catastrophic change:
        relationship between, 42–47
        conception of clinical information,
            45–46
    theory, 42
beta thinking, 93, 99, 121–122, 196
Bhagavad Gita, 19
Bible, 136
Bick, E., 13
binocular form of vision, 58
biology, 20
Bion, W.R. [*passim*]:
    "On Arrogance", 19, 23, 28, 31, 35,
        181
    "Attacks on Linking", 23
    beam of darkness, 21, 31, 37, 50,
        81–82, 92, 108, 223
    Brazilian Lectures, 20
    Cogitations, 5
    conception of probability clouds, 24
    concept of reversal, 63